ANOTHER ONE
BITES THE GRASS

Adweek Books is designed to present interesting, insightful books for the general business reader and for professionals in the worlds of media, marketing, and advertising.

These are innovative, creative books that address the challenges and opportunities of these industries, written by leaders in the business. Some of our writers head their own companies, others have worked their way up to the top of their field in large multinationals. But they share a knowledge of their craft and a desire to enlighten others.

We hope readers will find these books as helpful and inspiring as *Adweek*, *Brandweek*, and *Mediaweek* magazines.

Published

Disruption: Overturning Conventions and Shaking Up the Marketplace, Jean-Marie Dru

Under the Radar: Talking to Today's Cynical Consumer, Jonathan Bond and Richard Kirshenbaum

Truth, Lies and Advertising: The Art of Account Planning, Jon Steel

Hey, Whipple, Squeeze This: A Guide to Creating Great Ads, Luke Sullivan

Eating the Big Fish: How Challenger Brands Can Compete Against Brand Leaders, Adam Morgan

Warp-Speed Branding: The Impact of Technology on Marketing, Agnieszka Winkler

Creative Company: How St. Luke's Became "the Ad Agency to End All Ad Agencies," Andy Law

Another One Bites the Grass: Making Sense of International Advertising, Simon Anholt

ANOTHER ONE BITES THE GRASS

Making Sense of
International Advertising

Simon Anholt

John Wiley & Sons, Inc.

New York • Chichester • Weinheim • Brisbane • Singapore • Toronto

Published by John Wiley and Sons, Inc.

Published simultaneously in Canada.

The author wishes to acknowledge the following for permission to use previously published material:

Mill Hollow Corporation, for the incorporation of selections from his regular columns in *DM News International* into Chapter 8.

Henry Stewart Publications, for the incorporation of material from two of his papers published in the *Journal of Brand Management*.

Library of Congress Cataloging-in-Publication Data:
Anholt, Simon.
    Another one bites the grass : making sense of international advertising / Simon Anholt.
        p. cm. — (Adweek book)
    Includes index.
    ISBN 0-471-35488-0 (cl. : alk. paper)
    1. Advertising.   2. Advertising—Cross-cultural studies.
I. Title.   II. Series.
HF5821.A55   1999
659.1—dc21   99-37987
                                                                              CIP

Printed in the United States of America.

10 9   8   7   6   5   4   3   2   1

Contents

Introduction   vii

1. **The Trouble with Words**   1
   Language is often the first thing people worry about when
   planning an international ad campaign. Perhaps it should be
   the last.
   *How to avoid translation, how to avoid disasters, how to name global
   brands, and what's wrong with English.*

2. **The Trouble with Culture**   51
   If language is the tip of the iceberg, culture is what lurks
   below the surface. This is the stuff that really decides whether
   a global campaign succeeds or not.
   What culture is, why it's so important, and how to use it.

3. **Global Brand or Global Bland?**   89
   Your brand won't go anywhere unless it's equipped to travel,
   and that means building in the needs of your overseas markets at the beginning of the branding process.
   *How to make traveler brands, why provenance is critical, and why con-
   sistency is such a dangerous thing to strive for.*

4. **The Trouble with Creativity**   131
   Creativity gets more important with every year that passes,
   but on international campaigns it seems virtually impossible
   to achieve.
   *How to be distinctive, effective, relevant and memorable in countries
   you couldn't reliably point to on a map.*

5. **Network = Notwork**   155

The advertising industry's worst-kept secret: a psychopath in his worst nightmares couldn't invent a worse way of doing international advertising campaigns than an international advertising agency network.

How to achieve better results than a network, be faster, cheaper, and have more fun, all at the same time.

6. **The New International Line-Up**   187

An introduction to the concept of Smart Centralization, and the principle of World Advertising; working with multicultural creative teams.

How to get an effective global agency into one office, and where the global ideas come from.

7. **Going It Alone**   225

A closer look at the practical realities of doing without networks, and making a better agency.

How to plan, create, produce, and manage big global accounts without billions of dollars worth of real estate in 126 countries.

8. **More than Just Ads**   259

Everyone agrees that advertising needs an integrated, media-neutral approach. But what does this mean in the context of international campaigns?

Why the internet changes everything, why writing to strangers is rude, and how to research new product positionings in many markets without translation.

9. **Where Do We Go from Here?**   299

The future of brands is global, the future of the advertising business is murky, and some of the biggest global brands in the next century might come from some unexpected places.

Why branding is so important for the distribution of wealth, and how advertising can change the world.

Notes   309

Index   314

About the Author   326

Introduction

Not many people seem to realize it, but the advertising and marketing services industry is now facing—or may actually be in the middle of—the biggest crisis it has ever faced.

The problem is globalization: more and more companies are making the decision to market their products abroad, and the advertising industry is failing to keep pace with that growing demand.

It's fascinating to observe how the advertising industry persistently fails to recognize this, the growing demand for international competence, as the most significant challenge to its business.

So what exactly is going on here?

Somewhat more than half of all global trade at this point in time is international. All of this trade requires marketing, and much of it requires advertising. (I use the word *advertising* in its broadest sense of media and non-media marketing communications.)

Servicing this need are perhaps 50,000 advertising agencies worldwide, of which some 49,000 are domestic agencies, serving only the country, region, or city where they are located.

A friend at the American Association of Advertising Agencies tells me he now receives at least one call per week from independent agency members around the United States asking for advice on how to meet their clients' demands for international campaigns.

The twenty or so proper international agency networks are (a) full to bursting-point with clients in every product category; (b) diminishing in number as some merge and others fail; (c) fundamentally unsuited to the needs of a growing proportion of international client companies; and (d) beset with creative, financial, administrative, political, and structural problems.

In any case, many of the emerging international marketers don't need and can't afford a huge multinational organization to help them with their advertising: by and large, these first-time exporters don't start out with huge advertising budgets and big marketing departments in every territory. For such a business to contemplate hiring a global shop like Ogilvy & Mather or Young & Rubicam, and have their marketing staff outnumbered by their own agency a hundred to one in all but their home market, seems the height of absurdity.

What's more, a high proportion of these new exporters work in high-speed industries, such as information technology, where advertising a new product a week later than intended could easily mean the difference between success and failure: traditional network agencies, because of their geographical distribution and other problems which I will explore in Chapter 5, are often just too cumbersome to meet such needs.

And many others among our new exporters are selling to fickle and sophisticated youth markets, where low boredom thresholds, short attention spans, and highly developed brand awareness mean that knife-edge creativity is the lifeblood of their businesses: few network agencies are able to maintain that sort of risk-seeking passion in dozens of different countries for very long at a time.

Some quick solutions and some smart alternatives to the traditional networks are desperately needed: there simply isn't enough international resource out there to cope with the rocketing demand for global communications.

In this book, I describe a concept which I call *smart centralization:* a very simple, very obvious, very neat, and totally new way of creating *real* international communications for today's and tomorrow's traveler brands.

All this has a lot to do with who we are and how we communicate, so in the first two chapters I'll explore some of the *linguistic and cultural* dilemmas and quandaries which international advertising invariably raises, and try to put paid to some of the myths and misunderstandings surrounding these complex but critical issues.

And the best advertising in the world won't get you very far on the international stage unless your *brand* is fit to travel: Chapter 3 describes some fresh approaches to global brand development. It's all about the need to build a global brand with due sensitivity to the culture of its overseas consumers, and how this need should affect a company's thinking *right at the start* of its brand development process—not at the end.

Chapter 4 deals with the fundamental question of *creativity*, and talks about some new ways of finding ideas and executions which are relevant, meaningful, persuasive, and memorable in unlimited numbers of countries around the world.

Chapter 5 is a story which has never been told in print, yet it has been the advertising community's worst-kept secret for decades: the simple fact that *the traditional network system just isn't working.* I maintain that it almost never has, and probably never will work: that big, old-fashioned distributed structure is a mere accident of history, rather than a properly thought-out solution to the real needs of global companies.

My belief is that international advertising needs entirely new approaches to *planning, creative development, account management, production, and delivery.* In Chapters 6 and 7, I will describe some of these in detail. I also illustrate a revolutionary fact, which I hope will provide a major challenge to the dominance of the big networks: that small ad agencies, anywhere in the world, can manage complex and substantial international assignments through *smart centralization.* There is now, at last, such a thing as a *small international advertising agency.*

Chapter 8 explores how the techniques of smart centralization are more than just a neat trick for creating international advertising campaigns, but an approach which can and should apply throughout the branding and communications mix: in *direct marketing, interactive, content, and new product positioning work.*

Finally, in Chapter 9, I'd like to share some thoughts about how smart centralization and culturally-sensitive brand planning and communications could actually *make a difference* to the way people live in the next century and beyond.

This book aims to cast some much-needed light on the question of why a very small number of international advertising campaigns work quite well, and why the vast majority seem to bite the dust (or eat the grass, as they say in Germany).

It will also give a good deal of practical advice on how to ensure that your next global campaign makes your *competitors* eat your dust.

I hope that this book will provide help and inspiration to the marketers who need smart international communications; and I hope it will give courage to the smaller ad agencies who were beginning to think that the only possible route to growth was by selling out to the multinationals.

To them, I say: don't do it until you've read this book. You might end up buying *them.*

1

The Trouble with Words

Once upon a time, there was an airline which decided to run a special promotion on its busy route between Riyadh, Saudi Arabia, and London, England. Aware that here was rich potential for linguistic disaster, the marketing department decided to play safe and have their London agency devise a simple poster in English, which could then be safely translated into Arabic.

"Fly to London this Autumn," ran the line, "and save up to 20% on the normal return fare."

The posters were made, the campaign ran, and the promotion was a huge success. Such a success, in fact, that the following month, the people in the Saudi office decided to throw a party for their English colleagues.

At the party, the marketing manager for the Middle East drew aside his English colleague and said, "I'd just like to thank you for the excellent poster you created for us. I'm certain that it was the main reason for the wonderful success we've had. That famous English creativity! I've been saying it for years. We need a bit more of that over here!"

The Director of Marketing was flattered, and thanked his colleague, but the man carried on: "It was so unexpected, so . . . off the wall, so zany. I just don't know how you people keep coming up with these ideas."

The Director of Marketing began to feel confused: "Well, you know, we weren't even trying to be especially creative on that ad—you should see what we can do when we really pull out all the stops!"

But his Saudi colleague just replied, "Ah, the famous British modesty! No, in my book, it was genius. Especially the bit about the restaurant."

The Director of Marketing made an excuse, hurriedly left the party, and found somebody to translate the poster back into English for him. What it said was as follows:

"Fly to London this Autumn and save up to 20% on the normal return fare. AND while you're there, don't forget to eat at Ahmed's famous Kebab Oasis at 526 Edgware Road, where you will be treated like a prince."

Ahmed, it turned out, much, much later, was the translator's brother-in-law. He now owns two Kebab Oases on the Edgware Road.

A Word about Language

That story always goes down rather well when I tell it, I suspect because it plays so unerringly on the deepest fears of many international marketers: when you're responsible for communications in a language you don't personally speak, you believe that you know what you're running. But actually, it could be saying literally anything at all, *and you just wouldn't know.*

This fear is symptomatic of a very common but fundamental misunderstanding about the function of *language* in advertising, often characterized by an unshakeable conviction that language is a secret key for resolving every imaginable problem in international marketing communications.

Time and time again, I see clients and their agencies fall into the trap of believing that a British or American team can create an ad in the English language, and turn that into an Egyptian or Thai or Guatemalan ad simply by translating the English words into Arabic or Thai or Spanish.

You put it like that, and it seems obvious that it's not a very intelligent way to behave. Yet look at the way people create international campaigns, and it's clear that most of the time they're behaving exactly as if they believed that the *only* difference between an English or American consumer and an Egyptian consumer is that one speaks English and the other speaks Arabic.

A strange attitude indeed, especially since it is constantly confirmed and reinforced by the practices of global ad agencies—companies which style themselves as strategically-minded international communications consultancies. But there you go, and I don't see too many signs that this approach has changed over the years: every day, somewhere in the world, scarily junior people working on major global briefs in major global agencies are still treating the creative part of their international campaigns as nothing much more demanding than finding the cheapest translation company in the Yellow Pages.

If you'd like to prove for yourself that this is really not a language issue, just cut a press ad out of a British or Australian magazine and paste it into an American one (or vice versa). See? It looks totally out of place, and that's nothing to do with the fact that Brits spell "color" wrong. The whole ad actually *feels* wrong: it's designed, laid out, typeset, photographed, targeted, argued, written, *conceived* in a way which is totally alien to the American consumer. It sort of *smells* wrong. It has the wrong *pheromones*.

Consumers are, alas, not stupid: they have uncannily sensitive cultural antennae, and can detect an ad which was never really meant for them in the first place from about a hundred yards downwind.

A WORD ABOUT TRANSLATION

You don't need to work in international advertising for very long before you notice that *translation* is something which people lie awake at night worrying about a great deal. And, in my experience, very few of them have even the remotest idea what it actually is, and how singularly irrelevant it is to the whole business of creating international advertising campaigns.

Read any textbook on export marketing, overseas trade, global branding, or international advertising, and look up "translation" in the index. There is usually a short paragraph or modest section dedicated to it, in which the author shares with us some profound findings, gleaned over decades in the business, about this mysterious topic. Here's a fine example from one weighty tome, which is otherwise an extremely authoritative guide to the *practical* issues of export marketing:

> Translation is made easier if advertisements, sales letters, mail-drop leaflets and so on are drafted in simple English. It follows that colloquialisms, figures of speech, metaphors, technical terms, and humorous expressions should always be avoided. The people who put together the initial copy should attempt to *think* in a multilingual way, assuming from the beginning that the material will be translated. Short and simple sentences are preferable to complex statements.[1]

Leaving aside for a moment the fascinating philosophical quandary of how a monolingual person can think in a multilingual way, let me précis the author's advice: *the best advertising for any overseas market is the literal translation of a basic, formal, bookish, expressionless, non-technical, and humorless English text.*

Presumably, the author is not recommending that we adopt the same techniques for developing domestic advertising.

From another book: "Always make sure you have a native speaker check over the translations before you publish them"; "always make sure your translator is properly qualified" is another such gem from an equally respected source.

What *are* these people talking about, I wonder?

Translating advertising copy is like painting the tip of an iceberg and hoping the whole thing will turn red: what makes copy work is not the words themselves, but subtle combinations of those words, and most of all the echoes and repercussions of those words within the mind of the reader. These are precisely the subtleties which translation fails to convey. Advertising is not made of words, but made of culture.

Translating copy is like boiling lettuce. No matter how carefully you do it, the result is always disappointing. And you can call it what you like—I hear people using words like adaptation, transcreation, transculturation, transliteration,[2] even the spectacularly inelegant *transadaptation*—just as you can poach, scald, sear, or steam your lettuce, but it's still a culinary felony and it's still not going to make anyone's mouth water.

Translating copy is like picking fruit from one tree and trying to glue it onto the branches of another. The fruit will wither and eventually rot, and anyway, even if a miracle happened and you could find a way of grafting the living fruit onto the branches, the fruit would still be growing on the wrong tree, and nobody in their right mind would want to pick it and eat it.

Translation is like washing your socks on the wrong program—somehow, when they come out at the end of the cycle, the colors are fainter, they don't really fit you any more, and you might as well just throw them away and buy a new pair.

Enough silly metaphors. It's easy enough to show how little translation actually achieves. Take even the simplest, most basic of concepts: a cup of coffee. Surely, you might think, this can be simply translated from one language to another—after all, it's not a subtle piece of sophisticated creative writing. A dictionary will confirm that "a cup of coffee" can be directly translated into its precise equivalent in any language on the planet—for example, "una tazza di caffè" in Italian. What could be simpler?

"A cup of coffee . . ."

Nothing, except that it's not the same thing at all: "a cup of coffee," if you're British, means a half-pint mug filled with equal quantities of lukewarm dishwater, instant coffee granules, and sugar.

"Una tazza di caffè" is a different thing altogether: a tiny cup with a couple of spoonfuls of *espresso* — it's taken at different times, for different reasons, it tastes and smells different, and it's marketed differently.

(Actually, *una tazza di caffè* is something which Italians seldom say in normal speech: coffee exists quite happily outside its container in the Italian language, and a more natural translation of "a cup of coffee" would be "un caffè": in other words, "a coffee," which in turn would sound slightly unnatural if we said it in British English. The reason it's more likely to be heard in American English is probably connected with the strong influence of Italian and other European languages on American speech.)

The things you're actually saying are made of culture: words are just the way you say them, and fixing the language without fixing the culture is a very dangerous game to play — it's merely scratching the surface of a very deep mystery.

In fact, as people continue to beat their heads against the brick wall of translation, perhaps the most serious danger is that they will actually succeed. In the unlikely event of somebody finally managing to achieve the "perfect translation" of a piece of advertising, they might well find themselves in far deeper water than they expect, because of the expectations this degree of linguistic competence will raise in the mind of the reader.

Let me explain. If you get both your language and your cultural references wrong, people may well forgive you, because you sound like a foreigner, so they're not surprised if you say things which are kind of foreign too. But if you learn to speak like a local yet are still uttering foreign sentiments, you run a far greater danger: you may well kill your brand's chances in that country for years to come. Saying the wrong things in the right language is simply making it easier for consumers to understand how little you understand them.

A WORD ABOUT GRAMMAR

But perhaps ignorance on this difficult subject is understandable. Most people's formative experience of foreign languages was failing to learn one at school, where their sentences came back to them marked in red pencil as Right or Wrong. This was apparently because Spanish and German and other foreign languages had something called *grammar*, which of course most native speakers believe that English doesn't have. These other languages also had literally thousands of things called *verbs*, which were so difficult to remember that even foreigners didn't always get them right.

They naturally ended up with the idea that foreign copy and English copy are fundamentally different things. Writing a piece of copy in English is a creative issue: there are

7

thousands of ways of doing it, it's subtle and complex, and only trained copywriters have the necessary talent and experience. But when it gets translated for another market, it gets relegated from the creative department to the production department—and suddenly it's either right or wrong.

So when faced with the need to convert text into another language, people tend to believe that the safest thing to do is ask the translator to change the words as little as possible, and stick to a precise, correct translation. After all, the original copy works. Why change it?

This is in fact *the most dangerous thing you can do.* In the minefield of foreign languages and cultures, there is one certainty: sticking closely to the original text can only make things worse. But for people who don't know any languages, this is like telling them that the only way out of that minefield is by avoiding the path: it's neither helpful nor reassuring.

The reality is that advertising copy can never and should never be translated. This is surely one of the most important facts to learn when planning an international campaign: advertising copy can only be *written.*

A WORD ABOUT TRANSLATORS

In any case, the people who do translation for a living are usually academic linguists, and know nothing about the art of persuasion or the science of marketing. Quite apart from the fact that merely translating the words of an advertisement is ignoring its marketing function and consequently depriving it of its power to actually achieve anything, it almost certainly won't even sound like an ad either.

Asking translators to produce advertising copy, "because they do words," is like Pope Julius II going to his local firm of builders and asking them to decorate the ceiling of the Sistine chapel, "because they do paint." It's all very well for him to suggest they use some nice bright colors, go easy on the whitewash, perhaps put in a couple of scenes featuring the creation of man, the last supper, stuff like that, but it doesn't alter the fact that he's basically giving the brief to the wrong people.

Translation, no matter how carefully or competently it's done, and even when it's done by copywriters and called fancy names, simply never sounds like free writing: it always rings slightly false, it has a faint odor of foreignness about it which is anathema to successful selling and brand-building. Translated copy is copy with all its vital strengths removed: its slickness, self-confidence, dynamism, internal rhythm, intimacy, fluency, and persuasiveness. It has lost its sense of *purpose,* which is practically the only thing which will make people read it.

Translation is something you do when a valuable *text* needs to be made accessible to speakers of another language, and it is a process which aims above all to respect the sanctity of that original text: so poets translate poetry and novelists translate novels, but when translating, their first duty is to preserve as far as possible the integrity of the original author's words.

But advertising, unlike literature, is a primarily *functional* form: it has a definite commercial purpose, which is to communicate brand values and sell products. So attempting to preserve the text that was used to achieve this function in

". . . and mind you don't splash paint on my nice clean altar-cloth."

one culture defeats the point of the exercise: the point is to re-enact the *function*, not reproduce the *form*.

Unlike translation, copywriting is quite an *easy* thing to do: or rather, if you're any good at it at all, that's because it comes easily to you. You have a brief and a blank sheet of paper in front of you, and the freedom to express yourself as you wish. Once you've cracked the basic concept, you've pictured your target properly and you're familiar with the product, you just do the thing which comes most naturally to you, and write.

But if the piece of blank paper is replaced by the completed work of another copywriter, especially if it's written in another language, it messes with your mental processes in the most extraordinary way. You start to write things you wouldn't normally write. You find yourself constructing sentences in a strange and unfamiliar manner, just to accommodate the different thought patterns of another writer. It takes far longer to finish. You find yourself agonizing over how you would have expressed something which somebody else has expressed but which, in all probability, you would never have expressed at all if you'd had the choice. Naturally, you can change that thought or eliminate it altogether, but by this point all your fluidity and confidence and surefootedness—fragile qualities at the best of times—have abandoned you.

And if it's that hard to write, you can be sure it'll be hard to listen to or read. It'll sound like what it is: something cobbled together by a committee, and, for the reader or listener, a very bumpy ride indeed. The end result is that most consumers will sample the first sentence, register that there is no single, clear, authoritative voice addressing them here, and turn the page or flip the channel.

Advertising works when consumers believe they are being spoken to by somebody who understands them. Somebody who knows their needs, and talks and feels just as they do. Not a foreigner speaking to them with a phrase-book in front of his or her face.

A Word about Targeting

And of course there's more to the matter than just culture and style: advertising is so intimately linked with the social fabric, the laws, the advertising conventions, the buying habits, the aspirations, the sense of decency, the sense of humor, the mentality of a people, that without the weapon of free writing, creating advertisements becomes a doomed task.

There's an obvious point which is often overlooked by less experienced exporters and agencies, too: your brand's market position may well be different, whether you like it or not. A product may be brand leader in the States but unknown in Denmark. It may be unique in New Zealand but a me-too brand in Germany. It may appeal to a social group in Britain which simply doesn't exist in Peru. It will *certainly* be a domestic product in its country of origin and a foreign product everywhere else.

All these conditions inevitably dictate important differences in the way the advertising message is structured and expressed—just as they should form a key part of your entry strategy for that market, so your advertising communications should be given total liberty to cater for them. To allow this leeway for appropriate expression is nothing more than simple pragmatism; when planned for in advance, with proper analysis of the culture of the market, it is elevated to the level of strategy; to fail to allow for it is to perpetuate and amplify the error of the "naïve rule" of exporting.[3]

The only way to produce effective, distinctive and creative copy for any market is to brief a skilled copywriter from that market to *write* the thing from brief in his or her own language, ideally with no reference whatsoever to existing copy in other languages.

This doesn't mean that the work needs to be fundamentally different in each market, or that there's no such thing as a coherent and consistent international campaign. On the contrary, international campaigns can work very well—

indeed, as we shall see, they can work in ways which are far more powerful than campaigns which don't face the challenge of a transcultural journey—but what makes them successfully and intelligently coherent is adhering to a consistent *idea* whilst writing in a consistent *tone* from a consistent *brief* in order to present a consistent *brand image*, rather than clinging slavishly to one culture-specific form of words.

The words inevitably change, and it doesn't matter: they are merely an executional detail. Having the courage to let go of the words concentrates the mind wonderfully on the crucial question of what we actually want to say about the product, rather than wasting our time fretting about how to say it in languages we don't speak.

And finally, the reality is that people tend to read less and less, especially in mass-media consumer environments, and in the couple of milliseconds of his or her precious time which the average consumer is prepared to consecrate to the average ad, there simply isn't time to start delving into a mountain of words. If the bulk of the message isn't communicated visually, there's precious little chance it will get through, so agonizing over the correctness of the words rather than the correctness of the visual and cultural language shows fundamentally misplaced priorities (and a good deal of wishful thinking besides).

A WORD ABOUT BACKTRANSLATIONS

If you're responsible for what a piece of copy is saying, but unfortunately you don't know what it means because it's written in a language you don't understand, it's perfectly natural for you to try to find out. At first glance, it may sound as if a backtranslation is exactly what you need.

Phil Ray, the British copywriter, once told me a story about backtranslations which, I think, proves the riskiness of this assumption rather well.

In India, several hundred different languages and dialects are spoken, so any national campaign has to appear in quite a number of them. Whilst working in India, Phil once wrote an ad in English for Horlicks, a bedtime malted milk drink, and it was based around the idea that during the night, you get very hungry, except that because you're asleep, you don't know about it. Horlicks dubbed this perilous condition *night starvation*. Obviously, with such a powerful marketing idea, you hardly need to worry about creative trickery in the copy, so the headline simply read *Horlicks prevents night starvation.*

The ad was duly sent off to be translated into Urdu, Hindi, Tamil, Gujerati, and all the rest of them. Since he didn't know any of these languages, and he was anxious that the thought had been properly expressed, Phil thought it would be a good idea to get some other speakers of these languages to backtranslate the copy into English. Most of them came back with a rendition which more or less approximated to *Horlicks prevents night starvation,* apart from the Tamil, which read *twenty men asleep under a tree.*

If you're expecting me to explain how this happened, forget it. Even if I knew, which I don't, it would probably take six pages. But the point is a very simple one: there are usually at least fifteen or twenty different ways in which you can translate a simple sentence from one language into another, depending on your precise reading of the sentence, the shades of emphasis you give to each part of the concept, the tone of voice you use, the type of language, the linguistic style, the degree of grammatical correctness, the level of prolixity or brevity, the choice of simplicity or sophistication, and so forth. And with languages as different as English and Tamil, many of the *concepts themselves* may be entirely untransferable except in the most approximate way.

And once this is done, translating it back into the original language involves just as many choices all over again, so the total number of possible variations probably ends up in the thousands.

Which is just another way of saying that although backtranslation *looks* like a sensible precaution to take, and a relatively simple way of checking that nothing awful has happened to your copy, it really doesn't help too much. At best, it can merely tell you *what* each sentence says, not *how* or *why*, and these are considerations which, in creative writing, are often far more important. It may save you the trouble of looking up each word in the dictionary, but is absolutely no substitute for understanding the language and seeing the copy in the context of its new target culture.

Once you start getting into the process of "checking" foreign work, things can quickly get out of control. Some people go to quite extraordinary lengths in their attempts to make the whole translation process less opaque to the monolingual, and end up making it literally impenetrable: consider, if you will, the following excerpt from that excellent book, *Marketing across Cultures*, by Jean-Claude Usunier:

> The back-translation technique (Campbell & Werner, 1970) is the most widely employed method of reaching translation equivalence (mainly lexical and idiomatic) in cross-cultural research. This procedure helps to identify probable translation errors. One translator translates from the source-language into a target language. Then another translator, ignorant of the source language text, translates the first translator's target language text back into the source language. The two source-language versions are compared . . . Parallel and back-translation can be merged . . . When the two languages and cultures present wide variations, such as Korean and French, combining parallel and back-translation provides a higher level of equivalence (Marchetti and Usunier, 1990). For example (Usunier, 1991), two Koreans translate the same French questionnaire F into two Korean

versions, K1 and K2. A third Korean translator, who is unfamiliar with the original French text F, translates K1 and K2 into F1 and F2. A final Korean questionnaire K3, is then prepared by comparing the two back-translated French versions, F1 and F2. English is used to help compare them, as it is widely used and more precise than either French or Korean. This example could be refined: the number of parallel translations may be increased, or back translation processes may be independently performed. A more sophisticated solution to the problem of translation has been suggested by Campbell and Werner (1970). Research instruments should be developed by collaborators in two cultures, and items, questions or other survey materials should be generated jointly in the two cultures. After back-translation, or after any initial translation process has been performed, there is an opportunity to change the source-language wording. This technique, called decentering, not only changes the target language, as in the previous techniques, but also allows the words in the source language to be changed, if this provides enhanced accuracy. The ultimate words and phrases employed will depend on which common/similar meaning is sought in both languages simultaneously, without regard to whether words and phrases originate in the source or the target languages. . . . In any case, it remains absolutely necessary to pretest the translated research instrument in the target culture until satisfactory levels of reliability on conceptual and measurement equivalences are attained.[4]

I rest my case. Even though, to be fair, the above passage relates to research questionnaires (where translation is arguably an unavoidable part of the process), rather than creative work, it graphically and scarily demonstrates the importance of avoiding translation like the plague, for, as Shakespeare put it, "that way madness lies."

FLUENCY AND BILINGUALISM

The reality is that even if you know another language well, you only actually "touch" your mother tongue. I speak French and Italian fluently, sometimes well enough to be able to convince French and Italian people that I'm French or Italian too (at least for the first half of the evening), yet I'm always conscious when speaking or reading or especially writing those languages that I am dealing in a currency which can never be entirely my own. I feel like one of those scientists manipulating radioactive materials with asbestos gloves through a little brick wall: you can get extremely nimble at using the equipment, but the stuff you're handling is forever, frustratingly, on the other side of the wall.

Yes, there is something called bilingualism, which is rather different from extreme fluency. I have *learned* my other languages, whereas a truly bilingual person is *brought up* speaking more than one—usually because each parent has a different mother tongue. Yet even in these cases, unless the child spends equal amounts of time living in each country, has equal numbers of friends from each country, is educated for equal periods (ideally at each stage of her education) in both countries, and loves her mummy and daddy to the same degree (yes, this is crucial too, as the language of the less preferred parent may suffer a degree of subconscious rejection), then one language or another will always be slightly more "native" than the other.

Personally, when hiring creatives and especially copywriters, I avoid true bilinguals like the plague. The result of their perfectly split cultural and linguistic mechanisms often means that they have slightly less than 100% mastery of both, and they come over as being ever so slightly foreign whichever language they're speaking or writing.

Fortunately for them, the human brain has ample capacity for multiple languages, so bilingual people are far more than 50% fluent in each, but their allegiances are quite definitely divided.

A WORD ABOUT DISASTERS

When I speak at conferences on international advertising and marketing topics, I've often noticed an interesting phenomenon. It seems that whenever thinking people foregather and talk about these things, they always feel impelled to tell frightful stories about things going wrong.

Trouble is, they're always the same stories. If I had a dollar for every time I'd heard that story about how "Come alive with Pepsi" (or was it "The choice of a new generation"?) turned out meaning "Brings your ancestors back from the dead" in Chinese, why, by now I'd have about $27.

And it's such a half-witted story, anyway. The person who did the translation was obviously either a complete idiot or else working undercover for Coke. I mean, if he was sufficiently sentient to understand his own language, how come he didn't *notice* what he'd just written?

The same applies to Disaster Story 327b (It takes a tough man to make a tender chicken / it takes an aroused man to make a chicken happy); 228 (The ideal ink to prevent embarrassment / the ideal ink to prevent pregnancy); 138 (It's finger-licking good / so good it makes you want to eat your fingers); 124a (Body by Fisher / Corpse by Fisher); and on, and on, and on.

By the way, the numbers are catalog references from my vast private collection of disaster stories: I hear so many of them, I began collecting them years ago, much against my better judgement. I collect them with the same gloomy fascination as a burglar collects antique handcuffs.

I don't want to seem humorless, and I really do understand the attraction of disaster stories: to prove it, I'm putting one at the beginning of every chapter of this book, as a kind of *memento mori*, rather as Victorian scholars would place a skull on their desk lest they forget their own mortality. I frequently succumb to the temptation to tell them at conferences, too: but for me, the really interesting ones are those which prove that culture is actually more dangerous than language, and those are the ones I've chosen as chapter-headings.

These are the stories from which we can *learn* something, rather than fruitlessly quiver in our boots lest the same thing happen to us: they teach us valuable lessons about the real, profound challenges of international communications, rather than simply reiterating the empty truism that translation is a minefield.

A WORD ABOUT FEAR

It is interesting, though, that we all feel the need to tell each other these dreadful tales. It seems that there's no shortage of writers and conference speakers who are happy to tell you what *not* to do in international advertising, but very little advice that's actually any use.

I suppose it's because the emotion most commonly associated with performing acts of international commerce is fear: fear of the unknown. And the most frightening aspect of international commerce is almost certainly language.

There can be few things more alarming than being faced with another human being with whom one cannot communicate: not speaking a common language is like being suddenly struck deaf and dumb. And written communication is scarcely any better: someone hands you a sheet of paper covered in strange characters, and when you send it off to the relevant local office to have it translated, you're not even sure if you're feeding it backwards into the fax machine.

Some people mind this more than others, it has to be said. I often find that the people who are most highly-rated as international business practitioners are simply the ones with the thickest skins—they've often acquired their reputation because they've learned how to "deal with foreigners." Their behavior is characterized by a boisterous refusal to admit that national differences are anything more than polit-ical machinations on the part of disaffected country managers who weren't smart enough to land a proper job at headquarters.

These hardened cases get things done because they ride roughshod over other people's cultures. In a just world, they would be incarcerated in windowless rooms until they had read and taken extensive notes on the entire works of Geert Hofstede and Fons Trompenaars (two writers I shall mention again in the next chapter).

This global superiority complex—"I must be right because I'm the only one here who's not foreign"—is more commonly found amongst citizens of nations that have, or have had, global influence: Britain, France, and America are examples which spring readily to mind.

The British disease is imperial cockiness gone way past its sell-by date—a thick, ugly crust of superiority incompletely masking a howling, burning nugget of abject inferiority. It's the fatal combination of ignorance and arrogance: we think we know everything, and so will never learn anything.

Personally, for as long as I can remember, I've always experienced the most agonizing cocktail of humiliation, fear, and embarrassment when I travel to countries where I don't speak the language. The fact that my mother tongue, English, is so often egregiously well spoken in so many of these countries only adds to my sense of shame. But I'm probably just weird.

This sudden inability to communicate strikes at the very heart of our self-confidence, our ability to do business, our ability to do anything at all except gesture hunger, tiredness, thirst. It has the power to reduce your average Senior Vice-President of Global Marketing, who back home in the States could eat six brand managers before breakfast, to the level of a helpless babe—depending on the thickness of his or her skin, of course. No wonder so much international business gets delegated to junior people.

The reference to the Senior Vice-President of Global Marketing is not a casual one. I refer to an unforgettable episode from my agency days, which took place when I was traveling around Europe with a very senior client of mine, visiting his numerous marketing offices.

During the second week of our trip, we arrived early in Lisbon for our meeting with the Portuguese Country Manager, and so decided to stop in a bar for a cup of coffee. It seemed only natural that the Senior Vice President of Global Marketing should order the coffee, so I kept respectfully silent as he summoned the waitress. This diminutive woman (five foot nothing, but utterly sure of her station in life) was clearly piqued by his imperious manner, and decided that she didn't speak any English.

My client didn't speak any Portuguese, and I watched in fascination as this splendid man, one of the most impressive and self-confident individuals I have ever met (not to mention one of the tallest), quickly discovered that he was *completely unable to communicate,* and was as a helpless infant in the hands of one rather short Portuguese waitress, simply because she wielded the weapon of language and he didn't.

In the end she disappeared for twenty minutes before sauntering back to our table and slamming down a cheese sandwich, two vodka martinis, a lump of quince jelly, and a losing ticket for the previous week's lottery draw. The check, it goes without saying, was epically inflated, and I noticed for the first time that my client wasn't actually *that* much taller than me.

Perhaps because language is the first and most alarming of the barriers we encounter when we travel with our brands, it is often perceived to be the principal barrier. Wrong. It's merely the first of many, and in several respects it's actually the simplest one of the lot.

A WORD ABOUT HIPPOPOTAMI

Here is the tip of an iceberg, representing the dangers of language. Language, like the tip of the iceberg, is the bit you can see, and from that point of view it's a very simple phe-

The tip of the iceberg.

nomenon: it's difficult to get it right, but at least you know when you get it wrong.

In fact, you can be certain that the instant you get it wrong, you will hear from simply dozens of helpful individuals pointing out exactly how, where, and when you got it wrong, and just how foolish you now look for making such an elementary mistake.

There's very little complexity here. Ship bumps into iceberg, ship sinks. Company translates brochure wrongly, brochure is not understood. Soft drinks company translates slogan clumsily into Chinese, sentence in Chinese implies something unfortunate.

And the body of the iceberg represents culture. I forget what the exact proportions are with icebergs, but much of its bulk lies below the waterline, and this is the case with culture too.

I feel I ought to apologize for using icebergs as metaphors, since they have become as commonplace as disaster stories about Pepsi-Cola on the conference and training circuits: fortunately, I have an alternative metaphor up my sleeve.

A friend once told me that in certain African languages, they don't talk about the tip of the iceberg: what they say is *the ears of the hippopotamus*. I think this is a perfectly delightful expression, and of course very logical: after all, you don't see too many icebergs in Africa, or hippos in Iceland for that matter.

"The ears of the hippo" is also a better metaphor for the dangers of separating language and culture: one can imagine a confident brand owner going for a walk along the banks of the Zambezi. He or she spots these cute pink ears twitching

Disneylike above the water and cheerfully dives in for a swim, only to discover too late that they are attached to a large and dangerous beast.

The image of the hippo instills a proper sense of respect in all of us who have to deal with him. The iceberg, after all, is just a dumb lump of cold stuff. It sits there in the water without moving around too much, and so long as you avoid the hours of darkness and Hollywood scriptwriters, you can usually steer around it.

The hippo, on the other hand, is aggressive, unpredictable, and voracious. Just like culture, if you give him half a chance, he will *come and get you.*

A WORD ABOUT NAMES

Of course, no discussion about international marketing disasters would be complete without a glance at all the product names which ended up meaning something awful in another language. Some of them are true gems, and I will tell you a few, but it's worth pointing out that the one thing these are *not* is translation errors (they are usually errors caused by a *failure* to translate), or even terribly interesting cultural gaffes: in my opinion, they are shining examples of incompetent business practice.

After all, failing to research something as crucial as the name of your product in the relevant marketplace before you launch it is staggeringly idiotic behavior, and these companies deserve all the humiliation they get.

One of the best sources of ghastly names is cars: for some reason, there are literally dozens of automobile names in the annals of global shame.

Some are quite boring: the Rolls Royce "Silver Mist." *Mist* means dung in German. And the one *everybody* knows is the Chevrolet Nova. In Spanish, *no va* means "it doesn't go." Big deal. These are the brand-name equivalents of *brings your ancestors back from the dead*, and they have an extremely high "so what" factor.

But some are more noteworthy: there was the AMC Matador, which ran into trouble when they launched it in South America. Now, you might think (as AMC did), that since Matador is a Spanish name anyway, meaning "Bullfighter," you don't have any problems there. But you do, because "matador" in Spanish doesn't just mean bullfighter: that's "torero." Out of context, "matador" simply means *killer*. Pure and simple: "Daddy, will you buy me a killer for Christmas?"

This one is also pretty well known, it's true, but I find it interesting trying to reconstruct how such an accident might have come about—I think you'll agree that it's almost inconceivable that a major auto manufacturer could be so foolish as to launch a car in a country without asking *one single native speaker* what the name actually meant before they pushed the button which started the production line and stuck the badge on 56,000 cars costing $30,000 each.

The interesting thing is, they probably *did* ask a Spanish speaker, who probably *did*, quite correctly, assure them that *matador* does mean "bullfighter." The question they probably asked was *"matador* does mean bullfighter, doesn't it?"* to which the correct answer is "yes." But this was the wrong question: what they should have asked was "should we call this car *matador*?", to which the only correct reply would have been "no."

And then the curious case of the Mitsubishi Pajero, and this is one I simply can't begin to figure out. Look up the word *pajero* in a Spanish dictionary. Nothing to do with cars at all. *Pajero* is an extremely vulgar word used to denote somebody who masturbates; in some parts of the Spanish-speaking world it is used to mean a liar, and in others, a plumber. In one sense, this is all perfectly rational: after all, most of the people who drive big cars like that are either plumbers, liars, wankers, or all three at once. But I doubt that's what Mitsubishi had in mind.

And can I really be the only person who's noticed that the Ford *Focus* is really rather unfortunately named for the French market? Pronounced as a French word, it sounds exactly like *faux cul*—fake ass—and whatever you decide that means, it certainly doesn't sound very nice. And if you pronounce it as an English word, but with a strong French accent, it sounds *exactly* like somebody saying "fuck us" with a strong French accent.

In Europe, there's a Japanese car (d'you know, I believe it's another Mitsubishi) called the *Starion*. I once got stuck behind one of these things in a traffic jam, and out of boredom was trying to work out what on earth they were thinking of when they came up with this bizarre-sounding name. Was it a rather cultivated mélange of *star* and *Orion?* Suddenly, the truth hit me: this is a Japanese car, and there are two smaller models in the same range called *Pony* and *Colt.*

Get it? If not, read this sentence aloud with a Japanese accent: *"Pony, small horse. Colt, medium horse. Starion, big horse!"*

Some car manufacturers think that they can escape these perils by using meaningless combinations of numbers and letters instead of proper model names. But if it's written in your destiny that you will commit a gaffe, then the gaffe will find you. The Toyota MR2 needed to be renamed in France because if you say it quickly, *emme-erre-deux* sounds just like *merde.* (In England, they call it *Mister Two* but Toyota don't seem to mind that). The Alfa Romeo 164 is called the 168 in Hong Kong because if you read out the number 164 in Cantonese, *yut luk say,* it sounds like *yut lo say,* meaning "death all the way." (168—*yut lo bat*—is read as *yut lo fat:* "prosperity all the way"). And a Saab model is known as the 900SE, which, in Saab typeface, reads "goose," as plain as your nose: not a brilliant image for a manufacturer which spent years pointing out that it makes cars the same way it makes supersonic jet fighters.

Personally, I'm really getting fed up with cars named after horses and strong winds, and mock-Italian names. [Except when they go wrong, of course: there's a comical

Audubon on the Autobahn.

duo of Asian cars on the roads at the moment, very harmoniously but completely nonsensically called *Stanza* (room)
and *Piazza* (square)—presumably they're not marketed in
Italy under those names!]

In fact, using Italian or pseudo-Italian names for cars is
just about the most boring thing you can do, as the following
table shows:

MANUFACTURER	COUNTRY	NAME	ITALIAN MEANING
Austin (now Rover)	UK	Maestro	Master
Austin (now Rover)	UK	Allegro	Merry
Datsun	Japan	Stanza	Room (in a house)
Nissan	Japan	Serena	Serene
Nissan	Japan	Figaro	Opera title
Mazda	Japan	Piazza	Square (in a town)
Mitsubishi	Japan	Carisma	Charisma
Daihatsu	Japan	Cuore	Heart

Suzuki	Japan	Alto	High
Suzuki	Japan	Baleno	Lightning
Hyundai	Korea	Sonata	Ringing, Musical form
Daewoo	Korea	Leganza	≈ (Eleganza) Elegance
Ford	Europe	Mondeo	≈ (Mondo) World
Ford	Europe	Capri	Island resort
Ford	Europe	Cortina	Ski resort
Chrysler	USA	Pronto	Ready (or Spanish: soon)
Volkswagen	Germany	Palio	Siennese festival
Volkswagen	Germany	Vento	Wind
Volkswagen	Germany	Lupo	Wolf
Volkswagen	Germany	Corrado	Conrad (man's name)
Volkswagen	Germany	Scirocco	Sirocco (wind)
Mercedes	Germany	Vito	Man's name
Porsche	Germany	Targa	Plate (name of motor race)
Porsche	Germany	Carrera	Name of race-track
Opel	Germany	Corsa	Race
Aston Martin	UK	Volante	Steering wheel
Renault	France	Laguna	Lagoon
Vauxhall	UK	Astra	Star
Mitsubishi	Japan	Diamante	Diamond
Mitsubishi	Japan	Libero	Free
Mazda	Japan	Cosmo	Man's name
Mercury	USA	Capri	Island resort
Pontiac	USA	Fiero	Proud
Oldsmobile	USA	Firenza	≈ (Firenze) Florence
Acura	Japan	Integra	Whole
Chevrolet	USA	Monza	City, Race-track
Audi	Germany	Quattro	Four
Fiat	Italy	Strada[5]	Road
Plymouth	USA	Turismo	Tourism
Plymouth	USA	Volare	To fly; Italian song
Suzuki	Japan	Cappuccino	Milky coffee
Nissan	Japan	Largo	Wide
Toyota	Japan	Sera	Evening

Toyota	Japan	Corsa	Race
Toyota	Japan	Carina	(She's) sweet
Toyota	Japan	Caldina	(She's) a little bit hot

I remember reading somewhere that as many as 50% of all new brands in Japan are now named after Italian towns and rivers, although this has probably more to do with the glamour of European-sounding names, the fact that Italian words are not too hard for Japanese consumers to pronounce (like Japanese words, Italian words almost invariably end with vowels), and the musical sound of the language, rather than any strict association with Italian brand values.

This obsession that cars have to have something Italian about them is symptomatic of a general tendency to ascribe certain clichés to countries and their cultures, and then use that cliché as a branding tool. It's a very powerful tool, but like all tools, it can be used clumsily and destructively, or it can be used with great delicacy, originality and effectiveness. This is a subject I'll talk about in more detail in the next chapter.

On the whole, it's dull being like everybody else, and I applaud the manufacturers who have the courage to really stand out from the crowd, and name their products according to a different set of conventions. What those conventions might be is frankly anybody's guess, but the Japanese are terribly good at it, and with the sole exception of the Volkswagen *Rabbit,* they own the genre. Some of my favorites are the Mitsubishi *Fuso Fighter* (particularly comical, this one, because *fuso* is an Italian word used to describe a piece of machinery which has become inoperative by melting down or overheating), the Mazda *Bongo Browny,* the Nissan *Swingroad* (a car with excellent road-holding, I'm sure), the Nissan *Vanette Escargo* (not slow at all, and bears the same relation to a *Vanette Escargot* as a Porsche Turbo does to a Porsche Turbot).

Actually, Nissan have rather a special talent for this game: they also have a *Cedric,* a *Racheen,* a *Homy,* and, most spectacularly, the incomparable *Supreme Pantry-boy Deluxe* (sadly only available in Japan at present).

I think it's about time some European and American manufacturers spotted the limitless potential of weird names, and followed the *Rabbit*. I can picture this approach spreading rapidly worldwide, and a sparkling host of radically-named models in years to come: the BMW 9.7 Fishcake Deluxe, the Ford Pustule, the Rover Anabolic Steroid V8 Coupé, the Pontiac Ptarmigan Gti, the Alfa Romeo Tagliatelle alla Romana Super Sport.

One could go on *ad nauseam* about product names. I do have a small personal collection of comically-named products which forms an appendix to my disaster story archive — the air-freshener from Thailand called *Arsole*, the boiled candies for soccer-mad kids in Italy called *Dribbling* — but it's laboring a very minor point.

Somebody once told me that if you say *Wrigley's Spearmint Gum* it sounds spookily like the Latvian for "shark's sperm." With all these stories, it's difficult to know (without wasting weeks of one's life on futile research) where reality ends, and where modern myths, Chinese whispers, local politics, or pure fantasy start.

I mention local politics because these scare stories are often perpetrated by people who work for the same company that owns the brand, and they are a potent weapon. After all, if I was your Estonian marketing manager and I told you that your latest slogan was strongly suggestive of the Estonian for gang-rape involving moose, you'd probably believe me. Wouldn't you?

Nothing at all to do with the fact that I would rather you gave me some proper local budget so I could hire a proper local agency, create some proper Estonian advertising that people will actually understand, and make a proper career for myself as a proper marketing director rather than a glorified fax machine linked to Head Office. Nothing either to do with the fact that my knowledge of my language and my culture is the only piece of influence you've left me with, so I'm going to use it against you for all I'm worth.

Fact is, there's a bit too much of this disaster stuff around already: for some reason, people keep on e-mailing me the same (or very similar) lists of assorted translation errors and disastrous brand names which they've dredged up from the web—the same sad collection of linguistic shame which will probably continue swirling endlessly round certain back-waters of the internet until the end of time, like non-biodegradable plastic bottles trapped in eddies of dirty water under the end of Brighton pier. Perhaps they will now stop doing this.

A WORD ABOUT SMARTER NAMING

And, lest all this sound pointlessly destructive and critical, I hasten to add that there *is* a much better way of creating international brand names, which not only eliminates the possibility of Pajero-style disasters, but also brings the power of cultural sensitivity and linguistic sensitivity to bear on this much-misunderstood strategic and creative process.

If you look at the way that international brand-names are commonly created, it won't come as much of a surprise to find that most of them were never meant to travel in the first place—a domestic product may have existed quite happily for years until its owner suddenly decided to export it, and only then discovered that its name had undesirable connotations in other languages.

This is certainly the case with many of the disaster names described earlier in this chapter—indeed, some of them, like *Arsole* and *Dribbling*, not to mention (which I didn't) the French soft drinks *Pschiit!* and *Sic*, the Japanese toilet paper *Krappy*, and the drink *Pocari Sweat*, are hardly ever seen outside their home markets, where, it is presumed, they make perfect sense: so laughing at them is really rather unfair.

It won't come as a surprise either to learn that most of the brand names which are devised specifically for the international market are created using methods which closely approximate the way that international advertising campaigns are generated: the creative work is done by a "lead" agency in the "lead" country in the "lead" language, and the international bit is very much an afterthought.

Whoever is doing the work (most brand names are created by specialist companies—brand naming agencies, corporate identity specialists, design companies and branding consultancies—or by the client's advertising agency, or by the client company itself), the way in which the issue of other markets is addressed is depressingly familiar to anyone who knows the workings of international ad agencies.

What generally happens is that a single, monocultural creative team (or sometimes a computer program) in the lead market generates a large number of "raw" names, from which they pick a shortlist of favorites which seem to answer the brief most effectively. These are then "disaster-checked" by the naming agency's own international affiliates or by some other method, to ensure that they don't mean anything too awful in any other languages.

Now, the chances of the chosen names not meaning, looking like, sounding like or in any way resembling any other word in any other language are extremely slight (especially since there is currently a tendency to try to make all international brand names look like Latin or Italian), so this stage of the process will very often eliminate the shortlist completely. It will certainly remove quite a few of the best names.

So the agency has to go back to its "longlist" and pick some more, and disaster-check these, and so it goes on. Finally, there is a shortlist of names which doesn't mean anything too awful in too many other languages, and that has to go forward for legal checks—which usually eliminates this shortlist, because lots of companies with similar products have trodden this way before now, and registered all the most appropriate and internationally-safe names, so it's back to the longlist once again.

By the time a name is chosen and registered, it has usually come from so far down the original longlist, it's a minor miracle if anybody likes it at all.

But more to the point, its only international credentials are that it *doesn't mean anything bad* in any other languages than the original language, which is usually English. The question of whether it might actually mean something good, or indeed convey anything whatsoever, is hardly raised. That would really make the whole process far too complicated, wouldn't it?

The fact is that almost all brand names need to have some meaning to them, even the ostensibly "meaningless" ones. Of course, it's now virtually impossible to register real words as brandnames (either because they're already taken or because they're not considered sufficiently distinctive to be trademarkable), but even the most abstract coinings have some etymology, some reference-point.

And because this etymology must come from one language or another, and English is the best global lingua-franca we have, the result is that many of the international brand names in the world are moderately amusing or interesting in English and convey almost nothing in any other of the 100 or so major languages which are spoken by over 95% of the world's population: ThinkPad, 4Runner, Snapple, Baygon, Microsoft, Cornflakes, Frosties, Ray-Ban, Pop Tarts, Weight Watchers, DeskJet, NutraSweet, Duracell, Eveready, Maxfli, Dream-Works, and so on, are all names which are more or less completely mysterious to most people on this planet. Most continental Europeans I know believe that the Nissan *Patrol* is called by that name because it runs on gasoline (*petrol*) rather than Diesel. What's more, many of them are hard to pronounce, hard to spell and hard to remember if English doesn't happen to be your native language—they cause the same level of embarrassment and anxiety as asking for a product with a difficult French name does for most Americans.

While I'm on the subject, I really must have a little moan about a naming convention which American English is forcing upon the rest of the world: what I call TrainCrash words. TrainCrash words are formed when two words collide, and a capital letter is left sticking up in the middle of the wreckage like an upended locomotive. Almost every software package on the market has a TrainCrash name, thanks to MicroSoft and the pervasive influence of its creator, BillGates.

(Actually, having said this, I realize that Microsoft actually *don't* use very many TrainCrash words for their own products these days—in fact, if you type the word Microsoft with a capital "S" in the middle, as I just did, Microsoft Word's spellchecker will fussily correct it for you.)

I believe that I may be the first person to propose an etymology for the TrainCrash phenomenon, so please bear with me for a moment. This is important.

When the first big waves of Italian immigrants began to arrive in the United States in the nineteenth century, many had compound surnames, made of a partitive article plus their family name or birthplace (like Mario della Femmina or Antonio di Capri or Maria de' Curtis), which the primitive data processing equipment in use on Ellis Island was unable to cope with.

This was because these names had *spaces* in them, and the punchcard system suffered from the same bug as MS-DOS. Remember MS-DOS? If you tried to insert a space into a filename, the whole thing would crash, and you'd end up with a permanently unreadable, unaccessible, undeletable, unfindable file. So the immigration authorities began to *join up* the multiple surnames, but left a capital letter in the middle to show what they'd done: so della Rosa became DellaRosa, de' Vitis became DeVitis, and di Maggio became DiMaggio. And *that's* why American spelling has always had a weakness for these semi-Siamese words. Or at least, that's my theory.

Thank you for your attention.

IT'S ONLY A NAME, AFTER ALL

I won't go into detail about how to make better international brand names, because the creative principles are exactly the same as with advertising campaigns, and I'll be discussing this in depth in Chapters 6 and 7.

Suffice to say that using a genuinely international creative team to brainstorm the original "longlist" makes a huge difference: you get more "raw" names, because of the infinitely larger lexical stock which all of those different native languages bring to the mix; the needs of the speakers of those languages are considered at the start of the process rather than treated as a mere disaster-check, so there's a real chance of coming up with a name which might actually *convey* something in more than one language; and you don't lose 95% of your best work through language clashes, because that part of the filtering process is continuous throughout the process.

In the end, though, a name is just a word—a combination of probably not very many letters on a piece of paper, and it's important to appreciate how much it can do and how much it can't do.

For a start, there's what I call the *disappointment factor*. A name is an extremely difficult thing to appreciate at first glance, and the first reaction to a naming proposal is very often disappointment: until the name exists, the company's mind is agreeably humming with a sense of infinite, unexplored possibilities, and the temptation, when finally presented with those few letters on a page, to exclaim "is that all?" is almost overwhelming.

Some of the most powerful brand names in the world are actually little more than empty vessels, into which one pours brand equity through the diligent application of marketing. The very *least* one requires of such a name is that it should be distinctive enough for the company to own it unequivocally and without threat of confusion with other people's brands; and that it should be reasonably useable (spellable, pro-

THE TROUBLE WITH WORDS

nounceable, memorable, etc). The name will acquire an aura
of greatness around it as a result of the successful marketing
of the product it relates to, and that will make the name itself
appear to have magical properties. But the magic you're seeing is not the vessel itself — it's the brand shining through the
vessel.

Most of the really good names in the world work rather
like this. Imagine you're Bill Bowerman, it's 1971, and
you've just paid us a large sum to invent a brandname for
your new running shoes. After weeks of secret development
work, we're finally ready to present you with our recommendation. After due ceremony, we finally hand you a piece
of paper. On it is typed the single word

NIKE

You'd probably stare at this word for a while, and then say,
"It looks like you spelt Mike wrong."

So I'd say, "Actually, it's pronounced Ni-kee," and you'd
probably say, "So it's not pronounced the way it's spelled?"

To which I'd answer, "No, because it's the name of the
ancient Greek goddess of victory," at which point you'd
probably yell, "But for crying out loud, this is meant to be a
cutting-edge youth brand and you're talking to me about
ancient Greece?"

And in a sense we're both right. You're right to be disappointed, because at this point in time, the word is entirely
worthless. I can't begin to guess, and neither can you, how
magical that little word is going to look after it's appeared on
twenty million pairs of shoes in a hundred thousand city-
center stores from Mumbai to L.A., on a hundred advertising campaigns, thousands of billboards around the world,
and on the shirts and pants and caps and socks and shoes of
half the world's greatest athletes.

Somehow, you were expecting me to present you with
one of those great brand-names like *Snickers* or *Pepsi,* and it
would *leap off the page* at you.

But brand names only leap off the page for three reasons. One, because a company has already made them famous, and nobody can ever guess that in advance just by looking at the word. Two, they're so creatively clever that you marvel at how much smartness can be crammed into just one word: and the trouble with *those* kinds of names is that they only *ever* work in one language. Three, they've just got some kind of indefinable magic, or symmetry, or harmony, or beauty about them: they just *feel* right, and that's one *thousand* percent subjective. I can absolutely guarantee that if you feel that way about it, no more than four or five in every ten people you speak to will feel the same way. Internationally, it will be far less. This isn't a good reason not to use it: but it is a thing to remember.

In the end, the only things that matter are that it feels good to you; that it means something in at least a handful of your most important markets; and that it's a good, strong, unique vessel with no holes in it, so you can start pouring in that brand value, secure in the knowledge that it's not running out at the bottom as fast as you pour it in.

A WORD ABOUT SLOGANS

The desire to translate words as closely as possible is often most acute when it comes to expressions of *corporate* rather than product-based messaging: taglines, for example, are often forced to be more similar in different languages than is really good for them.

This probably happens because something as important as a tagline has usually been wrestled with and agonized over for many months at the highest level in the corporation, and the thought of having to go through even a small part of that approval process again for every export market, *and* in foreign languages too boot, is more than most people can bear to contemplate. What's more, a company's tagline has often been around for quite a few years, and the prospect of changing it for the first time in decades, just because some upstart foreigner doesn't think it works in his language, may appear unreasonable.

So if you want your key corporate message to speak to people in their own language, where do you start? As you might have guessed, having read this far, the closest translation of a tagline is almost by definition the solution which is least likely to be effective in another language.

Take Nike's famous tagline, *Just Do It.* This sentence or epithet is, for a start, almost literally *untranslatable:* to show why, try explaining in a couple of English sentences what the precise function of "just" is in this context. Or exactly what "it" refers to (curiously, in several European languages, an unspecified "it" in a sentence like this will almost always be taken to refer to the male reproductive organ). Or who it is addressed to. Or even what the whole thing *means,* exactly. Now, none of this means it isn't a good line in English: it's brilliant. But it combines remarkably little specific *meaning* with a great deal of general *power, tone, and style.*

When Nike began to advertise seriously in Europe in the early 1990s, we advised them that this was one of the few cases where we felt it was genuinely for the best to leave the line in English wherever possible—not because it was hard to translate, but because it was so important that the line should *convey* a great deal without actually *meaning* too much, and using a foreign language like English was an excellent way of achieving this.

Sentiments expressed in a foreign language are often seen by the recipient through a misty, glamorizing veil of partial comprehension, which in the right context can be extremely good for the brand. Using English in the case of Nike also served to reinforce a very important part of the brand's pedigree in Europe—that it comes from America.

The important point to remember about using English in non-English speaking countries (or, indeed, using any language outside its home market) is that what you gain in glamour by seeming foreign, you lose in precise communication, because people's understanding of your language can only be superficial. It takes a very high level of fluency indeed before a non-native speaker can begin to read the kinds of secondary and tertiary meanings, inferences, and echoes which are such an important part of key communications like taglines. But here was a perfect example of a line which was all about glamour, and nothing to do with precise communication whatsoever.

And everything would have carried on just fine, if it hadn't been that Jacques Toubon, the French Minister for Culture, decided to pass a law in 1995 which made the use of English or any other foreign language in advertising or other public communications an offence punishable by imprisonment.

So we were presented with a rather difficult task. Here was a piece of language which seemed the quintessentially American expression of a quintessentially American thought—obviously, you wouldn't want to translate it, but executing the same brief or communicating the same brand premise in another language becomes a virtual impossibility when the brief itself is so elusive and hard to define.

If it means anything at all, *Just Do It* means *get off your ass!* More properly, it is part of the Nike philosophy: you are in charge, you are the master of your own destiny. Don't sit around talking about it, it seems to be telling us, just get out and get running. That might make it sound like a brutish, anti-intellectual, aggressive sentiment, and admittedly Nike has had its aggressive phases, especially during the success-oriented 1980s: but because it's such a gnomic, brief, and mysterious utterance, *Just Do It,* said in a different tone of voice, could also sit quite happily on the Karmic, new age, meditative work that Wieden & Kennedy were creating for some audiences (especially for European women) in the mid-1990s.

Various members of our French team at this point suggested solutions along the lines of *Passez à l'action:* move into action. The trouble is, such a sentiment just doesn't seem to have the same potential for becoming a brand mantra as *Just Do It:* it doesn't have the same depth or simplicity, or the same potential for multiple interpretations. It is mainly physical, while *Just Do It* is also emotional, moral, and spiritual: somehow, it manages to sound more like an exhortation than an imperative: perhaps it's partly the effect of that untranslatable *just*.

Using direct commands like *Just Do It* always seemed to result in aggressive-sounding lines in French, and none of our French team felt happy using imperative sentences. For a start, there are very few antecedents for this—commands had never been used much as taglines in French advertising, and although we were keen to do something new, the French needed to sound natural enough to avoid giving the impression that the extremely well-known English line had been dragged backwards through a dictionary.

Imperatives in French sound so blunt because that's not how French people normally speak to each other—*do this, do that*. No matter how we tried to do it, it sounded like an order barked out to the multitude (and remember, last time someone got into the habit of ordering the French populace around, there was a revolution).

Normally, like any polite person, a French speaker who wants somebody to do something will *ask* them to do it, rather than simply telling them—and the courteous circumlocutions can get quite elaborate: a polite request in perfectly common language, such as *est-ce que vous pourriez me donner ce livre, s'il vous plaît?* actually means *is it that you could give me this book, if it pleases you?* In English, and especially in American English, we often use direct commands but make them sound like a request or a gentle exhortation just by modifying our tone of voice. But in French, as in many other languages, the difference between a command or a request or an exhortation is more often made grammatically or syntactically, and that makes it far too long-winded for a tagline.

There was also the important consideration that in the French language, as in many languages, we also have two ways of addressing people directly: *tu* (the informal or intimate address, such as you use for speaking to a single person with whom you have some intimacy, such as a child, a lover, a close friend, or relation: the equivalent of *thou* in the English of previous centuries), and *vous* (the formal address for people you don't know so well, and for groups of people: it's rather similar in this sense to the *y'all* form used in the Southern United States — developed, perhaps, because the descendents of French settlers were missing their *vous*). Standard Modern English is relatively unusual in *not* having this distinction.

The selection of which pronoun to use is one of the first questions which a brand needs to resolve when addressing its audience in countries where the distinction exists: does it want to sound like a young person speaking intimately and informally to another young person, and run the risk of sounding careless or intrusive or childish or patronizing or rude; or does it opt for the safer, plural form, and run the risk of sounding too formal, too cold, too elderly, and distancing itself from the very people it's trying to reach out and touch? Clearly, Nike had to be a *tu* brand, because its message was from a youthful brand to a youthful consumer, and the last thing we wanted was any suggestion of formality: one of the appeals of U.S. brands like Nike to young consumers in France is that their American provenance appears to promise freedom from a world where the adults are in charge.

In the end, the factor which ultimately dictated the direction we took was an observation from one of our French team about the French character: the French are, it is often said, intellectuals by nature and by habit. Well, this may not be the literal truth about *all* French people, but they certainly do hate to be treated like fools. So what we did was to split the whole *Just Do It* argument into its component parts:

1. You are in charge of your life.
2. Therefore, if you want to change something, you can.
3. It's a case of not thinking too hard about things.
4. So just do it.

We decided to honor the intellect of our French consumers, and merely set them out on the argument, so that they could deduce the rest for themselves. This, we felt was the solution which communicated the greatest sense of *empowerment*, without seeming like a petty or detailed command for how to live your own life. So we just gave them part 1 of the argument, which came out as *Ta vie est à toi* — your life is your own.

The trouble with something as well-known yet un-pin-down-able as *Just Do It* is that everybody has their own personal idea of what it means, and they don't like it if you overlay this with something different. Most French kids have only the vaguest idea of what *Just Do It* actually means in English, but they feel they understand it, and they happily cover their scooters with stickers bearing this slogan, and if you start telling them in their own language what you think it stands for, they will probably resent it. It's a bit like when the movie of your favorite novel comes out, and suddenly all of your own internal imagery is replaced with somebody else's, and you're sitting in the cinema and you feel like standing up and shouting out loud, "What are you talking about, you idiot? She had *red* hair, not blonde, and anyway, the farm was in a *valley*, not on the top of a hill!"

This little Nike story could easily have gone on for a whole chapter, and the complexities surrounding the transfer of one tiny utterance from one culture to another might seem out of all proportion to its size and importance. (I remember that the positioning document which we produced to support our final recommendations in French was over 20 pages long.) It's just like the amount of labor which goes into creating and producing a TV commercial: we might labor for months over the idea and the script, and shoot almost enough footage to make a feature film (not to mention spending more per second than most feature films spend per minute), all for the sake of perhaps 20 seconds of finished commercial, which one could argue that most consumers won't even notice.

It's all down to the principle of *concentrated value:* the more densely you pack your message with quality, the better your chances that somebody will notice it — at least in theory. A more pragmatic reason is simply to do with competitiveness, and the never-ending arms race of quality: everybody else is doing their stuff to this standard, so you have to keep on beating them. But I do sometimes wonder where it's all going to end.

By the way, the literal translation of *Just Do It* in Italian is *fallo*, which also happens to mean (a) phallus and (b) a sporting foul. Now *there's* a disaster story waiting to happen!

A WORD ABOUT ENGLISH

It is because agonizing dilemmas like this so often occur that companies and their advertising agencies so frequently take refuge in the English language. As I write, I can think of at least 12 British and American companies which use their English-language tagline on all their international advertising, even though in many cases it must be next to incomprehensible to the vast majority of ordinary consumers in those countries.

And even if it is broadly comprehensible, that's not at all the same thing as being *fully understood, appreciated and effective.* Take Nokia's current tagline, *Connecting People,* which is currently used in all of their markets worldwide. Now, the main reason why this line gives pleasure and works well in English is because of the two ways you can read it, syntactically speaking:

1. Nokia people are in the business of connecting (*connecting* used adjectivally, so *people* becomes the subject of the phrase).
2. Nokia are connecting other people (*connecting* used verbally, so *people* becomes the object of the phrase).

And this double read gives what would otherwise be a fairly bland statement a certain depth, a certain resonance.

Now I'd be prepared to bet that less than 1% of all Nokia's consumers outside the English-speaking markets would get these two reads, even if prompted. And I mean less than 1% of those among their consumers who actually speak enough English to be able to understand those two words in the first place—so the final figure could be very small indeed.

The result? Nothing serious, nothing like *brings your ancestors back from the dead:* but what has happened is fairly typical of international advertising. The English-speaking world gets a creative line, which is clever, memorable, and intelligent; the rest of the world gets something pretty boring, and not creative or distinctive at all. Consequently, the personality of the Nokia brand has missed an opportunity to express something very important about itself to the majority of its consumers: that it's intelligent, youthful, creative, and slightly different from the usual multinational corporation.

That line, read in a one-dimensional sense by a non-native speaker of English, will get a very different message: corporate, bland, and probably American,[6] since it's speaking to us in English, and something to do with helping people to communicate. Big deal, it's a phone company, what do you expect them to do?

And so English wins yet again, whether or not people really want it or understand it. I do have some sympathy with Monsieur Toubon, and although part of me wishes that he had a nice influential pan-European job in Brussels rather than a national one in Paris, I am also well aware that I am getting close to 40, and once people get close to 40, they always start bemoaning the erosion of culture and the pollution of language, and nearly-40-year-old people have been doing this for centuries, and nothing very bad has happened yet. The only really bad thing that can happen to a language is that it dies out, and this usually happens because somebody kills all the people who speak it, not through the gentle, natural processes of linguistic evolution.

All languages are greatly enriched by the influence of loan words from other languages (indeed, much of the reason why English is such a versatile and effective language is precisely because we have welcomed so many immigrant words from other languages over the centuries). There are rather more of these around than people often imagine, as this tiny selection suggests:[7]

Arabic	Assassin, azimuth, emir, harem, mohair, sherbert, zero, bazaar, caravan
Australia	Kangaroo, boomerang, koala, wombat, dingo
Brazil	Jaguar, bossa nova, piranha
Chinese	Bamboo, tea, tycoon, kung fu
Czech	Robot, pistol
Dutch	Bluff, cruise, easel, knapsack, landscape, roster, poppycock
France	Anatomy, cellar, chocolate, crocodile, cushion, entrance, grotesque, increase, jewel, medicine, passport, precious, sergeant, trespass, sculpture, vogue
Gaelic	Slogan, loch
German	Lager, hamburger, gimmick, waltz
Greece	Anonymous, catastrophe, climax, lexicon, thermometer, tonic
Icelandic	Geyser, mumps, saga
India	Catamaran, bungalow, curry, dungaree, guru, jungle, pajamas, pundit, shampoo
Irish	Blarney, brat, whiskey
Italian	Opera, violin, mafia, balcony, fiasco, giraffe, pasta, ciao
Japanese	Bonsai, geisha, haiku, hara-kiri, karate, shogun
Latin	Altar, circus, frustrate, include, interim, legal, monk, nervous, onus, quiet, ulcer, vertigo
New Zealand	Kiwi
Norwegian	Fjord, lemming, ski, slalom
Poland	Horde, mazurka, polka
Portuguese	Cobra, molasses, marmalade, albatross
Serbo-Croat	Cravat

South & Central America	Llama, quinine, puma, poncho, coyote, tortilla, barbecue, cannibal, canoe, potato, yucca
Spain	Banana, bonanza, cork, guitar, hammock, mosquito
Turkish	Coffee, jackal, kiosk, kebab
Welsh	Penguin, corgi
Yiddish	Chutzpah, kosher, nosh, schmuck, schlemiel

As my linguistics tutor at Oxford constantly repeated to me, *don't prescribe, merely describe.* Nothing is more fair or more natural than usage: if enough speakers of a language don't find a new word useful or pleasurable, it won't stick, and if it does stick, it's because it answers a need. And thus language continues to progress.

And yet it seems to me that some nations—I'm thinking particularly of the Italians, but they're hardly the only ones—suffer just a bit too much from Groucho Marx syndrome (I'd never belong to a club that would have someone like me for a member), and all too readily assume that just because something comes from abroad, it's necessarily superior to anything Italian.

The Italians' current love-affair with the English language is reaching epidemic levels, and (with due apologies to my linguistics professor) I think it's a terrible pity. All of these ornate, complex, and beautiful Romance languages—Italian, French, Spanish, Portuguese, Catalan, Romanian—find it extremely difficult to compete with English in the modern world. In an age of speed and science, English is perfectly equipped to survive and prosper, with its minimal grammar, its vast vocabulary (probably a million words if you count all the scientific neologisms), and its simple, robust, and logical syntax. You can bark out a comprehensible English phrase in fractions of a second, and because its words are generally quite short and its rhythm broadly iambic, it also happens to work extremely well in rock music. French, Spanish, and Italian lyrics always sound decidedly squashed in the relentless 4:4 march time of all rock music—their beautiful endings tend to get uncomfortably truncated—while English is perfectly at home when it's hammered out like a typewriter or a machine-gun.

I have a copy of *Amica* open in front of me (a popular upscale women's magazine from Italy), and a quick count reveals an average of 16 English words per page inserted into the editorial (and lots in the advertising too), and for no other reason than that it is thought to sound sophisticated. *In no case* is English used because there's no proper word for the concept in Italian.

People who work in ad agencies in Italy, for example, almost never say they work in *pubblicità:* they work in *advertising,* with the "r" rolled and the emphasis cutely misplaced on the third syllable of the word. Why? Because it makes it sound more glamorous, that's why. Exactly the same thing as ratcatchers telling people that they are in pest control.

And very often, over time, the English word begins to drift free of its moorings, and take on a subtly different sense: *il feeling,* for example, means something far deeper, more profound, than it does in modern American English: it's all about chemistry between people who understand each other deeply, a mysterious, instinctive bond of friendship—fellow feeling, in fact. For ages, the Italian tagline for Heineken beer has been *C'è Heineken, c'è feeling*—(where) there's Heineken, there's feeling. But this is *feeling* in its original sense of *one more time, with feeling.*

Or else there's the English word *water,* which is used in Italian to mean a toilet (it was originally *water closet,* an obscure Victorian euphemism, but Italians are convinced that it's short for *water closed,* whatever that's supposed to mean), but the expression has become truncated over the years for the sake of brevity, and instead of dropping the less important word (water) the Italians have dropped the critical word (closet). And they've done this by analogy with their own syntax: in Italian, as with all Romance languages, the noun comes first and the modifier comes second, so where we say "The White House" or "a big dog," Italians say "The House White" and "a dog big." It's logical, therefore, to drop the first word, as the noun is always more important than the adjective, which is why you often see gas stations in Italy called "self centers"—"self service" has been truncated to "self," and added onto another loan-word, "center," and hence a new piece of Italglish is born.

When a fragment of language becomes transported from its original home, the alien culture begins to accrete around it, and it undergoes a mysterious sea-change, like a rock with strange coral growing on it, until, eventually, it takes on an entirely unrecognizable appearance. This is also why no French person has the faintest idea what we're talking about when we use the expression *déjà vu* to describe that weird sense of having experienced something before: in French, the expression simply means something tired and *passé* (another expression that's not really French at all, by the way: the French would say *dépassé*).

Hardly any language on the planet is immune from this effect (and English is by no means always the source of the borrowing). In many ways, it's a metaphor for what happens with culture: we borrow from other cultures, we modify those borrowings to suit our purposes and tastes, and thus our culture becomes more "rich and strange"—to continue Shakespeare's theme—and the process is decidedly a journey towards wealth, not poverty.

So let us never feel ashamed or guilty about sending out our brands or our advertising into the world. The process is entirely voluntary: if people find what we offer of value, they will accept it, and if not, they will reject it.

A Word about Respect

Not long ago, I was discussing a proposed pan-European mailing campaign with an American client of ours, and we were going over the different variants on the standard pack which each country would require: different response mechanisms to allow for the vagaries of each consumer culture, different payment methods to cope with numerous currencies and banking systems (at least the Euro is making this simpler), different sizes and weights to comply with the oddities of certain postal systems, and variations on the basic promotional mechanic to match legislation in each country.

When we finally came to listing the eight or more languages we would need to write the copy in, my client smiled the first smile I'd seen on her face since the meeting started, and seemed to relax a little.

"Well, at least we can simplify things here," she said, glowing with pride. "I've had my people do some research on this, and we've found that over 60% of our target group in Holland, Germany, Denmark, and Sweden speak English. So we only need to have the copy in English, French, Italian and Spanish."

But I couldn't share her relief. As I've said before, however well a person may speak a second language, each of us really only has one mother tongue—the language we dream in, think in, the language which speaks to our heart and soul. Acquired languages go to the head; they may be understood, but they don't touch us deep down inside. Even in countries like the Netherlands and Sweden, where English is rapidly becoming accepted as the standard language of the workplace, there's a big difference between your mother tongue and your boss tongue.

The second, more practical reason for advertising to people in their native tongue is that we are in a very competitive business: every time we send a message to a consumer, that message is fighting for tiny fractions of mindshare in an increasingly busy environment.

Now, even for the consumer who speaks two languages, receiving and understanding a message in her second language requires more effort and more concentration than receiving one in her native language.

So when the question comes up, *why can't we just use English?* I always ask this question: do you think that consumers should make the effort to understand us, or should we be making the effort to be understood by them?

Are we more interested in being respected, or showing respect?

If nothing else, it's a question of mere politeness: if you want this consumer to fork out hard-earned cash for your product, the least you can do is write to her in her own language. A brand that has taken the trouble to communicate with consumers in their preferred language, as decades of successful ethnic marketing in the United States have shown, is a respected and treasured brand.

Expecting a Dutch consumer to read your advertisement in a foreign language—such as English—is hardly any different from expecting him to pay for your product in dollars instead of guilders or euros. Sure, he can do it if he really wants to. But why should he want to?

And there's another very important issue here: it's very easy to forget, in an increasingly bilingual world, in which English is more often than not the second language of choice, that it is still a *foreign* language for most people, and this is not a neutral fact. Using English in marketing communications says something very specific about your brand: depending on the sophistication of your target audience, it may no longer necessarily mean that you are from North America or Britain, and it may simply imply that you're an "international" company—which is, I suppose, what Nokia hope. But using English abroad means that the use of that language changes from being a transparent, even invisible medium of ordinary communication at home to being, in and of itself, a strong statement abroad. Quite aside from anything else, in non English-speaking markets, it confirms that wherever you come from, you certainly don't come from *there*.

For brands whose provenance is already a strong element within their brand personality, the use of English in their consumer marketing will reinforce this aspect of the brand, and it's crucial to be aware of *how much*, and *in what way* this is happening. For a brand which is already perceived as "very American," using all-English advertising may push its American-ness way beyond the bounds of what is considered attractive and welcoming by its European or Asian consumers, and may start implying "I just don't care whether you understand what I'm saying or not." For a brand which is not perceived as American at all, using English may confuse consumers, and even give rise to accusations of "pretentiousness."

It's certainly true that whenever research is carried out into levels of proficiency in English, the results seem impressive, especially amongst professionals, and my client was not at all unusual in leaping to the conclusion that this effectively licensed her to use English in all of her marketing.

However, it's worth bearing in mind that people's *claimed* linguistic preference, and linguistic expertise, may well be exaggerated in research groups. After all, speaking fluent English in most business environments is a matter of pride and a matter of status, so very few people are going to admit to unfamiliarity with the language, especially in a focus-group environment, where they are likely to be surrounded by their peers. Indeed, if asked whether they prefer to be addressed in their own language or in English, many will reply "English" automatically, since this merely provides further confirmation of their professional qualities and global mindset.

Fluent English is the ultimate executive accessory in most non-English-speaking countries, and as many publishers of English-language business magazines have discovered to their surprise, significant numbers of their readers may have considerable difficulty actually reading the magazine: they simply like having it under their arm as they stride through airports.

This is, incidentally, one of the many reasons why advertising English-language products in foreign languages is not as illogical as it may sound: in fact, there are remarkably few cases where it is genuinely in the best interests of the brand *not* to advertise to consumers in their own language.

Yes, we're lucky that English is the native tongue of our brands. It does make life extremely easy for us, because it's undoubtedly a widely-spoken language. So are Chinese, Spanish, French, and Portuguese. Our good fortune is that English is also spoken by many millions of non-native speakers, which is not the case with the others.

English works very well as a lingua franca because it's exceptionally easy to get started in: owing to its extremely simple grammar (its verbs hardly conjugate, its nouns and adjectives do not decline, and there are no genders to speak of), you can learn enough English to perform basic two-way communication in a matter of weeks.

To master it is an entirely different matter, because so many of the rules of colloquial English are unwritten. In this sense, it's the opposite of German, which is extremely hard to get started but relatively simple to perfect. Learning German is like learning the violin: it's very discouraging at first, because all you can produce is ugly scratching noises, while learning English is like learning the piano: you need only minimal technique to begin experimenting with it.

But these accidents of history and philology should not fool us into thinking that coming from an English-speaking nation gives us a fast track to easy and successful international marketing.

Nothing on earth can change the fundamental principle that when you want a consumer to buy your product, that consumer is your boss. And if you only do what suits you, rather than what suits your boss, you may find that real success remains forever, mysteriously, just beyond your grasp.

So where do we start figuring out how to treat consumers right, even if we know next to nothing about them? The next chapter is all about culture, which is where our journey begins.

2

The Trouble with Culture

This is my favorite international marketing disaster story of all time: the famous and ancient Gerber story. It's almost certainly apocryphal—but, true or not, it's a wonderful parable about the mystery of culture, and it's so good I retold it in the first house ad we produced for World Writers. It goes something like this:

Gerber once decided to sell their brand of baby food in a West African country. They exported the product and ran the same copy that had been selling jars for them by the billion since 1926. They put the famous label on the jar, with the baby boy wearing a big smile which, over the years, had helped them become a household name back home.

Reports soon came back from the distributor, announcing zero sales. Later, reports came back on the national news, telling of rioting in the streets, and casualties. Worried company chiefs watching television back home in the United States thought they glimpsed people burning copies of their poster in the background.

Much later, it transpired that in many African countries, there was a very real but hitherto undocumented assumption that what you see on the label is what's in the jar. This came over to consumers as a coarse hint that the little boy, far from endorsing the product, was the product: people thought they were being expected to feed their black babies with white baby. Sensibilities were naturally offended by this immodest proposal, and outrage soon gave way to violence.

Is your international advertising creating the desired effect?

The wonderful moral of the story is that you can get into big trouble without even opening your mouth.

SO WHAT IS THIS CULTURE THING?

Creating proper international advertising and marketing communications is the hardest challenge any of us ever face in this industry.

The whole issue is a labyrinth of administrative, financial, creative, client service, and logistical problems—even *moral* problems, once you start looking at the bigger picture—and in Chapters 5, 6, and 7 I will continue to analyze some of these problems, and start to propose some solutions.

But the problem I wish to talk about in this chapter is really the toughest one of all, and it's what the Gerber story is all about: getting to grips with *culture*.

It seems clear to me that the marketing and advertising industries' persistent failure to see culture as their biggest challenge—or a failure to understand that culture has anything to *do* with international marketing or advertising, or even a failure to acknowledge that cultural differences actually *exist*—is the main reason why, historically, there have been so many more failures than successes in international marketing programs, and why international advertising campaigns are so often so disappointing.

Exporters have known for years that culture is a factor worthy of consideration—at least in principle. Way back in 1960, the year before I was born, Edward T. Hall published a now-famous article in the *Harvard Business Review* entitled "The Silent Language in Overseas Business," which very powerfully described the influence of this apparently invisible dimension on international business.

The article was truly seminal: today, even the dullest Government information manuals for exporters always have a little paragraph in them describing what goes wrong when you clean your nails with your Japanese colleague's business card (it's usually the only bit of light relief in the whole book).

Exporters are now beset from all sides by dire warnings about culture. There are scores of books on the subject, some of which are very serious, very academic, and very heavy going, whilst many of the more popular titles aren't much more than endless lists of second- and third-hand scare stories. Some of these stories are so bizarre that one can only assume that they are wild products of the author's fantasy, or perhaps the result of certain "informers" in certain countries having a little joke at the American researcher's expense. Paul Herbig, for example, states with some confidence that products containing nuts cannot succeed in Europe because all Europeans consider nuts to be horse-food.[1] Ever since I read this sentence I've made it my life's work to find *one single European* who has any idea what the man is talking about, but so far I've asked about 11,000 Europeans whether they think nuts are horse-fodder and been rewarded with nothing but blank looks.

The more sensationalist titles seem to be designed with the sole purpose of proving how weird and touchy foreigners are, and putting people off international marketing for life: despite their tone of politically correct tolerance, and their constant hectoring of the parochial reader, many of them are little more than cultural freak-shows, the marketing equivalent of Ripley's *Believe It or Not.*

In order to prosper and thrive in different cultures, our brands have to learn, or at least to glimpse, the *source code* of these behaviors. Simply learning endless manifestations of them will merely paralyze us with fear.

However, most sensible people agree that nobody can ever really learn another culture. If you spend many years in another country, and most importantly, if you learn the language to a very high degree of proficiency, you can at least learn how to interact in a friendly and productive way with people from that culture. But one thing is abundantly clear: there's no way on earth that any individual within a corporation will ever be able to know, with any degree of breadth or depth, the cultures of *all* the countries where his or her product is sold.

One could argue that a more practical solution is for the corporation simply to hire marketing directors in each export market who are natives of those markets, and who also happen to be fluent in the culture of the *home* market of the corporation—at least this way, cultural exchange can actually take place, even if it's slightly one-way. In effect, this is exactly what happens in most international companies: those local managers are fluent enough in the "lead" culture to be sensitive to the real, underlying needs of the brand owners, and, in theory, able to "culturally interpret" their instructions back into the context of the overseas market. The real question is whether or not they *want* to: it certainly puts the brand-owner at a considerable disadvantage.

In fact, there is a very important middle ground between the very common state of total ignorance and the purely theoretical state of total global understanding: Simply knowing, and feeling, deep down, that culture *does* exist, and what it is in general terms, is an extremely worthwhile position to aim for, both for the corporation as a whole, and for the individuals within that corporation.

WHY IS CULTURE INVISIBLE?

For most exporters, culture remains frustratingly difficult to understand, or even to perceive, even after many skirmishes with it, and even if one has been on the losing side every time — or perhaps as a result of this fact. The mere fact of belonging to a culture oneself (and we all do, much as we might wish to resist it) actually blinds us to the notion that other, fundamentally different cultures and world views might actually exist.

This is partly because our own culture is so essential a part of our identity: because we've never experienced a moment of our lives without it, we don't even realize we have one.

It's a little like the point about language which I raised in Chapter 1: since most people are brought up speaking their own language, and they've acquired it by an undetectable process of osmosis throughout their early lives, they don't actually perceive it as a single, artificial construct in the way that they perceive other people's (unfamiliar) languages. This is why the whole concept of *grammar* comes as a bit of a surprise to most people when they first try to learn another language, and why children are often heard to observe that their own language is much simpler and far superior, because *it doesn't have all that stuff.*

Incidentally, this phenomenon also gives a clue as to why some nations tend to produce better linguists than others: in some countries, children are *taught* their own language at school, exactly as if it were a foreign language, even though they are already learning it "directly" as they interact with the other people around them. This prepares them with a whole raft of concepts connected with the nature, existence, and structure of language, which later on will make the concept of learning second and subsequent languages very much simpler for them. It's exactly the reason why I was taught Latin at school, and it stood me in extremely good stead: it's another way of learning *what a language is,* in the purest and most abstract form, without the issue becoming clouded with other concerns. It's a way of building the *structure* independently of its *content,* which is a very good practice.

I was about to say that one day, perhaps children will be taught culture in the same way, but of course this is, at least in theory, one of the main purposes of learning History and Geography. However, because learning how to live in the Global Village is now such a necessary part of learning how to live, perhaps we will start to see some of the *pure theory* of intercultural relations taught to our children.

Because our culture is as much a *means of perception* as it is a system of behaviors and attitudes, we can only observe other cultures through our own. *I think like this, therefore I am like this,* as Descartes didn't say, and in order to view another culture objectively, we would have first to abandon our own, and this is something which most of us, most of the time, just cannot do.

Sometimes, we are vouchsafed with a little glimpse of what culture actually is, and very often it happens because we are suddenly confronted with an objective, external view of our own.

For me, the first time it happened was the first time I met someone who'd never heard of England. I was in the north of Thailand, trying to get somewhere, and as I don't speak any Thai, was adopted by a girl who spoke some English. After she'd shown me the way to the station, she asked me which part of America I came from.

"I'm not American," I replied, "I'm English."

"Yes, I hear you speak English. But where you from in America?"

"I don't *come* from America. I come from England."

"What's that?"

There was a pause, and I began to explain: "England is part of a small island kingdom off the north-western tip of the European continent, with a long and interesting colonial past . . ." I stopped, struck by a hideous thought: England is *just another country*. Like Latvia, or Paraguay, or America.

I'm aware of how comical this anecdote must sound to most people—not least to Americans, Latvians, and Paraguayans. But to me it was a turning-point, because I suddenly realized that my view of the world was fundamentally distorted, and like people who are born with monochromatic vision, I had been simply *incapable* of grasping the concept of different colors. This was the filtering effect of looking at reality *through* the culture to which I belonged, but because I didn't realize the filter was there, I had never realized that what I was looking at wasn't the only possible reality.

Naturally, there is a good deal of political bias in my culture. Like many races which have had international influence at some stage in their past, the way we're taught history and geography and politics and everything else in England is *designed* to make us believe that we are somehow central in the world, special, better. But of course we're not.

And neither are you, *wherever* you come from.

True, the world's second most widely spoken language originated here. True, we once conquered a lot of other countries and rushed around the planet killing and stealing and subjugating as we went: but Latvia and Paraguay and America have histories and curiosities which make them special places too. Everyone is special, everyone is different, but nobody is ever much more important than anybody else except during tiny, brief moments of notoriety.

The other lesson in all this is that learning how to understand other cultures also teaches sensitivity, humility, and objectivity, which, contrary to much management teaching during the last couple of decades, are just about the most valuable qualities any individual or corporation in international business can possess in the modern world.

CULTURE AND ADVERTISING

Ask somebody who *doesn't* work in advertising or marketing (I can give you some names if you're stuck) to think of their favorite advertising campaign. I bet it's a domestic one.

Now ask them for their favorite *international* ad—one they've seen in at least three countries.

See? They think you're joking.

Personally, if I have to look at one more global ad where some loathsome international executive with round glasses is reading his child a bedtime story from a mobile phone in his Hong Kong hotel room, I may start to scream and break things.

It's trying so hard to say something to everybody which ensures that this kind of globaldegook says nothing to anybody.

People don't like it because it's a blunt instrument. Really good advertising, on the other hand, is distinguished by its *sharpness:* it speaks your culture as well as your language.

A creative director of mine once taught me a simple trick for writing effective advertising copy. As you sat down to write (according to his theory), you just needed to think of a friend or relative who corresponded to your target market, and *imagine you were talking to them.*

"So, Simon, me old mate," he would say, "let's pretend you're writing an ad for Gordon's gin. Now just imagine that your mum is sitting in front of your typewriter, and tell 'er why she's going to like it." Naturally, I was a bit offended at the suggestion that my mother might be the core target for such a product, but I let it pass. After all, when you're being given precious advice by a creative guru which you'll treasure for the rest of your professional life, you don't fuss over details.

The idea is that if you do it properly, every woman in the country who's even a little bit like your mum will instantly sense that she's finally being spoken to by a brand that understands her, understands her needs, her ambitions, her dreams, and knows exactly how she likes to be spoken to.

That fine silver thread of sympathy and understanding will magically string itself out and attach brand to consumer. And all those women will phone up their friends and tell them about that *nice* young brand they've just met.

But that's domestic advertising. What do you do if the target group is businessmen in Turkey or teenage girls in India? Summon up an image of your dad in a fez or your sister in a sari, there in front of your desk? Hardly.

There seems to be something fundamentally flawed in the whole notion of "lead agency." How can a bunch of British or American or French or German creatives possibly claim to be able to create messages—or even message templates—which would actually mean anything relevant or interesting or comprehensible to people in countries where they couldn't order a beer?

THE CULTURE BASKET

It seems to me that finding a good gag, theme, or look for an advertisement is all about picking the right toys out of the basket of popular culture, and playing around with them until you find a combination which people will find arresting and memorable.

Advertising, as I have said before, is actually *made* out of popular culture. Every time something happens in the press or on TV, a scandal takes place, a new personality emerges or an old one does something newsworthy, or the movie business or the music business provide us with new stimulus, then an item of popular culture has been forged, and the creative department has a new toy to play with.

Advertising very rarely *initiates* anything: sometimes it can draw our attention to something we hadn't noticed before, and sometimes it can remind us of something we'd forgotten, but its best trick is following so hard on the heels of changes in popular culture that you can hardly tell which came first.

Domestic ads work because their authors enjoy the luxury of being able to choose toys from a capacious, exciting, and constantly replenished domestic culture basket.

But when faced with a brief for a campaign which has to run abroad, the assumption of most creative teams is that they must look for their toys in some kind of common international culture basket. And frankly, this global basket looks pretty small, containing a very limited number of boring, broken, and over-used toys—no Barbies or Playstations here—these are old, painted wooden trains, the kind of toys you probably tell your children you were perfectly satisfied with when you were their age.

In any case, most of the international toys seem to have been previously used in Gillette advertisements: shirtless yuppies tenderly holding babies, more yuppies with round glasses punching the air outside the world's stock exchanges, impossibly good-looking girls standing around a scooter, discussing their shopping in some impossibly good-looking Italian piazza, and so on *ad nauseam.*

It seems obvious that when we're charged with creating an international advertising campaign, we badly need to find a way of building in the cultural needs of our overseas consumers at the start of the process, rather than clumsily attempting to bolt them on during the post-production phase, using the highly inadequate tool of translation. It's clear that they drop off as fast as we can bolt them on. Somehow, we need to *bake* that stuff *into the pie.*

Without even thinking about it too much, most of us still lazily subscribe to that hierarchical, top-down view of global marketing: we're constantly trying to sell American pie to the Germans by pouring German sauce over it just before we serve it up. Of course, that's a disgusting idea, and no German in her right mind would eat it.

Naturally, an averagely intelligent ad agency will use market research to tell it something of the demographics of its overseas consumers, and attempt to extract certain "key truths" about those consumers from the data and from its limited and inevitably prejudiced notions about the countries they live in. It may even speak to the local clients and listen to their views about the correct way to sell the product in their market.

But most of the time, it isn't really listening, because coming up with great ideas for ads is quite hard enough without worrying about this great mass of additional and contradictory information.

In any case, when you consider how *profoundly fluent* in the culture of your own country you need to be in order to do advertising in it, what difference can some consumer data and a couple of tourist's anecdotes possibly make? The fact is that it's not your country, and you can't begin to compete in cultural fluency or sure-footedness with somebody who was born and raised there, who speaks the language and knows the landscape, who is quite possibly a blood relation of several perfect examples of the very people which the message needs to reach.

Whilst developing the first Coca-Cola ads specifically designed for the Russian market, creative teams from Publicis in London traveled to Russia and spent time *trying to get under the skin of the Russians.*[2] This must have been a very valuable experience, and I applaud their serious-mindedness—in fact, the campaign they eventually devised was based on a Russian folk tale, which was a brilliant piece of intercultural behavior—but one can't help wondering how much nearer it actually brought them to making more appropriate advertising than a local agency could do. I know Russians who have lived for decades in Britain and still admit that they find our mentality, our way of life, and our culture almost impenetrable mysteries—and one presumes that the Publicis teams had some kind of deadline to meet, so can't have spent more than a few days in Moscow. And Moscow, as any Russian will tell you, is even less representative of the "real" Russia than New York is of America.

The other point, of course, is that unless they spoke fluent Russian, the team would have to have made their study via the imperfect medium of an interpreter, and language always seems to bring us back to a no-win situation: you can't access a culture except through its language, but you can't access its language except through its culture.

We should never forget that consumers give international advertisements no special allowances for being international: they have to compete for mindshare *on equal terms* with the best-loved domestic advertising in every single market they appear in. That's the bottom line, and unless their ads stand a realistic chance of achieving this aim, both client and agency should seriously question their rationale for running international work in the first place.

Very often, agencies respond to the puzzling problem of targeting foreigners by inserting some kind of "local" reference into the advertising, in a half-baked attempt to show that they realize who they're talking to—American agencies, for example, when asked to create a campaign for Europe, will often insert visual or verbal references to European cities or languages or lifestyles. But this is completely senseless: after all, people in those countries already know who they are and where they live. By pointing out that he is aware of this, the advertiser is merely underlining the fact that he is a foreigner.

The spread of international brands, and the consequent adoption of international advertising campaigns, has created an entirely new and very interesting cultural phenomenon: the creation of *national* acts of written and visual communication by *non-nationals*.

It has almost always been possible for nationals of one culture to access the acts of communication of other cultures (for example, an Indian can read an American novel); but as a result of the behavior of international brands, an American might now be creating an advertisement *for* Indians, *in* India: in other words, rather than people voluntarily reaching outside their own country to access expressions of foreign culture, foreign brands are now reaching *in* to other cultures, and attempting to create their own expressions of that *national* culture.

The only parallel I can think of in previous centuries is the figure of the writer in exile: Joseph Conrad, for example, one of the finest writers in the English language, was actually a French-educated Pole, but wrote in English for an English public. (Just to make things really polycultural, *Heart of Darkness* is a story of Belgian colonists in West Africa.) But in order to achieve this level of acculturation, Conrad had to live and work in England for many years, and immerse himself utterly in English culture (he even changed his name). A far cry from a couple of days in Moscow, of course: but that was definitely a step in the right direction.

PLANNING WITH CULTURE

Advertising and communications strategy is conventionally informed by observing and analyzing consumers: their needs, behavior, buying patterns, disposable income, lifestyle, aspirations, and all the rest of it.

The sum of these observations creates a set of parameters which we use to devise a communications strategy and define our messages; at best, it can give us a valuable and motivating insight into where and how our product can most dramatically and effectively be presented in the context of the consumer's life. (For the best book on planning I've ever read, see Jon Steel's *Truth, Lies and Advertising*[3] in this series.)

Although this kind of preparatory work is essential for any agency attempting to create a communications platform that's going to work in a large number of countries, global data has a tendency to become overwhelming, and in order to reach any kind of manageable conclusions, it is often necessary for the planner to simplify and refine it all down by such orders of magnitude that one begins to wonder whether it was worth generating all that raw data in the first place. In any case, as I've already pointed out, that data is fairly inaccessible—even useless or actually misleading—to people from a different culture, because they cannot, by definition, read the data in the context of the culture that it comes from.

So much difference has to be overlooked, so many factors have to be ignored because they simply won't fit the overall pattern, so many fascinating observations about the peculiarities of individual markets need to be sidelined for the benefit of giving the creative team a clear, single direction, that the exercise can easily become self-defeating.

This is, at heart, a navigation problem: we are trying to map a route through complex and unknown terrain, yet we only have two points of reference: the marketplace, and the brand itself. In order to get our bearings, just like any explorer, we need a third point in order to triangulate. Actually, what we really need is an extremely broad, yet robust and reliable *aerial view* of the consumer terrain: in the same way that modern cartography has been completely revolutionized by the ability to photograph entire continents from a satellite in addition to exploring the ground on foot, we need help in seeing the big picture.

I'm certainly not the first person in the world to have discovered that there is a satellite up there, and it's called culture mapping. At least *I* call it culture mapping, but in fact this whole branch of study appears not to have a name by which everybody knows it—is it social anthropology? Ethnopsychology? Ethnosociodemographics? At least culture mapping isn't an "—ology," so it sounds like something you can use, rather than just study.

Some of the most important works on Culture Mapping have been written by Geert Hofstede, a Dutch academic, who has devised and encoded a very thorough and robust system of cultural analysis, the 5-D model,[4] which for the first time, sheds much light on the mystery of diversity; and Fons Trompenaars,[5] another Dutchman, who with his colleague, Charles Hampden-Turner, a British academic, have developed a somewhat different seven-dimensional culture map, together with a methodology for actively and creatively resolving the cultural dilemmas which diversity brings.

The study of cultures is complex, it's academic, and much as everybody would like it, these are not systems which can be simplified down into a slim airport-bookstall bestseller called *The Ten Golden Rules of Cultural Difference*: no, if you want to use and understand these techniques, you have to study them in depth, or else you have to hire somebody who has.

Now the interesting thing is that much of the actual *business* that's done in the area of culture mapping takes the form of organizational consultancy and management theory: how to help employees from different cultures understand each other better, and work together productively without their fundamentally different backgrounds getting in the way or causing irreparable misunderstandings. For example, if you're a German auto manufacturer that's just merged with an American manufacturer, a transcultural consultancy will help to prepare your people and your systems to ensure that the two cultures merge effectively, productively, and harmoniously within the newly-merged corporation.

But because you're dealing with individual human beings, the usefulness of culture-based management theory is inevitably limited by the fact that individuals each have their own culture too: it's called *personality*, and this will affect their behavior and attributes just as profoundly as their national culture. So you could easily spend months in your Detroit office getting to grips with the cultural models which define the mentality, approach to work, relationship to authority, negotiation techniques, habits of communication, and social behavior of the German people, only to discover that it's next to useless when you're actually confronted by Herr Schmidt, because his particularly aggressive form of confrontation is just as likely to be caused by the fact that he's Herr Schmidt, and not because he happens to be German.

Using culture mapping in this way is arguably little more than respectable astrology: a useful framework for discussing people's differences, certainly, but nobody would ever pretend that it's a reliable means for predicting or even interpreting every aspect of their behavior. After all, Groucho Marx, Bruce Springsteen, and Oliver North are white American males, and that fact does tell you something about how their behaviors, actions, attitudes, and motivations might differ from those of three male Koreans of the same generation, but it's not *incredibly* helpful. In fact, it's about as helpful as knowing that all three of them are Librans.

The techniques of culture mapping are *extremely* helpful, however, in understanding your own behavior, values, and actions, and those of your corporation. This reason alone is sufficient to make it a valuable and worthwhile process for marketing managers to go through. You, it is supposed, know your personality, and consequently are able to perceive which parts of your attitudes and behaviors are modeled by your cultural background, and which parts are more the result of you simply being a different person from the people around you.

And for advertising agencies and their clients, culture mapping really comes into its own: it's absolutely *made* for mass marketing, an area where individual personality is of very secondary importance, and what you really want is reliable, true, but *gross generalizations*. You need to know what *most people* in a country are like, and how *most of them* will behave in response to certain stimuli. And because brands have personalities, so those personalities have a cultural fingerprint (it's often very similar to the cultural map of that brand's country of origin): culture mapping helps you to see how that culture can interface and interact with the cultures of its consumers around the world.

The five main parameters of Hofstede's 5-D model are as follows:

- *Power distance* (which measures how people within a culture handle the concept of inequality in society, in the workplace, etc.)

- *Uncertainty avoidance* (which measures how threatened people feel by ambiguous or unfamiliar situations)
- *Individualism/collectivism* (which measures how much people's loyalty and interest is limited to themselves and their immediate family, or extends towards larger groups or society itself)
- *Masculinity/femininity* (which measures the ratio between "masculine" values such as achievement and success, and "feminine" values like altruism and quality of life)
- *Long-term orientation* or *Confucian dynamism* (which measures forward thinking versus short-termism)

The Trompenaars model, as I mentioned, uses a different set of parameters, and its virtue is the way in which it concentrates on *creatively resolving* the differences which different values of these parameters create. His seven dimensions of culture are:

- *Universalism/particularism* (which deals with the degree of importance attached to the rights of friends as against the rights of society in general)
- *Individualism/communitarianism* (which corresponds to Hofstede's *individualism/collectivism* axis, and is the broader context of which the first dimension is really a subset or example)
- *Specific/diffuse* (which deals with the expectations people have of relationships)
- *Neutral/affective* (the degree to which people feel happy about externalizing their feelings)
- *Achievement/ascription* (the degree to which status is achieved through personal endeavor, or "inherited" by external circumstances—this dimension has something in common with Hofstede's *power distance* axis)
- *Time orientation* (whether a society bases its future on its past or not, and how tasks are managed across time, and is related to Hofstede's fifth measurement)

- *Internal/external* (which deals with a society's view of the relationship between man and nature, and the consequent degree to which individuals will tend to believe that they control, or are controlled, by their environment)

Like Hofstede, Trompenaars has further identified several different *corporate* cultures, which are driven by different combinations of these dimensions.

Another, older study of culture, the Kluckhohn-Strodtbeck Framework,[6] provides yet another set of cultural measures (Relationship to the Environment; Time Orientation, Nature of People, Activity Orientation, Focus of Responsibility and Conception of Space), some of which are close cousins of axes in the Hofstede and Trompenaars systems.

It's not within the scope of this book to go into detail about culture mapping: as I've said, it's a dense and complex discipline, and almost every author who has explored the subject has come up with his or her own entirely different set of "universal" and "fundamental" measurements for explaining the mystery of cultural diversity. It is interesting that certain areas are common to nearly all approaches—everyone agrees that people's relationships to status and power systems vary from culture to culture; so do people's views of their environment; so do their perceptions of time.

I also don't intend to explore the use of culture mapping as a planning tool for advertising and brandbuilding, because it quickly gets very complex and very academic. Bear in mind that each culture has to be assessed on the basis of at least three of the dimensions I described above, and consequently the ways in which these dimensions interact with each other, as well as with the cultural dimensions of the target consumer, means that you could easily fill a book with a single case study.

A few other authors have written on this subject: Marieke de Mooij and Jean-Claude Usunier's studies of the application of the Hofstede model on marketing theory are particularly interesting, and I warmly recommend their work to the reader who is interested in exploring this area further.[7-9]

Suffice to say that these cultural issues are fundamental to doing business abroad: recognizing their existence is an extremely important step towards resolving them, and ultimately, as one acquires confidence and experience, making powerful use of them.

They are one of our main tools for finding the areas of common human experience on which we can base a robust and universally applicable creative positioning. Where and how culture mapping best fits into the advertising process is described in Chapter 6.

ON BEING AMERICAN

Whilst we're on the subject of culture, a word about being American—because the fact is that most international companies *are* American (8 of the top 10 global brands are American-owned at this point in time), so this is the culture which, more than any other, has to learn how to adapt to the usage of others.

It is the success of the encounter between the culture of the brand and the culture of the overseas consumer which, perhaps more than any other factor, determines whether the brand will prosper abroad or not. And it's natural that many of these encounters will be indirect, via local representation, distribution, agency, and so forth: so the selection of these intermediaries is of crucial importance in determining the ultimate success of the encounter.

It's no accident that the Netherlands (the homeland of Geert Hofstede, Marieke de Mooij, Fons Trompenaars, and various other leading lights in the culture business) is being selected more than ever before as the principal intermediary for American and Asian multinational corporations as they move into Europe and beyond. International-mindedness is one of this country's chief exports—and since one of its main historical barriers to being considered a neutral stopping-off place, its difficult language, has become systematically and efficiently eroded by making the entire country bilingual, the Netherlands is now a serious challenger to the United Kingdom as "the marketer's Guam"—a strategically-located airstrip where American corporations can park their bombers before invading the continent.

The femininity of the Dutch culture (and the superior astuteness which this grants them) and the masculinity of British culture (and the dramatic, if costly success which this sometimes brings them) have long been recognized. A Javanese prince, in around 1780, observed "The British are like the strong rapid current of water, they are persevering, energetic and irresistible in their courage. If they really want to obtain something they will use violence to get it. The Dutch are very able, clever, patient, and calm. If possible they try to reach their goal by persuasion than by force of arms. It may well happen that Java will be conquered by the British."[10]

Still, when planning marketing offensives in Europe, the majority of American companies still choose Britain as their "lead" country for international campaigns. This is partly because it makes a certain amount of topographical sense (one might almost say a rerun, in reverse, of our commercial voyages westwards to America in past centuries); it's partly because the services and infrastructure available in the United Kingdom—especially in the area of advertising, media, film, and print production—are among the best in Europe; but at heart, it's because you tend to do business with the people who do business like you, and on the international stage, that means the countries with which you have most cultural commonalities.

The first great convenience for American companies operating in and from the United Kingdom is the fact that we both speak English, but language is of course nothing more than the external manifestation of the fact that we share many characteristics of an "Anglo-Saxon culture." This doesn't mean that our two cultures are the same, by any means: let's just say that these two hippos are cousins, and you can see that because their ears stick out in the same way.

To seek out kindred spirits when doing business internationally is entirely to be expected, and brings great benefits to both parties, but it may be counter-productive in the cultural sense: refining a global marketing or communications strategy within the context of a similar culture may serve to *increase* its ethnocentricity, assumptiveness, or two-dimensionality, rather than making it broader and more culture-neutral. In other words, we may just encourage each other to be bigoted.

For example, there are certain characteristics of the American way of doing business and promoting brands which are almost the direct opposite of what is considered acceptable (and consequently, what is likely to be most effective) in Scandinavia. Positioning a brand as big, fast, smart, powerful, and success-oriented may create considerable appeal in the United States—a masculine culture, according to the Hofstede model—but in Scandinavia, where a strongly feminine culture prevails, attributes such as small, slow, and wise could well create more trust and sympathy.

Now because British culture shares many of the same masculine characteristics as U.S. culture (and also, incidentally, scores similarly high on individualism), using Britain as a sounding-board, creative shop, foreign embassy, international sensitizing device, or cultural filter when promoting American brands in Sweden, Norway, Finland, Denmark, or Iceland, or indeed most other countries in the world, is likely to deepen and harden rather than moderate or correct this fundamental cultural disconnect.

It's not a reason to go elsewhere (I hasten to add, before I get put on the British Department of Trade and Industry's hit-list): but it is a factor to be aware of and to make allowances for.

IS AMERICA THE CENTER OF
THE KNOWN UNIVERSE?

By a strange quirk of geography, and despite its polyethnic urban populations, most Americans get fewer chances to explore and learn about cultural difference, by meeting real live foreigners on a daily basis, than almost any other nation on earth: America is simply *farther away* than most places.

Travel north, and you eventually meet Canadians, who at first glance appear to be pretty much the same thing as you are, but with different passports. Travel south and you get to Mexico, which at first glance looks decidedly third world. Try traveling east or west, and you'll get wet. Consequently, many Americans end up with the notion that all the foreigners they're ever going to meet conform to this pattern: they're either pretty much the same thing as an American (like Europeans, for example), or else they're pretty nearly savages (like Asians, for example).

Just as we British, in our little island kingdom, consider that most of the rest of the world is *overseas*, so do Americans. (The concept of *overseas* is, for obvious reasons, not at all the same thing as *abroad* in most other cultures—in Europe, for example, you're hardly ever more than a couple of hours' drive away from somewhere where they speak a different language. Actually, since the British Isles are now connected by tunnel to the European continent, we might consider adopting *underseas* instead.)

Americans definitely have a very distinctive view about their position in the world. I was interviewing an American candidate for a job as account manager recently, and he made a casual comment which I found very illuminating: he said, "Oh sure, I have plenty of international experience—*I've been there lots of times.*" This isn't the first time I've heard phrases like this used, and not always accidentally, by Americans. It's as if there's America, and there's *abroad*, and if you actually come from abroad, you are automatically an expert on other people who come from abroad, places, languages, cooking, and customs abroad: the only necessary qualification for being an authority on all global issues is not being American.

It's touchingly self-deprecating, in a way—the sense it gives of the rest of the world doing stuff which America isn't part of, and perhaps even having a big party that America hasn't been invited to. But these things are never simple: this attitude is in stark contradiction to the other American habit of having the "world's greatest" everything, as seen on the fronts of hundreds of tiny stores all over the United States: if you're the best in America, you are automatically the best in the world, because you are the best of the best. And I won't make that comment about the World Series, because it's been made before and we're all sick of hearing it.

While I'm on the subject, I really must complain about the current use of the word *local* to mean foreign. For some reason, *foreign* is now considered to be a politically incorrect word, and *local* appears to have been selected as its replacement in marketing circles. At a European marketing managers' meeting recently, I distinctly overheard the following surreal exchange in the men's toilet:

"Are you from a local country?"

"No, I'm from America."

Personally, I think *local* is far more offensive than *foreign*, since it carries strong overtones of *parochial, small-minded*. I suppose it has come about because of the common antithesis of local/global, but it's a very odd usage, and it will be interesting to see whether it sticks or not. I hope it doesn't, because then I can stop using it.

AT LAST: NEW HOPE FOR SUFFERERS OF IRONY DEFICIENCY

It could be said that the American culture *itself* makes it harder for Americans to recognize and allow for the existence of other cultures, even when exposed to them on a regular basis: this is because of a series of chance clashes between value systems which make equilateral sensitization extremely unlikely to happen.

American culture, for example, is strongly individualist, so direct speech and the forceful expression of personal opinions are valued; Japanese culture is collectivist, so humility, indirect communication, and the furthering of common aims are paramount. When an American expresses his or her personal opinion to a Japanese, expecting argument or capitulation, a Japanese is quite likely to smile politely and make a non-committal reply; the result is that the American may assume that the Japanese are secretive, ineffectual, arrogant, or even stupid, and the Japanese may have already decided that Americans are intolerably rude, aggressive, selfish, and opinionated. It's nobody's *fault*, of course, but neither is any the wiser about the other's culture, and they haven't made friends either.

Living in Europe and working for mainly American corporations, I sometimes get the impression that Americans, until they learn better, instinctively make a false parallel between the continent of North America, with its superficially distinguishable but basically homogeneous states, and Europe, with its superficially distinguishable and basically heterogeneous states. The fact that we Europeans all insist on speaking different languages, holding dramatically different opinions on almost every possible subject, behaving in a bewildering range of different ways, is seen as a conscious attempt to make life more difficult for Americans trying to do business in Europe. We still even use different currencies, for heaven's sake, despite the advance of our single currency (which some Americans infuriatingly insist on calling the *Eurodollar*).

I've worked with some Americans who talk as if Europe were a kind of theme-park, whose inhabitants put on a culture and heritage show during the day for the benefit of foreign tourists (and for the confusion of foreign businessmen), but that when we all go home in the evenings, we sink down on our sofas with a Budweiser in front of *Guiding Light* and gratefully lapse into American, God's own language, with our friends and families. For some Americans, it seems, Europeans are just Americans who haven't left yet.

Oh, and by the way, that last paragraph was intentionally provocative, and was designed to demonstrate (as if it needed demonstration) that despite many broad cultural similarities, there are also some quite acute differences between American and British culture — or, at least, in the ways we express those cultures. The completely unwarranted rudeness in that paragraph was actually *ironic:* that is to say, I didn't quite mean it, but I also didn't quite *not* mean it.

Now figure that one out if you can.

TWO NATIONS DIVIDED BY A COMMONPLACE

Here's a theory about the reasons why British and American speakers of English often fail to understand each other quite perfectly, despite the fact that there is remarkably little difference between their two varieties of the language.

The main function of British English is mystification and obscurity (because we're so exclusive, class-bound, snobbish, and tribal by nature, because we live on a small island and are constantly attempting to repel invaders), and we use language to define boundaries, and to *keep people in their place.*

The main function of American English is precisely the contrary: it is a true *lingua franca,* designed to enable people from a bewildering range of different backgrounds to communicate with each other as freely as possible: it is *inclusive,* rather than exclusive. Consequently, anything such as irony or wordplay which might cause misunderstanding, give rise to offense or otherwise obfuscate the precise expression of thought, is rejected.

The classic, tired, and very superficial comparison is that the Americans are convinced that the British are incapable of taking themselves seriously, and the British are convinced that the Americans are incapable of *not* taking themselves seriously. Like all commonplaces, there's a grain of truth in it, but like all commonplaces, it's mainly complete garbage. I *have* noticed in recent years that I always feel a strong sense of relief when there are Americans amongst groups of European business people—it's as if one can relax, because the grown-ups are here.

And as for seriousness, well, give me seriousness any day. For the past several years, I've taken part in an annual marketing conference on board a cruise liner, where marketers and marketing service people can meet each other via a series of pre-arranged appointments. For the UK version you need to keep your patience, and your wits about you: many clients will go to extraordinary lengths to avoid showing up for their meetings, will "accidentally" forget to bring their business cards (presumably because they're afraid of being contacted afterwards by hordes of ravenous vendors), will almost always arrive late, and stay up all night getting drunk like students who have just discovered alcohol for the first time, and are consequently seasick *and* hung over for most of the conference.

The U.S. version could hardly be more different: the delegates are sober, respectable, courteous and punctual; they give business cards, and they don't object in the slightest to you keeping in touch with them at regular intervals, for as long afterwards as you care to do so. It's got a lot to do with the different levels of respect for commerce enshrined in our two cultures: in Britain, as in many European countries, business isn't considered to be terribly posh: in America, the pursuit of wealth and success was written into the culture right from the start. Given the choice, I would rather do business with Americans than almost any other nation on earth (apart from the Sri Lankans, who are equally courteous but don't expect you to wear a tie, which as everybody knows, restricts the oxygen supply to the brain and reduces your ability to think straight).

And I'm not being *entirely* serious about this either, by the way.

IS THE WEST WINNING?

It is very easy to fall into the habit of believing that differences in culture are the main enemy of global brands, and it's not surprising that there is always an enthusiastic audience for those theorists and practitioners who claim that cultural differences are only a temporary problem, rapidly becoming erased by the irresistible advance of western civilization, western moral and ethical standards, western democracy, and western brands, as symbolized by the increasingly ubiquitous presence of McDonald's and Coca-Cola.

It's certainly true that, over time, conditions are conspiring to create a world market which is increasingly favorable to international marketing. However, it is important to re-emphasize what has been stated many times before by various authorities on the subject: this change is caused by the increased liberalization of global trade, the lessening of trade barriers of all kinds, the globalization of the economy, the rapid advance of global and "new" media, but most definitely *not* by the "Westernization" or homogenization of the consumer.

The view that consumers worldwide are gradually moving towards the universal adoption of American or European values is a myth, easily disproved, and self-evidently the result of interpreting other cultures from an ethnocentric Euro-American viewpoint. In fact, careful comparison of Hofstede's data over the past 20 years or so demonstrates that there is no perceptible "reduction" in national culture: if anything, there is a tendency for differences to become more marked over time.

When countries do set off down the road of embracing foreign cultures at the expense of their own, usually in a spirit of "modernization," such as that championed in Turkey by Kemal Atatürk in the 1920s and 1930s, however eagerly they start, it's never too long before there's a counter-movement. As soon as such a movement starts to become noticeably effective, and gets beyond the superficial level, people tend to

Culture is alive and well and living in Belgium.

step back rather smartly when they observe the risk to their own culture. In the heady excitement of becoming "world players," countries may abandon national dress, learn new languages, or even sideline their own, but that's about as far as people normally let it get before a reaction sets in.

We interviewed groups of Dutch teenagers on their preference for Nike's advertising in English and Dutch language versions in 1992 and 1998, and noticed a significant shift of opinion even over this short period: in 1992, a typical response was "if Nike speaks Dutch it can't be a cool brand," but in 1998, many respondents returned comments like "if you can't even figure out how to speak to me in my own language, you can't be too smart."

Culture is alive and well and living in Spain.

All around us, there are examples of cultures and subcultures which, threatened by the erosion of their specialness and difference, are fighting back: much of the religious fundamentalism which periodically resurges around the world is borne of such real or perceived threats to an older way of life which distinguishes the smaller or weaker culture from the dominant group. Nothing encourages the learning of languages more than the threat of their demise, which is why many of the native languages of the British Isles have been snatched back from extinction.

We may have lost most of our dialects since the day, barely 100 years ago, when Robert Louis Stephenson could travel around the country and find each county speaking mutually incomprehensible dialects of English; but we are incomparably rich in languages, many of which are undergoing a timely revival.

I won't trouble you with current figures for speakers of Erse, Gaelic, Welsh, Angloromani, Vlachromani and Welsh-Romani, Traveler Scottish, Polari, Cornish, Manx, Jerriais, or Dgernesiais, but these are all languages which have felt the cold wind of extinction.

Too late, alas, for Old Kentish Sign Language, the ancestor of Martha's Vineyard Sign Language, which, I grieve to learn, is now officially extinct. (At least it's for a good reason: the endemic deafness which created it in the first place has also, happily, become extinct.)

But elsewhere, the rise of Basque, that extraordinary language which bears no relation to any other tongue on this planet, and the violent passions stirred up by the threatened erosion of this and other tokens of its people's cultural separateness; the seemingly endless and often bloody fragmentation of the peoples of the Balkans and central Asia: all this is about culture as much as it's about land. Politicians may worry about land, because they see things on a macro level: land spells tax revenues, population, military power, and international influence; but people care *desperately* about their cultural identity.

Nobody's going to abandon any of that passion just because they happen to like the taste of Chicken Mc-Nuggets.

WHAT IS CULTURAL SENSITIVITY?

Cultural sensitivity is pretty much a prerequisite for living in the modern world, but it's specially important for people who wish to sell their products (or their clients' products) in other countries.

There are probably four degrees of sensitivity to other cultures:

1. *Ignorance and intolerance* ("Because you are a dirty foreigner, I hate you and everything about you.")

This is a sub-base state—in other words, it's a state of actually *lower sensitivity* than the average human being in a condition of complete ignorance, with no education, no religion, and no particular moral system would naturally inhabit: to reach this level, people must be ignorant, uneducated, godless, amoral, *and* pretty nasty too. There are plenty around.

2. *Political correctness* ("Because you are a local-country individual, I have been programmed to respect you, whatever I may personally think about you, and we will celebrate our differences in a joyful world community, whether you like it or not.")

Some people might find it surprising that I rank political correctness only one level above total ignorance and total intolerance. The reason is that political correctness, in its worst form, is not *sincere,* and is based on ignorance and condescension. It's ignorant, because it applies blanket rules of tolerance in an intolerant way, and it has very little to do with understanding or wishing to understand the *nature* of the "minority" it's meant to be protecting. It's much more to do with oppressing the overdog than with protecting the underdog, and I call that oppression.

It's condescending, because it assumes, again blanket-fashion, that (a) all underdogs want and need your protection (an underdog-blanket?), (b) that they can't stand up for themselves, and (c) that you are using your superior influence to protect them: they are therefore your inferiors. The subtext of political correctness is that it's an affliction to be different, so referring to people's difference in any way is *de facto* insulting. Now don't get me wrong: I'm not saying we should all go round calling people names, but political correctness always runs the risk of turning into a kind of intolerant liberalism which borders on racism and fascism.

Political correctness comes from the political organ (whatever that is—the gall bladder?), rather than from the heart.

3. *Tolerance* ("Well, we're certainly different from each other, but that's okay, we're both human beings, and I guess it's because we were brought up differently.")

Ah, true tolerance. There's nothing fancy about this, but it is, I firmly believe, the natural state of civilized humanity. Almost all good and kind people think this way.

4. *Cultural sensitivity* ("I want to find out more about you, and tell you more about me, so that we can understand each other better.")

This is the state which people who work in international fields actually need to reach: a benign (not intrusive or pathological or selfish) curiosity about what makes people different from each other. It's superior to mere tolerance, because unlike tolerance, which is basically a static condition, cultural sensitivity *makes things better*: it is a condition of virtuous striving. If everybody were culturally sensitive, actually, there would probably be no wars—but then again, if everybody were simply tolerant, that would cut down the numbers a bit too. (If everybody were politically correct, we'd be constantly bashing each other over the head, screaming that *our* pet minority was more oppressed than *your* pet minority.)

Cultural sensitivity is something we can all attain: you don't have to be born bilingual or live abroad or even know a single foreigner. Indeed, one of the most interesting aspects of studying culture is the picture which begins to emerge that there is a little of the "foreigner" in all of us: in reality, there are relatively few cultural patterns which one simply can't empathize with at any level. After all, we're all human beings, and although culture occurs at a deeper level than language, it's not the core of our being.

Fons Trompenaars uses the example of Asians saying "yes" even when they are not in agreement: this is often explained by "experts" on Asian culture as a "yes, I am still following you," rather than a confusing euphemism for "no." Trompenaars says that it's nothing of the kind: it's exactly the same kind of "yes" which he uses when his wife appears in a horrible dress and asks him whether he likes it. It means "yes, I like you—in fact, I like you too much to tell you that the dress is horrible."

All it takes to understand other cultures is a little application, a little study, a harder look at ourselves.

I have always admired Lafcadio Hearn, a now largely forgotten writer, who traveled much in the East during the second half of the last century, and wrote very sensitively and evocatively about rural Japan. Perhaps because he was born of mixed race—he was half-Greek and half-Irish, which is a particularly romantic combination—he had cultural sensitivity in bucketloads, and eventually took Japanese nationality, married a Japanese, and lived there for the rest of his days. (Somebody should really study the high coincidence of cultural sensitivity and mixed-race ancestry.) In the preface to his best-known book on Japan, Hearn writes:

> This is the life of which a foreign observer can never weary, if fortunate and sympathetic enough to enter into it, —the life that forces him sometimes to doubt whether the course of our boasted Western progress is really in the direction of moral development. Each day, while the years pass, there will be revealed to him some strange and unsuspected beauty in it.[11]

This, I believe, is the true voice of cultural sensitivity speaking.

People who acquire or are naturally blessed with cultural sensitivity make the most *fantastically* successful international marketers, politicians, diplomats, film directors, business people, writers, philosophers, economists, journalists, travelers, and so on. And it is the *true* Holy Grail of all global brands in the twenty-first century.

Your cultural sensitivity is what defines whether your first contact with foreigners will do you and your brand good, or do you both harm.

Varying degrees of cultural sensitivity is the reason why the effects of globalization, increasingly global communications and increasingly common international travel will tend to increase idiot nationalism in some people and companies, and humility, tolerance, and understanding in others.

For instance, a country has no reason to have strong feelings about its national football team until it competes abroad — then, suddenly, that country's separate and different entity is thrown sharply into relief by comparison with other countries, and the result can be positive or negative, depending on the level of tolerance within that country.

This is also why travel is good for you, and why people who live abroad or travel a great deal often come to understand themselves better. Living in your own country is like being permanently dressed in clothes which are the same color as your own wallpaper, so you can't really see where you stop and where the background starts. The first time you stand in front of wallpaper of a different pattern, your own outline suddenly stands out as never before.

This is another reason, incidentally, why I believe that "westernization" won't happen: exposure to the "global" culture of Western brands can actually provide the catalyst for people to realize that their own culture is different, and special, and worth striving to protect. "Global" culture, because it is developed for, and purveyed through, mass media, is necessarily quite gross: it is undeniably attractive, but the attraction tends to be superficial. The products of global culture are adopted, and the brands on offer are bought, but they seldom entirely replace "local" cultures: they live alongside them, as a McDonald's in Paris or Tokyo will trade alongside a bistro or a sushi bar.

Perhaps most importantly, there are many other elements of cultural inspiration and influence besides the global/American, and the chances are that on the *other* side of that McDonald's in downtown Tokyo, there will be a Chinese restaurant, an Irish pub, or a Mexican grill. What is actually happening all over the world is *not* the creeping spread of American-dominated cultural imperialism, but a general process of omnilateral, polycultural *mixing*, and this can only be a good thing.

The explosion of international communications means that people all over the world are free as never before to observe, learn, adopt, imitate, embrace, and reject elements from a wealth of different cultures, and it's certainly true that one of the consequences of this exposure appears to be that many people are now acquiring a *layer* or patina of "international" culture (or fluency in international culture) over their native culture, which means that they can and will "culture surf" to their hearts' content. It's also true that those layers do mix to some degree: but my sense has always been that they co-exist, rather than one eroding or replacing the other, because people have a great capacity for acquiring more and more richness in their world view, in their language, in their sense of style, in their philosophy and their observations.

(And richness is a good thing. The Victorian poet, Gerard Manley Hopkins, characterized better than almost anybody else how true beauty derives from complexity and diversity: he called it *dapple*—the pattern of light and shade, the satisfying richness of differing and even conflicting textures. This profoundly humane belief is the diametric opposite of the rather baneful view that only purity can create lasting beauty, and it is central to the principles of international creativity which I will describe later on.)

Ultimately, elements of foreign cultures fall from favor or become acculturated by degrees, in much the same way as loanwords from other languages pass imperceptibly out of use or into unrecognizable, localized hybrids. In other words, people have a *choice*, and nothing could be more democratic, more fair, or more unstoppable than this kind of wholly pragmatic natural cultural selection.

Being exposed to other cultures is good for us and good for our brands because meeting other people helps us to understand ourselves: wisdom is made of such experiences. Each person we meet will draw his or her own portrait of us, and as long as we keep remembering to look, we can see that portrait in the way they behave when they are with us. When foreigners from different cultures draw our portrait, this can be even more revealing: seeing the River Thames as painted by Turner, Kokoschka, Canaletto, and Monet helps Londoners to see the true aspect of their own city in ways they could never have done on their own.

As long as we *listen* carefully to the way people respond to us, and do our best to understand the nature of that response, we can grow in understanding, richness, stature, and confidence.

International brands can succeed because people have always loved to have foreign visitors in their midst, and as long as they are pleasantly exotic but respectful and well-behaved (*if fortunate and sympathetic enough to enter*, as Hearn puts it), they will often be granted special privileges which the indigenous population don't receive—they are often viewed in some instinctive way as *lucky*, perhaps because their different background is thought to give them a special objectivity which is close to divine wisdom. Indeed, in very primitive societies, foreign visitors are often mistaken for gods or spirits.

This is surely one of the great advantages of export marketing: by moving our brands to countries and cultures where they *don't* belong and *don't* fit in, we are giving them a priceless opportunity to gain a very special status and importance which they could never enjoy in their natural environment.

Neither the risks of getting it wrong, nor the rewards of getting it right, can easily be overstated.

If we get it wrong, we can kill our brand's chances abroad for generations to come. But, as I will start to show in the next chapter, if we play the game wisely and confidently enough, who knows, we might even be taken for gods or spirits.

3

Global Brand or Global Bland?

Here's another disaster story. Not a funny one, I'm afraid, but this time I know it's true, because I was there.

Once upon a time, there was a large international corporation in the tobacco business, whose newly-appointed Worldwide Director for Brands had a bit of a thing about consistency. One of the first tasks he undertook when he joined the company was to produce a comprehensive design and corporate identity "bible" for all of the company's brands, which was duly sent out to all of their offices worldwide, and their several hundred design, advertising, and sales promotion agencies.

Some months after the program was complete, the Brand Director was traveling in Poland, when on impulse he dropped into a small tobacconist's shop in Katowice. He was gratified to see, prominently displayed in its proper dispenser, a sheaf of take-me leaflets relating to a promotion for their top of the range brand, a luxury king-size cigarette.

But as soon as he took one of the leaflets, he realized that something was badly wrong. It was printed on paper which was quite definitely on the thin side. The paper was positively slender. It crackled unpleasantly between his thumb and forefinger, and drooped limply as he held it up to the light. No question: they had used a paper stock which was well below the weight specified for this brand in the design manual.

Feverishly, the man scurried around to the nearest stationer's, where in broken Polish, between sobs of emotion, he managed to ask what weight of paper this might be. Sure enough, confirmed the stationer, as he stroked the paper with a practiced thumb, it was around 100 gsm. The Brand Director knew as well as if he had the manual in front of him (unlikely, this, since the complete volume weighed nigh on 10 pounds) that the minimum prescribed weight for paper used in promotional activities for this particular brand was a comfortably upmarket 200 gsm.

He got on the phone to his Marketing Director and arranged for the Polish Sales Promotion agency to be sacked. Then he got on the phone to a consultancy and ordered a complete, worldwide audit of all the company's printed communications, for all of their brands, covering the last year.

It cost him a great deal of money, but the results were fascinating. I'm simplifying here for dramatic effect, but basically he was told that the whole of his communications program was in disarray: there was practically no adherence to his guidelines, the brands were pitched all over the place, and it was as if the brand bible, that magnum opus, had never been produced.

With one solitary exception: Poland. In fact, a certain Sales Promotion agency in Katowice, recently dismissed, was just about the only company in his entire organization which had showed any interest in maintaining corporate standards, or used any intelligence in their application.

And one of the best examples of that intelligent application was the way that they had not slavishly followed design guidelines to the letter, but interpreted them in a way which suited the realities of the Polish market.

And the best example of their intelligent approach to compliance was a certain promotion for the King-Size luxury brand. In a country like Poland, where paper is generally thinner and of poorer quality than in Western Europe, a weight of 200gsm is more than upmarket: it's shameless luxury. Using it to advertise this promotion would have implied a brand which was not so much aspirational as downright unaffordable. In Polish hands, 200gsm is practically cardboard. The exact cultural equivalent, in Eastern European terms, it turns out, is around 100gsm, which the Katowice sales promotion agency had very intelligently used.

Who Defines the Brand?

The agency was reinstated, and a program of inspired, personal implementation and training was started the following quarter, in order to communicate not just the rules, but also the thinking behind the brand standards, worldwide.

The moral of this disaster story is fairly obvious, I think: obedience is good, but thinking is better.

———

Who Defines the Brand?

Although this book is mainly about advertising and other forms of brand communication, it's impossible to talk sensibly about ads without talking about the nature and structure of the brands behind them. The most internationally sensitive advertising in the world can't do much to help a brand which is fundamentally ill-equipped to travel, or, indeed, one which is owned and managed by people who don't understand how to *make* it travel.

To put it in another way: marketing communications are the ears of the hippo, but if you want to see them poking cheerily out of the water in a far-away lake, it's the hippo that has to move first.

Sometimes, like the tobacco man in the story, people in international marketing departments get these momentary feelings of panic: after all, they are personally responsible for communications appearing around the world in dozens of incomprehensible languages, and sometimes the stuff that actually appears in front of the consumer on the other side of the world seems rather far removed from decisions they make back home.

In many corporations, international brand development is made vastly more complex because of the long chain of command—or, sometimes, the total disconnect—between the people who decide brand policy and the people who actually give the brand the power of speech in each market. It goes without saying that this chain gets even longer, and

91

the process even more opaque, when a manufacturer is operating overseas through a third-party marketing channel.

There's a good parallel in Greek philosophy for the way that brands are directed.

Plato describes the creative acts of ordinary human beings according to a system of archetypes, using the metaphor of a table: there is, he argues, only one true table, and that is the archetypal table, existing only in the mind of God. The archetype is the pure essence of tableness, unfettered by any materials or dimensions. When a carpenter sets about making a table, he will attempt to reproduce his understanding of the archetype in the limiting form of three-dimensional wood; and when a painter paints a picture of the carpenter's table, his painting is doubly imitative, and two steps removed from the pure concept of tableness. (Of course, a great artist will attempt to paint directly from the archetype—which is why Van Gogh's tables suggest tableness so beautifully without looking much like the "real thing" at all.) The theory is that anyone who understands the nature of the archetype will be able to reproduce tables which will be true to form.

For table, read brand. In most larger corporations, there is usually a small group of godlike people who understand the brand's personality very fully because they work on it and with it every day: they are in possession of its archetype, and any expression of it which they choose to make is likely to be true to brand. They are the "authorized dealers" of brand value, licensed to answer questions about it, reproduce it, use it.

The trouble is that these demigods are seldom the people who are actually responsible for providing the brand with a voice: they merely direct operations from a distance. Sometimes, they have a fairly direct line to the *corporate* communications people, but frequently not to the product marketing people, and the consequent enhancement of the split between *those* two functions is really in nobody's interest.

So their understanding of the brand's personality must be communicated down through many layers of carpenters and artists before it actually reaches the consumer in the form of advertising: and the original, pure character of the brand is often diluted and distorted by the time it gets this far, especially when the brand needs to communicate with consumers in many different cultures and in many different languages.

Obviously, these issues have big implications for the way a company hires its people: arguably, learning how to manage a global brand is as much about culturally sensitive human resources management as it is about systems and practices. And because, as I have frequently observed, the most powerful brands are usually the ones with the most effective internal communications, it's also a great deal to do with the way brand values are *taught* within the organization, and there are important lessons here to be learned from the world of education.

I once had a job as an English teacher, and made the same mistake which I imagine many beginners in that profession make: I started out with the assumption that teaching was all about me, the teacher, possessing a certain body of data which my students needed to share, and finding ways of passing that data on to them.

I soon realized that this isn't the point at all: the quantity of information which students need to acquire after primary education is simply too great for it to be handed over, piece by piece, from teacher to pupil, and in any case, it is enormously hard to digest information given in this way.

No, real teaching is making people want to learn. Teaching is about having a passion for your subject, and knowing how to *make that passion contagious.*

And this fact is as true for communicating brand essence amongst a large group of marketing, sales, and advertising people around the world as it is for teaching Shakespeare to teenagers. Give them the raw data, and they will discard it the moment your back is turned. But explain *why* it's there, *how* it got there, *why* it's important, *why* you love it, and *what* they can do with it, and you'll generate a hunger for acquiring more and more of that data which will last them for the rest of their lives.

DESCRIBING BRAND ESSENCE

The archetype of a brand is not a simple thing: if it could really be described in a few words, then none of these problems of communication would exist.

A great many convenient formulae have been devised over the years which purport to make advertising and branding activity simpler, more scientific, more effective, and more controllable. Perhaps as a result of this mass of advice, I sometimes observe, even amongst experienced and marketing-literate companies, that there is confusion about some very fundamental issues, and distinctions between very different things become blurred.

For example, when companies are quite properly attempting to define the personality of their brand before embarking on an advertising or marketing exercise, I often see them struggling to reduce its essence down to the shortest, simplest communication—they sometimes even give themselves the brief that it should be expressed in a single sentence or even a single *word*.

This strikes me as being a rather difficult and rather unwise thing to attempt. The notion that "if you can't say it in one sentence it's too complicated" probably derives from teaching about USPs or positioning statements—but these are consumer communication briefs, which undoubtedly benefit from being clear and simple.

It's perfectly true that the average advertisement or mailer is more likely to work if it isn't packed with too many promises or ideas. But a brand is a rather different creature from an advertisement, and simplicity as an aim for a brand seems more likely to stunt its growth than encourage its effectiveness.

ABOUT RICHNESS

If you compare *Fortune* magazine's table of America's most admired brands today and 60 years ago, you will find that in many categories, the same brands occupy the same position.

One could make a whole series of interesting hypotheses based on this fact (not least that the role of dedicated brand manager can't have very much to do with a brand's success, since the job was only invented halfway through the lifetime of most of these brands). But mainly it proves that big brands have quite a strong tendency to survive, and even survive fairly aggressive mismanagement.

This is probably because consumers want to believe in big brands and need the reassurance and guidance which they offer, and are inclined to forgive and forget all but the grossest aberrations.

And this is surely possible only because such brands have become rich and complex over the years, and small imperfections and deviations have little effect on the whole picture. A younger and hence simpler brand, which is associated with only one or two qualities in the consumer's mind, is far more at risk: a single anomaly might contradict half of the brand's character and cause the whole edifice to crumble.

It has been said many times before that brands are like people—the common use of the expression "brand personality" shows how general this assumption has become—and personality, almost by definition, is a complex thing which will not respond well to being reduced down to a single sentence.

If you ask me why I like my friend Mary, I will probably have trouble answering your question. I may try a few different answers without much success and end up rather lamely saying, "I don't know, I just like her, that's all." If you insist on me naming her qualities, these are likely to appear vague and even contradictory: I might say, "well, she's great fun, really lively . . . but she can be very quiet and sympathetic if you're feeling depressed," or, "she's really deep, but most of the time we just crack jokes."

If you ask some of her other friends the same questions, they will probably say quite different things about her too, especially if you ask some of her friends in other countries. You might end up with the impression that Mary isn't one person at all. But she is: she just responds differently to different people, as we all do, and responds differently to different situations. The thing which makes her one person is her personality: the archetype which governs her choice of response to people and situations.

Richness is very much the essence of that personality: rather than a simple, single rule which defines Mary, Mary is the sum of a great many characteristics and behavioral tendencies, which gradually, over the years, we come to understand as being the fabric which make Mary up.

And because she's so complex, our relationship with her is flexible and forgiving. We can allow her weaknesses and failures—we can even like her more for these if they confirm other parts of the picture which we find likeable.

The one thing which might really throw us would be if she ever did anything which was genuinely out of character. People, almost by definition, can't do this—they can't be untrue to their own archetype, unless they consciously will it. You could argue that such an effort of will is no less an expression of our personality than our involuntary actions. Brands can, because they are steered by inexpert human drivers, and not by God. Maybe *that's* the argument for brand management.

WHEN BRANDS TRAVEL

So richness rather than simplicity in a brand is to be desired, so long as it's always true to archetype; and it follows that richness is especially desirable when a brand needs to appeal to different groups of consumers in different countries.

If our brand is to gain in equity by showing reasonable consistency around the world, it becomes especially important that it embraces many diverse qualities (as long as they are all true to type) so that even people from entirely different cultures, speaking different languages and inhabiting widely different market situations, can still find elements of durable and relevant appeal within the same personality.

Again, of course, these things cannot be decided on or constructed from the center: the international characteristics of a brand need to be inspired by or learned from the actions and views of consumers in each country. No company official, irrespective of his or her godlike understanding of the brand's personality, can possibly hazard an opinion about how and whether it can be fully, relevantly, and attractively expressed in all possible market situations and all possible languages.

So even when the branding divinities think they are describing universal personality attributes for their brand, all of which will evoke precisely equivalent responses in all of their consumers around the planet (subject, of course, to accurate translation), they are kidding themselves.

The reality is that brand attributes are inescapably defined by words whose meanings are uniquely linked to the brand's home culture. For example, a brand book for an American company might list personality attributes such as *warm, human,* and *authoritative,* but the associations of these terms are neither straightforward nor universal, however easy translatable they may appear to be. Consider what *warm* implies to Latvians and to Maldivians, or *authoritative* to North Koreans and to Southern Italians. And you could write a substantial thesis about what *human* implies to the Japanese and to the Australians.

About Hierarchies

Most international companies have a lamentable tendency to devise their communications and marketing actions according to an invisible, unspoken, unacknowledged, but very real hierarchy. All actions and thought are generated by the lead country, in the lead language, in the context of the lead culture, and that relatively unimportant side-issue—the rest of the world—is relegated to the status of post-production. This would be fine, and very convenient, if it wasn't for the fact that the company's consumers and sales and marketing people around the world have an uncanny ability to sense when they're being treated as an afterthought, and they don't like it.

Avoiding the problem soon boils down to a question of politics. It's clear that internationalness needs to be built into a brand from the ground up: just as an advertising campaign devised for one market and "adapted" for another will seldom fool consumers into believing that they're being given first-hand communications, so a brand personality described and charted by a group of American or Japanese branding gods will lack real bite and relevance to Polish or Greek mortals by the time it's converted into consumer advertising or internal communications guidelines. Clearly, the brand's

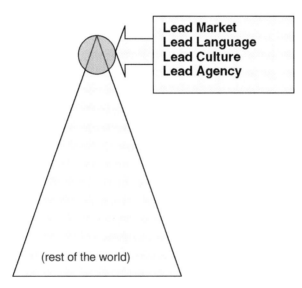

The hierarchical approach to international communications.

Mount Olympus must be a multicultural and multilingual place—I'm tempted to say that *every single export market* should have its representative at this stage of the process.

But not only must the needs of each market culture be built into the brand: the brand needs to be built into corporate strategy. In a commercial age where brand becomes the main competitive advantage of more and more organizations, the representation of branding and marketing at board level becomes more and more valuable; and since global branding requires global thinking, an international, brand-literate or brand-driven Olympus becomes a vital necessity.

And it goes almost without saying that the brand book which this group develops should be, at the very least, an interactive, polylingual, polycultural brand CD, rather than one of those boring folders of rules and regulations, invariably written in English ("because we're an English-speaking company"), which just end up on country managers' shelves, gathering dust.

But it's the same problem that the networks encounter when trying to create international advertising campaigns: few can honestly say they've managed to collect together such a group in one place at one time, and not ended up with a riot on their hands.

Many of the brand-owners who have tried it quickly and gratefully revert to the cozy hierarchy which was their previous default mode, thanking their lucky stars that they belong to the lead culture, and weren't born foreign.

The *winners* in this race, on the other hand, have just started out on a long and very tortuous voyage of discovery.

WHO ARE YOU, ANYWAY?

It's important to underline that understanding the culture of the markets where you hope to advertise can and should affect your brand's behavior, its actions, its language, but it cannot and should not try to affect *who you are* as a corporation, as a brand, or as a citizen of your nation of origin.

This is a distinction which many companies (and individuals) do not make at all naturally, but a simple hierarchical model from neurolinguistic programming (NLP) can help to resolve the issue with very little difficulty. I'll take a page to describe this model, as I find it extraordinarily useful for prioritizing all manner of information, both personally and commercially:

- At the highest level lies our *identity.* This attribute or set of attributes really doesn't change very much at all during the course of our lives: it is the sum of those really fundamental characteristics which make us *who we are,* rather than somebody else, or nobody at all. In branding terms, this is the essence of the corporation's personality.
- At the next level lie our *beliefs* and *values.* These may change over the lifetime of an individual or corporation, but they tend to evolve very slowly, and are closely linked with identity. In corporate terms, these are the company's *mission* and *vision,* and, like identity, are often intimately related to or inherited from the personality of the CEO or founder.
- Below beliefs and values are *skills* and *talents:* the stuff that we do particularly well or particularly willingly. We can learn new skills, and abandon old ones, but it takes time for such changes to occur, as much of this is innately connected with our inner qualities. Our skills and talents are what make us perform differently from other people; in companies, these are our core competencies, our traditional operations.
- One stage below the abilities we're born with or painstakingly acquire are our *behaviors:* this is simply the stuff that we happen to be doing at any given moment. Ideally, it should match the level above, but often it doesn't, and this can cause tension and unhappiness: an observation which applies equally to individuals and to companies.

- At the bottom lies *context:* this is what surrounds us, and the stuff which happens to us. We exercise more control over this than we sometimes imagine (we can always move someplace else if we don't like it). Again, it should ideally be in harmony with the levels above it, and if it's not, it can cause problems.

Now, whenever things happens to us, it can be very valuable simply to measure the experience against these parameters, and consequently to decide how important it is, and to what extent it really affects us, and to what degree we can control it.

A brand, just like a person, really cannot control *who* it is: that is a reality borne out of historical accident and genetics. Even if a company one day decides that it is going to *change* its brand, the perception of that brand actually resides with its consumers, so it will probably create confusion and achieve little else.

The fact that brands exist in the minds of consumers is actually quite a useful thing: it almost literally *outsources* part of the company's value, which provides great stability as long as you don't fight against it. It's like a diesel-powered generator: even if the lights go out in the office building, there is still value inherent in your customers' perception of you for a short period, and life carries on until the problem is resolved.

But, just like a person, one of the most valuable exercises that a corporation can go through is to learn exactly *who* and *what* it really is. And that starts from understanding how it appears to others; and how it appears to others is largely determined by the ways in which its values and beliefs, its actions and its competencies, differ from those of its competitors, both international and domestic.

One of the most significant individual factors about brands which operate on an international level is also the one which is most often overlooked by their owners, because it seems so obvious: where they come from.

Where Are You Coming From?

The provenance of a brand is perhaps the first thing which overseas consumers want to know about you, and it will drive their perceptions and their prejudices right from the very start. It is a phenomenon over which you have extremely little control, not least because it's an objective fact which you cannot change.

Which is not to say that people don't try. There are plenty of examples of brands (and individuals) which *lie* about their provenance, because they think it will make them appear more exotic or attractive: what I call *cuckoo brands*, because they lay their eggs in other people's nests.

Italy's number-one selling chewing gum, Brooklyn, its packaging emblazoned with a reasonably accurate image of the eponymous Bridge, is manufactured in Milan by the Perfetti company, and has never been near the States in its long life. Saisho Electronics, the mock-Japanese house brand of a U.K. white goods retailer, Dixons, has no cultural roots, heritage or history outside Great Britain—although the product itself might easily be manufactured in China and assembled in Thailand.

Sometimes it's the consumers who make false assumptions about a brand's provenance, not the brand owner who lies about them. I'm certain that part of the reason why the American laser/fax supplies and photofinishing company, Nashua, has prospered abroad is because so many people believe that it's a Japanese company—a provenance which, in Europe and other regions, has carried more associations of hi-tech competence in recent decades than American provenance (Nashua is, of course, the name of the New Hampshire town in which the company is located, and the word is, I guess, Algonquian).

The provenance of brands can also switch with a change of brand owner: characters like Winnie-the-Pooh, Mary Poppins and Alice in Wonderland, all of which were once quintessentially English, are now perceived by children around the world as being quintessentially American, thanks to the power of their Disney overbrand and Disney makeover; likewise, Quasimodo, Anastasia, Snow White and Hercules are no longer French, Russian, German or Greek, but all come from the same global-American culture stable as Mickey Mouse and Donald Duck.

This phenomenon is the converse of the cuckoo brand effect: here, the cuckoo steals eggs from other birds' nests and hatches them in its own. I've just taken my children to see *Mulan,* and I'm still in shock: what this company does, in my opinion, is absolutely piratical. It travels around the world stealing scraps of culture from different countries; then it simplifies, dilutes, sterilizes and packages up those scraps, dips them into a tacky sauce made of totally ethnocentric and heavily sentimental American values, and *sells* them back to their rightful owners.

And yes, I know that paragraph has cost me whatever slight chances I may have had ever to get some work out of the Disney Company, but I feel good about it. At least I've had my say.

THE ASSOCIATIONS OF PROVENANCE

Something even more dramatic can occasionally happen with provenance. If a country begins to produce and market enough powerful brands in a product category which was previously associated with another nation, the perceived provenance of the entire category is liable to switch: for example, outside Europe, pizza is now generally associated with America, simply because so many of the global pizza *brands* are known to be American, even though pizza was originally a national product of Italy.

Interestingly, this process hasn't occurred with pasta, which is still understood to be Italian. Perhaps this is because dry packaged goods have been in commerce, and hence branded, for very much longer; consequently, Italian brands had time to become established long before the product became adopted as a "world food." In other words, pizza was "taken up" by brandowners whilst it was still non-proprietary *cultural freeware* (it was something you cooked at home or ate in a restaurant, and was consequently part of the social rather than commercial fabric of its native culture), and before it became somebody's intellectual property. Branded pizza has really only existed for as long as people have had freezers, and most of the "Italian" pizza brands on the market are cuckoo brands, claiming phony Italian provenance.

But with very few exceptions, the really successful international brands come from countries which have a brand image of their own, and the product is often strongly linked with that image. It's an Italian car, associated with the Italian qualities of style, speed, innovative design. It's French perfume, sold on French chic, classiness, wealth. It's a Japanese TV, majoring on the Japanese virtues of high-tech expertise, miniaturization, value for money.

Just like corporate brands, provenance brands evoke certain values, qualifications and emotional triggers in the consumer's mind about the likely values of any product which comes from that country. In the United Kingdom, we're happy to buy banking services from Sainsbury's, a supermarket, because there is a healthy and attractive match between the values, qualifications and emotional triggers we already associate with the Sainsbury's corporate brand, and the attributes which we demand from people who handle our money.

Likewise, Europeans and Americans are happy to buy outdoor clothing from Australia because the country which produced Crocodile Dundee is surely well qualified to protect us from weather and wild animals; and there's a good emotional match with the perceived Australian qualities of rough and ready, humorous, unselfconscious masculinity.

Perhaps the most compelling aspect of provenance-as-brand-attribute is the fact that, if used wisely, it can represent an almost unassailable competitive advantage. Take, for example, the rather familiar scenario, where manufacturers in an overseas market develop the expertise to produce goods of equal or superior quality to imported goods — perhaps at a lower price than the imports, and with the added reassurance of a domestic brand name. In such a situation, imported brands will stand little chance of survival — unless, that is, there's a quality within the brand which appeals more to consumers in that marketplace yet cannot be credibly imitated by the domestic manufacturer.

That quality is provenance. When Japanese companies began to develop the expertise to produce their own high-quality electronic, optical and automotive products in the 1950s and 1960s, they all but drove American and European brands out of the market, through a combination of nontariff trade barriers and a simple consumer preference for domestic products,[1] which was no doubt partly driven by the strongly communitarian element in the Japanese culture.

Apart from the global superbrands, the only Western brands which are now left with a significant market share in Japan are those upmarket luxury brands whose provenance is strongly linked to their brand: Scotch whisky, French perfume, Italian fashion, Swiss watches, Belgian chocolate, German cars. These brands continue to prosper because their provenance is unarguable, indispensable and irreplaceable: in such cases, consumer perception is that all other product or brand attributes are insignificant compared to the primary requirement of authentic provenance.

This is the kind of positioning which not only brand owners, but countries too, need to work hard at developing and maintaining around the world. It is a kind of *intellectual protectionism* which gives that country's brands the biggest boost and the greatest protection in international markets that one can possibly imagine.

But it's not easy, and it requires constant investment and constant vigilance. As I've said, provenance can be faked, so part of the skill of building and maintaining provenance attributes within a brand is about establishing *authentic* heritage in ways which are meaningful in the context of the target culture, and which pre-empt and prepare the consumer against the inevitable arrival of local "cuckoo" brands. The other danger is from shifting consumer perceptions and beliefs: as French wine-growers and European automobile manufacturers have discovered to their cost, other countries can quickly steal away the "compulsory provenance" position.

WHICH KIND OF INTERNATIONAL?

Many brand-owners, if you ask them, say that whilst they wouldn't want their provenance to be completely erased, they are also nervous about coming across as *too* "local." Many of them say they want to be perceived as "international," but this seems like a rather inexact concept, and it's important to specify what exactly is meant by *international*.

I can think of at least three entirely different species of international brand, and there may well be more: I call them the *polynational* brand, where consumers all around the world are convinced that the brand is native to their own country (such as Mars, Heinz, Dove, Colgate and Esso); the *intranational* brand, which is perceived to "come from international," and if it inhabits any physical region at all, it's the empty space between airports (these are typically luxury brands like St Moritz, Ambre Solaire, Alfred Dunhill, Hilton and Rolex); and the *supranational* brand, which is not perceived to have any particular provenance at all, but simply exists (these are usually big corporate brands behind long-established and thoroughly internationalized products: like Kodak, Lego, Kellogg's, IBM and Reebok).

There are, of course, many shades of national provenance too. Nike, for example, is a more Euro-American brand than Pepsi, Timberland seems definitely more mid-

Atlantic than Levi's, and Sony is Japanese in a very different (more "global") way than Suntory.

It's interesting how the impression of a brand's provenance is often in contradiction to the *language* of its name, so strong is this element of its personality—Heinz is a perfect example.

If you ask British consumers about Heinz, they will wax lyrical about it being a quintessentially British brand, how they grew up with it, and so on. Heinz advertising in the United Kingdom is based on enhancing and exciting the brand's deeply-rooted local cultural associations. For American consumers, there's a rather similar reaction, and if you told them that across the Atlantic people thought of it as a typically British company, they'd be amazed. And the British conviction is all the more surprising when you consider that *Heinz* is an almost pantomime German name: not an issue for Americans, whose names come from all over the world anyway, but British people are exceedingly sensitive to the apparent provenance of names, and a German or Italian or Swedish surname normally sticks out like a sore thumb: here, the brand aura surrounding Heinz completely screens this factor out.

Even direct references in the logo to a brand's origin can be mentally discarded by consumers if they run counter to what the consumer wants to believe about its provenance: Reebok's old Union Jack logo, for example.

BRAND EXTENSIONS, BRAND PAIRINGS

Look around, and there are many powerful parent brands which haven't yet explored the rich potential of unexpected yet compelling brand extensions: Boeing suitcases? Greyhound Bus sunglasses? Swatch skis? NATO computers? And of course, the associations these brands have in their home market may be totally different from the position they occupy in the minds of foreigners: Greyhound Buses, for example, are viewed by many Americans as being a pretty skuzzy item, but by Europeans as an intensely romantic icon, redolent of Route 66, road movies, Kerouac, and the land of freedom and adventure.

It's a game which is almost as amusing to play as the converse, where you try to mis-match parent brands and brand extensions as horrendously as possible: Boeing toilet paper? Greyhound Bus air freshener? Swatch cough syrup? NATO pizza? Of course, it's more than a game: it's an exercise we often use to help companies get their own heads around what their brand is, what it could be, and what it definitely shouldn't be.

In exactly the same way, when you try to match provenance with product, there are some pairings which clearly make brand sense, and others which just don't. People might well buy Indian accountancy software or a stylish Lithuanian raincoat, and although I'm tempted to say that they probably *wouldn't* buy Peruvian modems or Dutch perfume, attitudes can and do change awfully quickly. Ten years ago, who would have believed that we Europeans could be happily consuming Japanese beer, Malaysian cars and Danish mozzarella?

It's not surprising, though, that so many of the world's successful commercial brands come from the Top Ten "country brands"—America, England, Scotland, France, Italy, Spain, Sweden, Japan, Switzerland and Germany.

Certainly, when we talk of the "brand image" of a country, it can easily sound like a list of shallow clichés and facile prejudice, and may prove depressing, even insulting, to the people who actually live there: but these commonplaces are a fine platform on which to build a believable global brand. Mass communications, and especially international mass communications, need to deal in a currency which is at heart quite gross: it is one of the more tricky and rewarding tasks of advertising and marketing to manipulate the clichés into something more creative, more substantial, more fair, more true.

The reality is that harnessing the power of provenance brands is a time-honored shortcut to establishing brand equity in new products. It's doubtful whether Daewoo would have enjoyed such rapid success in the United Kingdom if other Korean manufacturers had not first helped to lay the groundwork of establishing a credible set of provenance attributes for Korea in popular British culture; Coca-Cola would certainly be half the global brand it is today were it not so inextricably linked with Brand USA, the world's most valuable country brand.

America has become such a powerful brand over the years because it's been marketed so well—having the best advertising agency in the world (Hollywood) pumping out feature-length Brand America cinema commercials for nearly a century has certainly helped. And they also have that wonderful sales promotion agency, NASA, which periodically sends a rocket into space, in order to demonstrate the superiority of American technology.

Having a parent brand as powerful as the United States gives you a significant head start: commercial brands from Top Ten countries merely have to attach themselves to the equities implicit in their provenance, and a cultural trail is instantly blazed for them around the world. It's like hitching your trailer to a dragster.

USING PROVENANCE WISELY

The ultimate purpose of culturally-sensitive international advertising is certainly *not* to disguise the brand's provenance and have it masquerade as a local brand—this can, in fact, be extremely dangerous to the integrity and survival of foreign brands when they travel abroad.

The brand's real origins may or may not be considered an important facet of its personality and brand equity, but advertising is seldom in the business of making brands seem less exotic than they really are. Sometimes, the very fact that

the brand is sold in so many countries is a point worth celebrating, and it's a dangerous fallacy to assume that just
because somebody lives in one country they don't want to
hear about other countries.

These days, there is hardly any topic which people find
more fascinating than other lands and other cultures: so,
paradoxically, the most international theme can sometimes
be created through the use of the most intensely "local" subjects. One good example of this is the long-running global
press and poster campaign for Jack Daniel's bourbon,
which becomes effectively international by being decidedly
local: rather than try to tell you who you are, it tells you who
it is, and talks about where it comes from, rather than where
it's going to. This approach, if done sensitively and without
arrogance, communicates a very attractive sense of *self-
confidence* in the brand: I know my worth, I'm proud of my
origins, but not in a way which attempts to aggrandize me or
diminish you. These are *tolerant* ads.

Whether or not we choose to celebrate the fact that a
brand comes from somewhere else is one thing, but it is certainly possible to go too far in the direction of local cultural
immersion: a brand could end up looking so indigenous that
it loses any equity which its real provenance might have
added to the brand; or it could simply appear to be trying too
hard, and irritate consumers.

The provenance of your brand is one of the characteristics which determine your *right* or license to communicate
fluently in your domestic market. But that license becomes
slightly limited when a brand travels, and if you allow your
communications to display *intensely* local familiarity with the
culture of your export markets, this might even set up
uncomfortable tensions. This is because your consumers
know where you really come from, and might be confused or
offended if you suddenly stop behaving like an outsider.
Indeed, the fact that they'd had you down in their minds as
an outsider may have been a source of comfort and reassur-

ance to them, and if the brand begins to become too well acculturated, it may lose respect. Don't forget that there's always the risk of what I call *Groucho Marx syndrome.*

Sun Microsystems, for example, are currently running an international campaign based on the concept *we're the dot in dot.com,* and it includes a number of locally-created executions. In London, for example, there is one poster in the campaign which features a mocked-up London street sign, bearing the words "Square Mile," followed by the suffix ".com" in handwriting. (The "Square Mile" refers to the City of London, where most financial institutions are based — it's our equivalent of Wall Street.)

Now, there's no actual *street* in London called "Square Mile," so the street sign visual is a bit of creative license, which, if it had appeared in the advertising of a domestic brand, would probably not have seemed out of place. But coming from Sun Microsystems, a company which like most significant players in the IT field is perceived to have a very strong U.S. heritage, it seems decidedly odd. In fact, I discovered from talking to a few people who had seen the poster, we all assumed that they had simply made a mistake because of their lack of local knowledge: we thought we'd caught them out, and sneered.

As it happened, the poster came from a U.K. agency, and was devised by people who know perfectly well that there's no street in London called Square Mile. But because, from the consumer's point of view, *the person (brand) talking* was American, we interpreted it as a mistake.

Interestingly, when I realized that the gag was fully intentional and fully conscious, I was even less happy about the messaging, and actually felt quite offended that this foreign brand should come here and start taking creative license with *my* culture. It's a bit like when you meet someone at a party who behaves as if they know you better than they actually do: most people find such behavior extremely offensive. Or it's like playing with a language that you're in the process of learning — you're starting to get more confident, and one day make a rather clever joke in the language, but it simply causes puzzlement: people assume that you've made a mistake, even though exactly the same joke made by a native might have caused much mirth. It's all to do with people's expectations of their interlocutor, conditioned by their knowledge of his or her provenance.

Then the next poster in the campaign appeared: a huge, full-color Union Jack, with a ".com" after it, and my outrage knew no bounds. There's almost *nothing* more despicable than a foreign company trying to ingratiate itself in an export market by cloaking itself in that country's flag: it makes itself a turncoat, and one doesn't know whether to dislike it more for laying claim to an identity to which it has no right, or despising it for having so little loyalty to its own.

I know it sounds a bit old-fashioned, but one should never underestimate the importance of traveling brands having a *proper sense of humility!*

EMIGRÉ BRANDS AND PRIDE OF ORIGIN

Taking pride in one's origins, as the Jack Daniel's example shows, needn't be an act of cultural aggression, superiority or ignorance: often it's simply a mark of self-confidence and self-knowledge, qualities which are extremely valuable in brands. Just as we tend to admire the people who seem to know who they are, so we admire brands which have a proper sense of their own identity.

Even émigré brands which have been abroad for a century or more can sometimes find a new pride and a new sense of purpose from rediscovering their provenance. One wonders what impact it might have if some of the pioneers of global branding—companies like Singer, for example, which was a global brand long before the term was coined, and which, over the decades, have lost all trace or recollection of their actual origins—were now to reassert ownership of their national heritage too.

The parallel with human émigrés is irresistible. A century ago, immigrants to the United States happily traded in their native languages and cultures in order to become Americans, but their descendants are now rediscovering those roots as a source of much pride and comfort.

Actually, this process often occurs within the lifetime of an individual: the children of immigrants frequently reject their parents' culture because they find it socially uncomfortable being different from their peers (children are so strongly inclined to recognize and victimize nonconformity within the group that even the possession of a second language — surely an asset to be admired and envied rather than looked down on — tends to be seen as a mark of social inferiority).

But once those children become young adults, and start to take stock of their independent existence from the group, and take pride in their individuality, they may find that the things which make them different are to be cherished, rather than thrown away — this tends to be the case in societies where individuality is prized: in countries like Japan and Korea, where conformism to the majority is seen as a virtue, such a counter-reaction might never occur.

Madonna and Sylvester Stallone don't even pronounce their own surnames in a way that a first-generation Italian could understand, yet Madonna wears a T-shirt with the slogan "Italians do it better" and Stallone rather likes being known as the Italian stallion.

The fact is that belonging to a group of a quarter of a billion people hardly feels like belonging at all, and people need to belong. (How long before we see Arnold Schwarzenegger in a "Proud to be Austrian" sweatshirt, I wonder?)

THE DRIVERS OF CONSISTENCY

So you have a brand, and by the use of multicultural representation at the highest level, you've defined its fundamental essence in a culturally-neutral way, and you've figured out how you want to make use of its provenance.

You now know exactly who you are, and where you're coming from. Let's suppose that you also know who you want to talk to, but the trouble is, there's this stuff called culture getting between you.

One thing is constant: the brand itself. Its global audience is the opposite: it appears to be totally inconstant. So, the thing which links the two together—your communications—should they be as constant as the brand, or should they be as inconstant as the consumer?

If you make communications entirely consistent, they will accurately reproduce the brand, but not in a form which the consumer can consistently comprehend; on the other hand, if you make your communications as various and diverse as the consumer, they will no longer mirror the constancy of the brand.

The correct answer is almost always a combination of the two, but not in a spirit of weak compromise: the *subject of discourse* relates in a constant fashion to the brand, and the *mode of discourse* is flexibly tailored to the varying needs of the consumer.

Companies which practice consistency in their international communications cite many reasons for the policy, and in many cases it really is because looking at consumer diversity around the world is like opening Pandora's box: the results are so bewildering and far-reaching, that you quickly shut it again. In such cases, consistency is simply a metaphor for control: if a company can't cope with all that difference, it comes naturally to try to impose some kind of order.

EXTERNALLY AND INTERNALLY-DRIVEN CONSISTENCY

The pursuit of consistent communications isn't always a free choice made by the brand owner.

Sometimes, for example, a consistent brand positioning may be driven by consumers, and consistent communications are the natural consequence of this. Ever more mobile consumers, the globalization of media, the spread of the internet, and the adoption of the Euro are making it more and more difficult for brand owners to sustain different positionings — and consequently different price-points — for their brands in different markets.

In the past, many manufacturers have been able to create and maintain lucrative niche positionings for their products in certain countries, and enjoy the high margins, albeit lower volumes, that such a policy brings. But in other markets, perhaps because the brand has a different history, or because of a different deal with distributors or local producers, or because the product itself has always been consumed by a different target group with different levels of disposable income, the positioning may be quite different, the price much lower, and so the volumes need to be much higher.

The trouble is that holding two positionings is becoming an extremely risky business, because consumers are now very likely indeed to find out about it, and *mind*. The rapid spread of internet-based third-party product data (not to mention a company's own sites), constantly scanned by ordinary consumers as well as the consumers whom Faith Popcorn calls the "vigilantes," means that in situations like this, you can run but you can't hide. Suddenly, people can see stuff they weren't ever *meant* to see.

At best, a loyal consumer from a country where the brand is positioned as an upscale, exclusive choice, will feel confused and disappointed that the brand seems to lose its self-respect in the countries where it's positioned as more mass-market (and this sense of disappointment can be fatal to that consumer's attachment to the brand). At worst, she will feel ripped off, and realize that the premium she has been paying for the brand at home, far from being a compliment to her superior taste, a mark of her status, or a reassurance that she has selected the brand for the discerning few, is simply spent on expensive advertising designed to make her believe these empty promises.

The companies right in the firing-line are the ones making or selling smaller, lighter, lower-cost, non-perishable or digitally transferable items, which can easily be bought direct from the internet or other international media and shipped, if necessary, from abroad. A CD is the classic example: when I find that I can buy the same CD in a record store in London for £13.99 and on the internet for $8.50, and it can be mailed to me within three days, I will simply move my custom. My local retailer won't even know what has happened to me: I'm a customer one day, and gone the next.

On the other hand, if the goods are unshippable or perishable, I can complain, and if there's a vigilante streak in my nature I'll make it my duty to stamp out this unfairness using whatever tools I have to hand, but since I'm usually quite busy and don't feel *that* oppressed by large corporations, I'll simply accept that I have lost any loyalty I may have felt towards that brand, and be on the lookout for an alternative. My local supermarket or auto dealer won't lose *all their* customers straight away just because they've found out that people over in France are paying 40% less—at the least they have a certain amount of time to justify their prices or drop them before they lose too much business.

A typical example of the culturally unavoidable but commercially untenable dual positioning is single malt whisky, which is positioned in the United Kingdom as a solitary, expensive, upscale indulgence for older men, but in Italy as a much more affordable drink for younger men and women in lively social situations. How long can such instability last? All that has protected brand-owners until now from paying the price of these equivocal situations has been geography, a phenomenon which the internet has effectively killed.

In such situations—and there are many—a great number of existing international brand-owners are driven, often against their will, into creating global positionings for their brands as fast as they can: and in price-driven scenarios like

116

this, the downwards pull tends to be the strongest. If there's one thing you just can't hurry, it's pushing a product upmarket and into a higher price bracket.

Many globalizations are driven by competition, and in a rapidly shrinking world, against a pattern of increasing convergence, competition can come from almost literally anywhere, and from almost any type of company.

There are many cases of highly successful and profitable domestic manufacturers which have been put out of business by other companies operating far away — not even necessarily "muscling in" on the manufacturer's domestic market — but which are simply available on the world market, and offer lower price, better specification or service, more choice or more attractive brand values.

A corporation's decision to create global advertising campaigns may also be driven by structural change within the corporation, rather than as a result of direct pressure from the marketplace: global advertising campaigns can be directed and created centrally, which is very useful if the marketing department has been centralized. And the reason that the marketing department has been centralized is often quite simply because other departments in the company have been centralized too: distribution, legal, manufacturing, IT, HR, and so on — perhaps, on the advice of consultants, some major restructuring or re-engineering has created this situation, and marketing simply didn't occupy a prominent enough position in the corporation to point out that it's the odd one out, and *can* suffer profoundly from being directed in too centralist a manner — especially when centralization and standardization are believed to be synonymous.

SNAKE SOUP AND STILTON

Another very common reason for choosing the standardized international campaign route is to do with "quality control":

often, this is just a nice way of saying that the global marketing people don't rate the "local" markets' ability to do *good enough* advertising—nothing to do with its suitability for the market. This probably causes more unnecessary and counterproductive centralization than any other single factor.

It's very common for American or British companies to hire a multinational ad agency, yet invariably choose the work produced by the U.S. or U.K. offices because it seems like the best work, and is the most accessible to them: work seen out of the context of its original culture can often just seem *plain bad*.

It took me many years before I realized that this apparent difference in quality is often (but by no means always) a piece of distortion caused by cultural differences, not an objective truth. It's actually rather unfortunate. On many occasions in past years, I had experienced this phenomenon myself, and completely failed to see what was actually happening.

For example, I'd be in Scandinavia, and somebody would tell me about a new creative startup, and rave about their amazing originality, wit and creativity, and insist that I should see their showreel, because this was surely the hottest shop in Scandinavia. So we'd go round with great excitement and meet them and watch their reel, and invariably I'd be privately aghast to discover that it was just the usual weird Nordic stuff—fat, middle-aged men with mustaches rolling around in fields, speeded-up slapstick scenes, a lot of comic business with cows, a lot of talk I didn't understand even in translation, and fat, middle-aged women throwing large round cheeses at young men in suspenders.

And all around me, the Scandinavians who'd made this stuff, *and* the Scandinavians who hadn't, would be *demented* with laughter. It made me feel very lonely, and very anxious: after all, for a man in my position, supposedly an expert on culture and international creativity, admitting that I detested foreign advertising might prove to be a bit of a problem, but there was just no getting away from the fact.

So I thought I'd better spend some time on this problem, and see if I could learn to like the stuff. Then I noticed something which gave me a glimmer of hope: when I was watching British advertising in a room with people from other countries, the same thing would happen in reverse: I'd be in fits of laughter, and the Germans or French or Argentineans in the room would be looking at me as if I'd just sprouted an extra head.

Aha, I thought: perhaps this is a *perception* thing. Next thing I noticed was that when I watched Italian advertising, because I am reasonably fluent in the culture, I found *some* of it quite amusing, and didn't exactly split my sides, but did chuckle gently: the Italians were in hysterics, but the other English people, who didn't know Italy well, were looking rather bored and embarrassed.

Well, it's a simple point, and I apologize for laboring it, but I think it's extremely important. Most domestic advertising, because it's such an intense dose of culture, is completely inaccessible to people from outside that culture. But the strange thing is that most of the time this doesn't just make it look boring, or weird, or unfunny: mainly, it makes it look *incompetent* — plain bad. For some reason (perhaps somebody would like to write a thesis on the subject) the symptoms of cultural miscommunication in advertising most frequently resemble the symptoms of *bad* communication. Actually, maybe I know why: perhaps instinctively, we interpret our own failure to *decode* messages properly as the creator's failure to *encode* them properly. It's always more natural to put the blame on someone else.

At a simpler level, much of this is simply down to *taste:* it's hard to explain in rational or scientific terms, for example, why Chinese people like to eat things which English people don't, and vice versa. Yet Britons will categorically state that snake soup is repellent, and Chinese people that

Stilton cheese is not edible (or even approachable) by normal, decent human beings: yet millions of Chinese happily eat their soup while millions of Britons eat their cheese, so clearly neither is *right*.

For all these reasons, the whole business of judging international creative awards and selecting work to appear in advertising annuals and halls of fame is fraught with appalling dilemmas. How can a panel of jurors from one country possibly judge the quality of work from another country except by their own standards?

Every time I have to judge international creative awards, I'm conscious of the fact that hundreds of talented and hopeful agency people from around the world are voluntarily offering up their precious creations to the most unsuitable, ignorant, unsympathetic and biased audience they could possibly find. And despite our best efforts to award at least a modicum of foreign agencies, the proportion of winning campaigns is *invariably* 80% British, 15% other English-speaking countries, and 5% for the rest of the world. And we remain utterly convinced that this is nothing more than an accurate reflection of the fact that 80% of the best advertising in the world is British.

Perhaps it's not so odd that British and American advertising are almost the *only* species of advertising in the world which are regularly admired by people from other countries. I suspect that this fact may not be an absolutely reliable, objective measure of its quality, but rather a reflection of the fact that advertising, being a relatively new medium, still displays very strongly the roots of its own cultural provenance. Most of us who create advertising, anywhere in the world, learned how to do it by observing the work of Bill Bernbach, David Ogilvy, David Abbott, John Hegarty, and their ilk, and that has impressed an anglocentric currency and world view on the very medium itself. It would be a great thing if, over time, alternative traditions of advertising culture were to emerge, stemming from other national traditions of communication.

LET'S GET CONSISTENT

Whatever the reasons a brand-owner may have for wanting consistent positionings and consistent messaging, they're almost always for the benefit of the company rather than for the consumer: after all, there is such a thing as an international marketing director, but no such thing as an international consumer. It's a trivial point, but one which people tend to forget.

It's true that more and more consumers travel around a lot, and as I've said, if your target market happens to be frequent travelers, it makes sense to ensure that they see the brand positioned and communicated in a recognizable way wherever they go.

But—and this is where inexperienced international marketers often leap too far, too fast—this doesn't have to mean identical *executions* of that positioning. After all, your consumers are hardly going to sit down and compare the copy on your French ad with the copy on your Greek ad and instantly stop buying the product if there's any difference between the two. In fact, if they're interested enough to want to look that closely, and smart enough to be able to read both those languages, chances are they'll give you more credit for having had the sense to adapt the message intelligently to two different cultures rather than slavishly translating it into two different languages.

As an abstract notion, consistent communications may look like an attractive quality to aim for. For a start, it looks as if it might be an awful lot simpler than tailoring the message specifically to each market—at least, it looks simpler from the creative point of view, even if it tends to give rise to much tension and unrest at the country manager level.

Consistency also enables *some* cost savings: developing one campaign to run in lots of countries is likely to cost less than developing lots of campaigns running in lots of countries—but the cost argument tends to be marginal, because even though the savings on creative and production fees may be significant, especially on TV work, these are still tiny sums compared to the overall cost of media. Standardizing creative and production is merely scratching the surface of the financial issues, and a single misjudgment in the way media is bought can wipe out in one stroke a whole raft of painstakingly accrued creative and production savings.

In a broader sense, and over the longer term, consistency ought to be good for the company's balance sheet: when the brand is demonstrably the same in a large number of different countries, that makes the brand more valuable—assuming, of course, that it has not achieved this consistency at the expense of competitiveness and profitability in each market; assuming the company has the necessary accounting and evaluation systems to measure this; and assuming that such evaluation is part of its accounting policy.

The other large category of companies which tend to opt for consistent executions are the first-time and emerging exporters: for them, the cost of carrying out market research and tailoring their messages market by market, when they often have no physical presence in those markets, is simply inconceivable. Many of these companies are really just "trying their luck" overseas with a single product and a single marketing approach, and in many cases would probably be better advised to negotiate marketing deals with their local agents or distributors in each market, in order to build their overseas sales in a less risky, wasteful, and haphazard way.

True, using third party marketing does make it harder to control one's brand, but since most really successful brands develop as a consequence of successful products being successfully sold to a large number of consumers over quite long periods, it may make more sense to worry about building sales and distribution first and consistent brand equity second. If the product is good, and the brand *deserves* to succeed, this will happen more naturally (and more cheaply) on the back of successful market penetration than on pure brand marketing.

STAYING ON TOP OF THE WORLD

Trueness to the culture of the brand is all too often achieved at the expense of trueness to the culture of the market. Somehow, brand owners need to be able to weigh up both sides of the equation, and with equal understanding of each, decide on the best compromise—or, ideally, the perfect marriage—between the two.

Because one man or woman usually has ultimate responsibility for the brand in all its markets, that individual's personal judgment inevitably comes into the equation. But even the most experienced global marketing managers can only have one native culture and one native language, and as I've pointed out before, they can only confidently and accurately "feel" the rightness of the advertising and brand communications work which is created for their own market.

When it comes to the minor detail of those couple of hundred other markets which they *don't* know intimately, where they *weren't* brought up, where they *don't* speak the language, they're simply guessing. Naturally, neither the company's local marketing teams nor their agencies are to be relied upon for an objective opinion—after all, it's either your work you're asking them to assess if you've imposed a centralized campaign upon them, so they are quite likely to criticize it, or else you've let them create their own work, which they are rather *unlikely* to criticize. So where does our Senior Vice-President of Global Marketing turn for a second opinion?

In most cases, he or she usually has three options:

1. *The "trusted foreigners" network.* After many years working on international business in various multinational corporations, our global head of marketing has built up an impressive network of friends and ex-colleagues around the world, who speak various languages and know various markets. Trouble is, these people work for other companies now, and have full-time jobs, so

123

they simply don't have the spare time to be sufficiently briefed on the project in order to give a worthwhile response. Consequently, their view will be personal, prejudiced, subjective, hurried, uninformed, and quite probably extremely misleading.

2. *Local research.* This can only tell you about the average consumer's comprehension and liking of the work, and make a guess at how effective it's going to be. Consumers are not, on the whole, best qualified to comment on whether messages are "true to brand" or not, especially when the brand's not a well-established one.

3. *Cloning.* In the end, benchmarking against domestic advertising is the commonest technique of all, because it's the quickest, the cheapest, and because it enables the Global Marketing Director to exhibit the least possible weakness or uncertainty to the world in general. (It has to be said that most job titles containing the words "international" or "global" are pretty hard to live up to.)

Basically, technique 3 is all about finding out (inevitably, through backtranslations) how closely the various country versions match the "official" version as run at home. If they're the same, they're good. If they're different, they're not. Now, if you state it as baldly as this, it seems incredible that any intelligent marketer could possibly subscribe to such a system: but a few really do, even if it's seldom as clearly expressed or as clearly visible as this.

Of course, the people from Brand Headquarters are in a better position to judge whether work is right for the brand than whether it's right for each individual market. What could be more reassuring for our VPGM than to get off a dozen planes in as many countries and be greeted by a poster advertising his or her brand, accurately translated into the local language, identically art-directed, and containing the same double meaning in the tagline, the same colors, and ideally the same number of words in the headline?

One factor alone makes this ruthless technique less than childishly simple: the infuriating fact that certain really hardened foreigners actually insist on using *different writing systems*, rendering their work completely impenetrable to people from headquarters. Sorry, that was British irony at work again, but I know at least one old-school international marketing director who is perfectly convinced that the peoples of Asia and Central Europe and the Middle East evolved non-Roman writing systems with the specific intent of making his job harder to do.

This particular breed of international marketing executive was once quite common, although increasing familiarity with global business practice is mercifully driving it towards extinction. However, you still occasionally meet marketers who get sold on the idea of cloning because it gives them such an aura of machismo. Being able to produce a long string of apparently identical ads, each one with its headline obediently translated into an exotic-looking language, rather as certain men on street corners pull out a concertina of dirty postcards on a street corner, demonstrates that you have real *grit*. If you've been able to impose this kind of consistency on all those foreigners, despite their notorious cussedness, you are obviously a cross between John Wayne and Henry Kissinger, and it looks *wonderful* on your résumé.

Using the cloning technique to measure consistency, the diagnosis may be simple, but the treatment is slow and painful. Indeed, the fact that globally consistent advertising is such a difficult thing to achieve probably reinforces the sense that it's a quality worth striving for: the trick of teasing out the commonalities from a riotous collection of proudly, often aggressively different cultures, as I've mentioned before, is no easy one.

But lest anyone leap to the conclusion (as many do) that the supreme expression of a truly global brand is the creation of a smoothly homogeneous set of neatly cloned global communications materials, let me stress that the crucial issue is that consistency is not an end in itself: after all, the ultimate aim of any marketing process is surely to create maximum impact, maximum efficiency, maximum effectiveness, and maximum loyalty in each individual market. These aims are often in direct conflict with the struggle for consistency: almost by definition, the most effective approach for any given market cannot be the most effective in all other markets.

This sounds negative, but it's merely realistic: international advertising is extremely hard to do well, and it's best to start out with a clear and complete picture of the difficulties involved. Then you can start to figure out some systems and tricks for getting it right.

THE MARKETER'S ARROW

So it's definitely a worthwhile exercise to start off by dividing every element within the marketing mix into two groups: the parts which will benefit more from sensitivity to the culture of the brand, and those which will benefit more from sensitivity to the culture of the market. And rather than slavishly adhering to the absolute aim of perceptible consistency in all things, we should in every case consider the *underlying* issue—does consistency in this instance ultimately benefit the brand?

Often, there are natural divisions within the same medium. For example, when dealing with classic print and TV campaigns, clients and their agencies often treat words and images as comparable instruments, and in the effort to create a demonstrably coherent international campaign will force *both of them* to be as similar as possible across all markets. This is usually achieved by taking a successful campaign created for the domestic market by the lead

Wedding or funeral?

agency, and using this as a template or "master" which everyone else is required to "adapt" to local market conditions. Most commonly, there is a decree that the art direction can't be changed at all, and the copy may be translated into the language of each market, but the arguments, the structure, the positioning, and wherever possible the same creative devices used in the copy must be retained in translation.

On an instinctive level, this probably feels like sensible and reassuring behavior. But actually, when we split each advertisement up into its component parts, we soon discover an interesting fact: images work completely differently from words. For a start, images are more robust and usually travel better. Of course, everybody has their pet disaster stories about how certain images and certain colors mean dramatically different things in different markets (for example, white is traditionally associated with purity in the West but with death in the East; an owl is a symbol of wisdom in

France but of bad luck in Italy); and almost all forms of non-verbal communication carry different meanings in different cultures. The Texas Longhorns' "Hook 'em horns" gesture will get you into *big* trouble in Italy for implying that the person you're doing it to has an unfaithful wife or husband. The thumbs-up sign, that apparently universal gesture of friendly approval, will create dire consequences in Australia or Nigeria, because it happens to mean "fuck you."[2] Sorry, I have been trying to avoid scare-mongering, but I simply wanted to demonstrate that managing to communicate by avoiding words doesn't always mean that you've successfully avoided the need to modify your message.

All this is real enough, but as long as such issues are considered early enough in the planning and creative cycle, and the needs of each export market — social, cultural, economic, legal, etc. — are brought to bear at the conceptual stage, there is no reason why such differences should present overwhelming problems. They only become a problem if they're left until the end of the process.

If we accept that one of the underlying purposes of consistency is to present consumers as they travel between markets, with a recognizable "face" to the brand, as well as giving the manufacturer efficiencies of scale in developing advertising, packaging, and other promotional materials, then associating a set of colors, a photographic style, a logo, or a "look" with the brand is a pretty simple way of achieving that aim. The visual elements are where most of the production money gets spent, anyway: photography, illustration, film, design, and color printing. But this is clearly an argument for producing and adhering to an international *corporate identity* standard, not for cloning the entire communications vehicle.

So standardization of images is both possible and practical, as long as they're properly checked out by an international team at the start of the process, or ideally, dreamed up by an international team in the first place.

Words, on the other hand, don't like being homogenized,

and even the most valiant attempts to respect linguistic and cultural differences at the conceptual stage of the creative process usually can't prevent serious conflict between global brand needs and local market conditions occurring at the execution stage.

In reality, words are the marketer's finest and best instrument for achieving *difference*. For the very reasons that they don't work well as an international communications tool, they are an absolutely ideal tool for showing true sensitivity to the consumer's cultural environment. Images are good at achieving consistency at the expense of cultural sharpness, while words work well for building that sharpness back into the communication.

Images are the feathers on the shaft of the global marketer's arrow, but *words* are the point.

And giving a freer rein to words certainly doesn't mean that we can't create a consistent personality for the brand, as long as that freedom is given to people who are intellectually, philosophically, and even physically as close to the brand as possible. After all, we're not trying to make the *means we use* to express brand personality consistent, but the understanding and acceptance of that personality consistent amongst consumers in many different markets: As we shall see in Chapters 6 and 7, one of the key benefits of smart centralization is that it ensures that the necessary amount of *freedom of expression* is allowed within an environment which is strictly controlled and brand-driven, yet culturally sensitive to the marketplace in question.

The solution to the dilemma of consistency is surely a question of seeking to refine input, rather than control output. What becomes crucially important is that the people who are responsible for directing global communications and the appointed communicators of the brand fully understand the real personality, the deep essence of the brand, so that their expressions of that brand conform properly to its archetype.

Maintaining that perfect balance between control and freedom is very much the essence of international brand communications. Control, as we have seen, is not an easy thing to achieve.

But if that sounded hard, just take a look at how you achieve *freedom.*

The next chapter is about how you set people's thinking free: free enough to be global.

4

The Trouble with Creativity

──────

Here we are, then. A new chapter, and time for another disaster story.

This one concerns a brand of mosquito spray whose manufacturer decided to market it in an African country (it may have been Sénégal, but as is always the case with these stories, you can never find anybody who actually knows when and where it happened, so it's impossible to check).

The client's Paris agency was selected to create the launch commercial (probably because French is the official language of Sénégal), and, sensibly cautious about the dangers of over-sophisticated messages, decided to go for the non-verbal dumbshow approach.

The ad opens on two Senegalese men sitting in a room, slapping their arms and faces, where the mosquitoes are biting.

Jolly music starts, and a third man dances into the room, smiling and spraying the product into the air. One by one, his friends stop slapping themselves, stand up, and join in the dance. After a few seconds, all the men are dancing the conga around the room, smiling, and not slapping. The conga snakes out of the room, the door closes, the light switches off, a simple sales message appears on the screen, and that's the end of the ad.

The distributor reported disappointing sales, which were close to zero in the areas where the commercial had run.

Focus groups were duly conducted, and the following reaction was recorded:

"We understand that this new mosquito spray is supposed to be

special. But why should we pay more for a product which, in order to make it work properly, you have to dance?"

CREATIVITY: THE IMPOSSIBLE NECESSITY

The reaction of those respondents wasn't so surprising, really, in a culture where medicine and magic are pretty much the same thing, and where a special dance might indeed be the most natural way to ward off biting insects. The modern, Western product in its aerosol can was expected to provide a scientific solution to the problem—and yet the message seemed to be suggesting that it couldn't work without the aid of some old-fashioned magic.

Another way to view the moral of the story is this: people don't just read messages differently in different civilizations, they also read the media differently. Commercial television is a relatively new medium in Africa, and in rural areas viewers often do not distinguish readily between educational, political and promotional messages. Although this is changing very rapidly now, in cultures where the narrative tradition is largely oral, there is still a risk that any message may be taken to be *the literal truth.*

Moreover, to most tribal Africans, each ritual dance is its own complex and eloquent language: miming out the history of the tribe, appeasing the gods, choosing a mate, making rain, threatening violence. To the urban Parisians who created the commercial, if people are dancing, that just means they're happy. So in a sense, this is a translation story after all: one which proves that there are more kinds of language than we generally imagine.

Good. I think I've pretty much killed that story now.

The point I wished to make is that in international advertising, creativity is the impossible necessity. We can't do advertising without it, and yet it's the thing which makes

Another kind of language.

international work so dangerous and so hard to manage. If the mosquito spray commercial had simply shown the product and said *buy this, it's good,* then it might have weaseled around some of the worst misunderstandings and cultural traps, but it probably wouldn't have been especially memorable or effective advertising either.

And these days, making advertising is definitely harder work than it used to be. The emphasis placed on creativity—surely the hardest part of making an ad—has steadily increased over the last few decades.

This is partly because advertising is now a far more pervasive phenomenon in people's lives than it used to be, and people have gradually built up resistance to it. Once, consumers were prepared to put some effort into reading and understanding commercial messages, because it is a natural tendency to listen to what people are saying to you: but once they learned that there was seldom much value to be derived from these messages, consumers acquired the trick of shutting their minds to them. Consequently, advertisers now need to use more and more sophisticated tricks in order to persuade people that, contrary to all expectations, this time the message really *is* worth listening to.

People in advertising circles are very fond of dredging up old advertisements made by people like Bill Bernbach and David Ogilvy in the 1960s and saying how amazingly creative they were: *You don't have to be Jewish to enjoy Levy's*, or the picture of the Volkswagen with the word *Lemon* written underneath it. As a junior creative, I was always too respectful to admit that I didn't really get either of them, but the reality is that few of these ads would stand a chance in today's crowded media.

Of course they were creative *for their time*, and probably shocked people half to death in New York in those days. In 1913, the audience at the first performance of Stravinsky's *Rite of Spring* in Paris were so outraged they practically wrecked the concert hall: my five-year old daughter thinks it's "boring classical music."

In the fifties and sixties, creativity in advertising was really just the icing on the cake. If you did an ad which showed the product, gave the information, looked good, and was well placed, that was good enough—but if you also managed to communicate the message in a winsome, witty and original way, then you'd really hit the jackpot.

Now, Big Creative is the *cost of entry* into most markets. Unless every advertisement we create is the most astonishing advertisement ever created in the history of the universe, it fails because no-one will even notice it: it just won't register on the consumer's radar (as Kirshenbaum and Bond so eloquently put it)[1] and will vanish without trace, along with the considerable investment our client has made in developing and exposing it.

Consumers (and that includes us, so we can look around to check this) are bombarded every moment of the day with astonishing graphics, astounding utterances, the diligent application of unbelievable amounts of intelligence and hard work onto every tiny marketing problem.

I've always believed that there's a hidden pact going on between consumers and advertisers: consumers are only prepared to give us a moment of their increasingly precious attention if in return we reward them for it by genuinely *informing* them, genuinely stirring their *emotions,* or genuinely *entertaining* them.

This is the price of their voluntarily parting with some of their hard-won spare time in order to hear us try to persuade them to part with their hard-earned cash. And over the last half-century, as the consumer's attention has become a more and more valuable commodity, its price worldwide has steadily risen.

So which reward should we pick when planning an international campaign?

PAYING WITH INFORMATION

Giving information in advertising has always presented a particular challenge, for the simple reason that it's so easy for companies to forget a crucial fact about their product: *they are more interested in it than their customers are.* Reams of detail about a product may be utterly captivating to a person who spends most of his or her life working on that product, but are likely to exercise little fascination in the mind of the busy punter.

It's also useful to bear this point in mind when planning corporate advertising campaigns: nothing could be more boring for the average reader than companies talking about themselves. The trouble is that heads of corporate communications and public affairs, CEOs and the like are rather prone to assume that just because they eat, sleep, dream and smoke their own corporations, the rest of us must be on tenterhooks to hear them declaim their "vision," their "mission," or their "values."

Well, we're not.

As everybody is thoroughly sick of hearing, our biggest problem these days is an excess of information. Gone are the

135

When creativity was an optional extra.

When creativity was an optional extra.

days, I suspect, when minute observations like David Ogilvy's ticking clock in the Rolls Royce ad really achieve much stand-out—quite aside from the fact that this particular advertising technique has now been so energetically and enthusiastically imitated so many times over the years by disciples and admirers of the Ogilvian pen, it's hard to imagine ads like this stopping anybody in their tracks these days. The reality is that almost all the products you can buy now work pretty much perfectly, and do far more than you would ever expect or want them to do. (Of course the glaring exception to this rule is service companies, whose "product" is far, far harder to get right, because of the frustratingly intractable nature of the raw material, and all too often fails to live up to its promise.)

Yes, there is undeniably a strong temptation to make international campaigns product-based: in the absence of any useful commonality between their overseas target groups, companies often take sanctuary in talking about the one undeniably consistent element in the whole exercise: the product they're selling.

Trouble is, advertising which merely talks about product features, rather than user benefits, is extremely unlikely to achieve any lasting effect on the consumer. Indeed, ads based on lists of features are scarcely more than one-page brochures.

Paying with Emotions

Stirring emotions can be very dodgy terrain indeed, and international advertisers should be absolutely sure of their ground before setting out into it. Let us never forget that at heart we're still just trying to sell stuff to people, and sometimes, that sits uneasily with serious or important sentiments.

Benetton's campaigns have explored this terrain quite thoroughly, and people are frequently heard to comment on the striking mismatch between the big issues which Benetton's posters cause us to confront, and the fairly banal activity of selling brightly-colored sweaters to teenagers.

This criticism seems to be missing several points: firstly, that this advertising, like much youth advertising, is not designed to sell a product, but to make the brand famous— and this it does extremely effectively. Secondly, there is not *meant* to be a rational, logical link between the message and the product: the target group of this advertising neither looks for nor wants one. They wish to subscribe to a mindset, a philosophy, and this needs only to be linked to the brand, not to the product. The fact that the product bears the brand on its label will, ultimately, encourage sales of that product, but at the point of message, is almost incidental.

Actually, if you listen to Oliviero Toscani talking about his Benetton campaigns, he swears that the purpose of this advertising is not to sell sweaters, indeed that it's actually *risky* for the brand: it is, he claims, a genuinely disinterested attempt to use the power of advertising to increase public awareness of important issues. Benetton, we are expected to believe, are literally *donating* their vast marketing budget to the downtrodden in society, in a glorious, karmic gesture, to the lasting benefit of each and all of us.

Call me a cynic, but I suspect that this is only part of the story. It may not be entirely accidental that the images which Benetton use seem very accurately targeted at the *parents* of Benetton's core target market, and calculated to shock them as much as possible. Now, young adults want to rebel, as we all know, so hearing their parents fuss, fret and fulminate about this dreadful company could scarcely be better calculated to make their offspring rush off to the nearest Benetton and purchase armfuls of brightly-colored sweaters (doubtless with their parents' credit cards).

(It raises, incidentally, a fascinating concept: that one aspect of marketing a style brand can involve *actively repudiating* an unwanted target segment. In such a scenario, it is not enough merely to use advertising to encourage the most appropriate audience to accept the brand: it is also used to encourage the *least* appropriate audience to *reject* the brand.)

Benetton have somehow managed to get away with it, but attempting to move people by referring to major social issues in advertising, unless you're selling in the voluntary sector, is much more liable to annoy and alienate your audience than anything else.

But there are many ways of stirring the emotions without hanging the product onto a cause-related peg: every conceivable product or service has at one time or another been sold on some kind of emotional platform: for cars, insurance, banks, corporate brands, soft drinks and almost all sport-related products, the emotive approach has become practically *de rigueur* in Europe.

The technique is to identify a strong or uncommon emotion which can be credibly associated with the product or with its use, and concentrate on this rather than on the product itself, which may be quite mundane.

For example, paint sounds like a pretty boring product, and one which has traditionally engendered trivial/comic entertainment advertising or straight-faced product benefit communication—but the English paintmaker, Dulux, realized a few years ago that the most interesting thing about paint is the sense of pride and achievement you feel when you've finished decorating your home and making it more beautiful. Dulux merely needed to identify this feeling and portray it in a believable and attractive way in their advertising, in order to "own" it outright, and consequently take a very dominant stance in the whole home decorating environment.

All this has been discussed many times before, of course, but the key issue here is how well this emotive stuff travels. There are at least four significant factors in the equation:

- Whether the emotion, as portrayed, can be reliably decoded by consumers in each new market
- If they correctly read the emotion, whether they find it credible to link it with this product
- If they read it correctly and accept its link to the product, whether they are happy about advertising which concentrates on an emotional rather than a rational "benefit"
- If they read it correctly, accept its link to the product, and are happy with the principle of emotional benefits,

140

whether this approach is likely to prove an effective, distinctive, legal, and competitive way to enhance the brand or sell the product in each country

In other words, it ain't simple. And it should never be forgotten that the way consumers in any given culture react to advertising *in general* is a highly significant factor: do they *like* advertising? Are they *interested* in advertising? How much *time* are they prepared to give to advertising? What do they *expect* from advertising? All of these factors have fundamental implications on the appropriateness of harnessing emotions and entertainment in the service of marketing.

Interestingly, the two countries which generate most of the creative work for most of the world's international campaigns—Britain and America—are probably the two countries where *consumers most actively enjoy advertising*. A recent European survey[2] showed that more than 75% of British people find advertising entertaining and more than 80% think it is useful to consumers (by comparison, only 30% of Germans think advertising has a positive effect and more than 80% think it is boring). In Britain, consumers love advertising so much, we have prime-time TV shows dedicated to showing curious or interesting advertising from around the world.

Whether all this is cause or effect, it is probably idle to speculate, but it does raise a very real dilemma about the difficulty of using American or British creativity as the basis for global campaigns. Anglo-Saxon consumer advertising is targeted at a highly marketing-literate, almost "professional" audience—something you won't find in too many other countries. Advertising has been around here long enough for the advertiser and the advertisee to build up an extremely sophisticated dialogue together—like many Britons, the moment I see an ad, I'm prepared to spend time and effort on understanding it, extracting the cleverly-encoded or even hidden messages, study the images, and read the body copy until they give up their secrets. If an ad only gives me stages a and d in a four-part argument, I'm perfectly happy to fill in b and c for myself: in that sense, it's thoroughly interactive. It's got to a stage where if I ever see an ad that simply states the bald facts about the product, I can't believe it's for real, and might waste entire seconds of my life trying to find the missing gag, or end up assuming that the irony is so subtle I've failed to appreciate it.

It's a far cry from countries like Germany, where consumers consider the primary function of advertising to be giving reliable and factual information about products, and where if you start cracking jokes or trying to stir people's emotions, your target group may well assume that you have absolutely nothing worthwhile to say about your product and are simply trying to distract their attention from this embarrassing truth. (Mind you, if 80% of German consumers find advertising boring, it's probably high time agencies attempted to shift this paradigm somewhat.)

Yes, the heightened sophistication of the British and American advertising industries does also mean that theirs is often the *best produced* advertising, where most trouble is taken over the conception and execution of advertising messages, where the best production skills and resources are located, where the advertising community employs some of the best and brightest talents in the land (in most "normal" countries, those people work in the arts, academia, or government) — and this is certainly an important part of the reason why we continue to win the lion's share of international accounts and international awards.

The other half of the reason is as I mentioned earlier: most of the clients and most of the awards judges are either American or British themselves. Those that are not are often strongly Anglophilic, or else are prejudiced by the power of the *provenance* of the creative product into believing that it is equally powerful.

But it does all make a super-sophisticated, super-rich mix for most other countries in the world, and Anglo-Saxon agencies need to make a conscious effort to simplify their thinking for audiences which, quite simply, don't care about advertising very much.

This simplification isn't "dumbing down" and it isn't about "avoiding wordplays," or—as we are about to see—abandoning our sense of humor. It's about endless refining and purifying and distillation of the idea, and the use of more skill than ever before.

Paying with Entertainment

When I'm advising ad agencies on developing effective systems and practices for creating international campaigns, I like to start by seeing how they've been doing it up till now. I'm always interested in their creative briefs, because in the section called "Any Special Requirements," I so often find a comment like this:

NOTE: this campaign is global, so no puns, plays on words or anything else that may cause translation difficulties, and NO HUMOR.

Excuse me, did you say *no humor?*

International or not, advertising without humor is scarcely advertising at all, despite the fact that various attempts have been made to eliminate it in the past: David Ogilvy, for example, once made the famous observation that nobody buys from clowns.

Yet 30 years on, still nobody seems to be taking his advice. A quick poll of campaigns currently running in Europe reveals that a large majority—perhaps two-thirds—appear to be trying to make us laugh. Even advertising in Germany, the country most often believed to be a laughter-free zone, is as full of puns and wacky visuals as anywhere else. (There's just a lot more product detail in the small print.)

Maybe it's natural for humor and advertising to go together: maybe advertising needs to be funny for the simple reason that consumers aren't obliged to pay any attention to it. As I have already mentioned (and I don't think this point can easily be overstated) advertising is about asking people to part with money, so the onus is definitely on the advertiser to offer some reward for their attention. Without that reward, advertising is ignored or resented, and without humor or ingenuity, our finely-tuned sales pitch starts to resemble the whine of a beggar.

Laughter also goes together with advertising because it's an important part of social intercourse everywhere: if you're trying to get to know somebody, it's natural to try and raise a smile.

This is an almost universal habit. The only race I know which appears not to conform to this pattern of behavior are the Finns, a nation often reputed to be somewhat dour and taciturn. [There's a rather telling Swedish joke on the subject. A Swede and a Finn sit down to share a bottle of beer. The Swede opens the bottle and murmurs "Skål" (good health) to his companion, whereupon the Finn replies crossly, "Listen, are we going to drink this damn beer or are we going to sit here chattering all day?"]

I once heard a Finnish film director describing his countrymen in an interview: he said, "You'd be like this too if you lived in a refrigerator where the light is broken for half the year," neatly proving that the Finns are, in fact, far from humorless.

Certainly, there are countries where laughter is discouraged, or even *forbidden,* but it's not because people don't want to laugh—it's usually because the laws are made by a very few extremely powerful, extremely conservative, and extremely old people who happen to believe that just because they don't enjoy laughing, nobody else should either. Take Iran, where a popular magazine, *Ardineh,* has recently been closed down by a group called The Headquarters for Combating Vice and Promoting Virtue. *Ardineh's* crime was to publish an article entitled "Is Joy Lost in Our City? Is Laughing A Sin?", in which the author describes how her family, whilst enjoying dinner in a restaurant, were sternly rebuked by a small boy who told them they should be ashamed to be laughing.[3]

Clearly, even though this is an extreme example (and anyway Iran is one of the places where we are least likely to be running our global advertising campaigns), we must always be acutely aware of the social and moral framework which prevails in each culture, and how it affects the expression of basic human instincts. In a country where mirth arouses disapproval, laughter is not only a more unusual phenomenon (and consequently, to many, a more welcome one): it takes on a positively revolutionary flavor.

But whatever the environment in which people live, laughter disarms people and defuses situations, and as advertising messages proliferate, it becomes ever more necessary to win over consumers before lethargy or resistance set in.

Of course, and fortunately for the Iranians, we don't only smile at jokes: we also smile at wit. Wit flatters the audience, creates a smart people's club where speaker and listener are instantly fellow members. The French philosopher, Henri Bergson, called these two kinds of laughter *ha ha!* and *aha!*[4]

The advertising you like, although it depends to some degree on your age and sex, is more likely to be based on *aha* humor than on the *ha ha* variety. (I can state this with confidence only because I'm assuming, gentle reader, that you are over the age of 10.) It depends on your age because your taste for intellectual and linguistic humor should increase as you grow up, and on your sex because women often have less patience with advertising that is merely comic: they appear to be more receptive to certain combinations of wit and style which are exquisitely hard to achieve in advertising. Perhaps that's what Ogilvy meant about people not buying from clowns.

Pure comedy is often quite simple: it's visual rather than verbal, and physical rather than intellectual. It's fat men hitting each other with ladders and people hurting themselves in the *Laurel and Hardy / Mr. Bean / Tom and Jerry* vein. This kind of humor is almost completely universal, both culturally and intellectually—it amuses small children in New Guinea as much as university professors in North America. This would seem to make it an ideal ingredient in international advertising campaigns—assuming we overlook the fact that it's somewhat childish.

NO CANNES DO?

Personally, I have learned many valuable lessons on the role of humor in international advertising by going to the Cannes Festival.

Once a year, as you probably know, the global advertising community gathers in the Cannes sunshine to vote for the best television commercials of the year, eat a lot, pretend to be the movie industry (which is what many advertising people actually spend most of their lives doing), drink $20 Martinis and hang out in the Ritz-Carlton lobby. It is in this grim and joyless setting that many basic truths about advertising begin to emerge.

I'm not joking when I say it's grim. Those who have never been to the International Advertising Festival may not appreciate just what an unpleasant experience it is to sit in a darkened room and watch several thousand TV commercials in a row.

This is not just because most of the ads at Cannes are awful (although most of them truly are): TV commercials are a very concentrated and *ardent* form of communication, and after the 20th attempt to convince you that, contrary to all probability, this company really *does* have something to say, you feel as if you've been beaten over the head with a heavy stick.

But only strong aversion therapy can cure us advertising folk (temporarily) of our professional interest in the medium, and fleetingly teach us what it feels like to be an ordinary consumer and *not to care.* Only then can we really judge what's good and what's not, and the really exceptional work begins to stand out.

Cannes is also interesting because the ads *and* the audience are international, so watching the audience is an absolutely unique opportunity to see *live* global responses to global advertising—admittedly from a rather specialist audience.

And, sure enough, the winning ads at the Advertising Festival are almost always funny ones. Trouble is, many of the ads which don't win were trying to be funny too, and doubtless had people rolling around in front of their TV sets in Turkey or Korea or Germany. So it's not simply that humor doesn't travel: clearly, some kinds do and some kinds don't.

So what species of humor is universal enough to win over the multicultural Cannes jury? It's hard to see much method in their approach: in past years, they've awarded gold medals to bizarre Japanese pot noodle ads featuring grunting cavemen being chased by improbable dinosaurs, and showered honors on Australian press ads for jeans showing eviscerated sharks (not really funny at all, you might say, but the group of Australians next to me were practically wetting themselves), and sitcoms about a British woman whose annoying mother constantly sings the praises of a supermarket.

And yet, to the outrage of the Italian press, the same jury completely ignored the Italian campaign most Italians love, where a famous comedian poses as a grocer, cracking jokes with his female customers as he weighs the ham, and many more like it from many other countries. No doubt there's a good deal of the "snake soup and Stilton" syndrome going on, as I described in the last chapter, and much of this is simply down to the random vagaries of taste.

On the whole, it's easier to explain why this kind of humor doesn't travel than it is to explain why the other kinds do: verbal humor is local humor, almost by definition. The

Italian ads died in the translation, and unless you know the comedian and find his Roman dialect funny, there's not much left to laugh at.

Yet the grunting Japanese caveman has somehow blundered into some truly common ground: it's *simple* and it's *graphic*. For a very similar reason, everyone loves the Norwegian airline ad where a man bursts naked into his drawing room with a rose between his teeth, only to find that his wife has flown her parents over on a cheap weekend return: here, the pain is social rather than cranial, but our laughter still derives from his discomfort. Everyone in the civilized world, it seems, is attuned to the rich potential of the banana-skin and to the spectacle of people hurting or humiliating themselves.

Those stylish Levi's ads which Bartle Bogle Hegarty used to make for the European market were always popular, too: the young man who discovers that his girlfriend's father is the drugstore owner who sold him a condom; the young woman who provocatively strips in front of an apparently blind man, who, it turns out, is only looking after his dad's white stick and shades and isn't blind at all.

But for all their glamour, the Levi's ads are pure Benny Hill (another perennial international success). Those wry tales of double-entendre, whether they're enhanced by hip rock music and Hollywood gloss, or jerked out by a little fat bloke with round glasses and a bevy of dolly-birds in bikinis, are as old as the hills. No humor, it seems, is as universal in its appeal as *schadenfreude*.

Filth, too, often wins at Cannes, like the Argentinean ad for spicy tuna sauce which brought the house down a couple of years back: a lingering shot of a pair of male underpants on a washing line, with a ragged hole burned eloquently through the rear.

Laughing at pain, embarrassment, sex, and bodily functions: how childish can you get?

Culture—the stuff we learn as we grow up—is basically what prevents audiences around the world from laughing at the same jokes. As education takes away our innocence, our sense of humor becomes more cerebral, less physical, more intimately linked to our immediate cultural environment, less international. It gets interested in playing with words and the meanings of words.

Childhood is the last moment in our lives when it's more true to say that we're members of the human race than we are citizens of a nation, and consequently it's the most childish humor which travels best: of course, you're free to dress it in adult clothes if you wish.

Treating your international audience as children (an approach which the international advertising community, with commendable insight, has adopted for decades) is perhaps the smartest thing you can do — or at least learning how to speak to the child within that audience.

But forget this at your peril: children, like foreigners, aren't stupid. They're just different. Talking to the child within your audience is about discovering the simple stories which move us all, and separating them from their telling. There's more about the critical concept of *stories* in Chapter 6.

THE TRICK OF INTERNATIONAL CREATIVITY

Most creativity has really very little to do with inventing new things, but a great deal to do with finding unexpected angles on familiar things.

Real conceptual newness in advertising is extraordinarily rare: perhaps, given the rate at which it has proliferated over the past decades, it's virtually extinct, although they were probably saying that in 1883. Actually, the French philosopher, La Bruyère, observed as long ago as 1688, *everything has been said, and we're about seven thousand years too late to be original.*[5]

Incidentally (and it is decidedly incidental to the subject of advertising), much great art works this way too: there often wasn't anything new about the *subjects* of most Renaissance painting, Baroque music or Jacobean drama, but the genius of the artist lies in reviewing familiar themes with a new insight, clarity, wisdom, profundity, faith or humor, which has the power to *illuminate* the theme in a way which is revelatory to ordinary people.

Many equally important works of art derive their new-ness not from the concept or even the artist's perspective on that concept, but on the *means of expression* itself: much archi-tecture, for example, is distinguished not because the build-ing has a new function, nor because it revisits the principle of that function from a new perspective, but because it is built in a new way: new forms, new materials, new colors, or the use of new techniques.

This kind of creativity, in the context of advertising, is perhaps the most commonly used — perhaps because we are working in media which are in a state of constant develop-ment, like video and interactive — but there are definite restrictions on the potential of this kind of creativity to travel between cultures. Sure, an amazing new digital post-production treatment will probably help a commercial to achieve even more standout on Bangladeshi TV than it does in North America, but it's generally not adequate as a replacement for an idea: and we also need to ask ourselves whether it is sustainable, memorable, effective, and whether it contributes to the *effective communication of brand personality.*

The type of creativity which we tend to aim for in inter-national work is therefore *conceptual,* rather than *executional.* Conceptual creativity is quite rare. It happens when you actually have an *idea* which is strong enough to make the way you express it an almost secondary issue. Ideas of this kind can even transcend the cultural and linguistic differences of which I have already spoken. These are the ideas which entirely subvent the superficial incompatibilities of the coun-tries we happen to live in and the words we happen to use.

A fine example of this is the old Avis line, *We try harder,* whose particular genius derives from the simple and straightforward expression of a remarkable positioning idea, rather than a remarkable expression of a simple and straight-forward positioning. I've never tried, but I'm sure you could use an almost straight translation of the *We try harder* ads in almost any language without diminishing any of their power.

You could put it another way, and say that conceptual creativity is nothing more than *good marketing*. "We try harder" is a marketing strategy, a company mission state-ment, a staff training mantra and a corporate brand vision, long before it becomes an advertising slogan.

Executional creativity is, unsurprisingly, far more common. At worst, it's used when you can't think of anything particu-larly interesting to say about your product, so you try to say it in an interesting way. I recently saw a perfect example of the lowest kind of executional creativity on a large poster near where I live. It was an ad for an airline (I honestly for-get which), showing a photograph of the generously-spaced seats in business class, and bearing the headline

Actual sighs.

The positioning is, of course, identical to every other company's in the business, so my choice of that airline rested exclusively on how much I admired them for having noticed the existence of the English homophone size/sighs. But is this scrap of wit really enough to justify attracting the con-sumer's attention and wasting his or her valuable time? I think not.

And, of course, this kind of advertising makes a notori-ously bad basis for an international campaign: what's the brief? We're an airline that likes our little joke? Or—don't tell me—we're witty and irreverent.

Perhaps the most compelling reason for always aiming for conceptual creativity is that it will almost certainly increase the effectiveness of our advertising. Advertising, we should never forget, is not an end in itself, and not an art form: its purpose is to build brands and sell products: conse-quently, if it grows out of a deeply-rooted and robust proposition which is closely informed by marketing strategy and brand personality, it is far more likely to drive the brand forward than an execution which is only casually and superficially linked to the ultimate purpose of the task in hand.

As I'm forever reminding companies, small armies can defeat really quite large armies, as long as all their soldiers march *exactly* in step: if every aspect of a brand's communication is confirming the same core message, then brands can frequently outsmart competitors who outspend them by orders of magnitude.

Whatever tricks we use to achieve it, creativity is nothing more than an attempt to make our message more striking, more memorable, more effective. A simple fact about our product, however true, is usually ineffectual unless worked on: like a gemstone, its worth is merely putative until a skilled craftsperson has cleaned it, polished it, and cut facets which will reflect the light through the stone to its best advantage. The cutter's skill is important, but the worth of the raw material is fundamental. The finest artist can't make a worthless stone more valuable; yet it takes a true craftsman like Bill Bernbach to recognize a rare gem and have the sense and good taste to display it, almost entirely unadorned, in the simplest setting.

GETTING UNDER THE SKIN OF CULTURE

The art of true international creativity is a two-stage process: finding the themes which lie *below* culture—the moments of human truth which are not merely meaningful to all of us, but also, because of their profundity, *highly significant* for all of us—and then finding the most appropriate cultural expression of that theme for each market or group of markets. First you dig down, then you burrow up.

First, here's an example of how to dig down.

One of the scenarios which Fons Trompenaars frequently uses in research groups to assess the balance of universalism and particularism is as follows: "A close friend has to appear in court, charged with hitting a pedestrian. You are the only witness, and know that he was exceeding the speed limit. If you testify that he was not speeding, he will avoid serious consequences. To what extent does your friend have a right to expect you to lie under oath on his behalf— no right at all, some right, or every right?"[6]

Broadly, as one would expect, individuals in strongly universalist societies (such as North America and Sweden) *tend* to cluster towards the "no right at all" end of the spectrum, whereas particularists (such as Russians or South Koreans) will tend to favor the response "every right"; and, if they are also told how badly the pedestrian is hurt, their likely responses tend to shift along the scale in opposite directions. But the reality is that very few respondents indeed, from any country, can answer this question straight away, without hesitation. Everybody, regardless of their culture, recognizes this as a dilemma, and the answer is never simple or obvious.

This fact is, in many ways, more significant and thought-provoking than the responses people give, because it points to a fundamental truth about culture: we all *recognize* dilemmas and threats as members of the human species, but we all *respond* to them in different ways, as dictated by our culture and our personality.

Dilemmas, threats, choices, and quandaries are a fundamental aspect of human existence (hence, probably, the universality of *schadenfreude* as a source of mirth). As Trompenaars points out, our lives are threatened every 5 to 10 seconds by imminent oxygen starvation, and the threat is only lifted if we breathe.

These, and similar observations about where the human condition stops and where culture starts, often aren't advertising ideas in themselves, but they are part of our roadmap for planning international campaigns: they help us to recognize when we've dug down as far as we need to dig in order to reach areas of more universal truth.

The essence of this approach is all about *doing interna-tional for the right reasons:* not primarily because it's simpler (although this might be an attraction), nor primarily because it's cheaper (although in many cases the savings are well worthwhile), nor primarily because of an abstract desire for control or neatness (although this desire can easily be satis-fied), but because when international advertising is done properly, it's the best advertising in the world.

The aim of this book is to show how to *harness* the power of language, culture, brands and creativity in order to achieve the best advertising in the world — it's about ways of celebrating and exploiting the enormous difficulties they represent, rather than seeing them as obstacles to be jumped over or weaseled around at any cost.

Clearly, this needs a new philosophy of international advertising, and it needs new structures.

For advertising agencies in particular, it means a dra-matic change of corporate and personal culture, because, as the next chapter will show, the old models simply can't pro-vide answers to all of the challenges which global business now throws at us every day.

5

Network = Notwork

This is an absolutely true story of global advertising politics, corroborated by three unimpeachable sources: I've simply changed a few names and a couple of other details.

Once upon a time, a major drinks manufacturer appointed a global brand chief, who quickly became known as a stickler for worldwide adherence to corporate communications standards. Let's call him Bragg.

Bragg's philosophy was very simple: nobody was allowed to create any materials for use in their own markets, and to deviate from the centrally-produced global campaigns in any way was to risk losing your job.

But the Country Manager in Mexico (we'll call him Suarez) repeatedly found that the work he was being sent from New York was unsuitable for his market in all kinds of ways, and every time he attempted to raise this issue with Bragg, he was reminded that his was a very small market, that much larger issues of global brand equity were at stake here, and anyway the agency which had created the work was one of the most creative in the whole United States.

Eventually, Suarez decided that he would secretly brief his agency (the Mexico City office of the global network which the company used worldwide) to create a one-off promotional campaign to his own brief, and the dramatic increase in sales he confidently expected would serve to persuade his bosses that allowing some local initiative (to the right people, of course) was much better for business in the long term.

But his agency found themselves in a dilemma: if they met his demands, they risked annoying Bragg, and possibly losing the whole global business for the network. So after much soul-searching, they decided to contact Bragg and ask him what he would like them to do. Bragg listened with interest to their story, expressed gratitude for their well-placed loyalty, and told them not to worry: he'd talk to Suarez himself.

The next day, Suarez received a call from Head Office, telling him to be in Bragg's office in New York the next morning at 9 sharp. This wasn't easy, but by dropping everything and leaping on the next flight, Suarez managed to make his appointment. Arriving at Bragg's well-appointed offices at 10 to 9, Suarez was asked to take a seat.

Time passed. Suarez sat patiently in reception, and read all the magazines on the table. He asked for coffee, and was brought some in a plastic cup. People came and went, but nobody that Suarez recognized. It was getting on for 12. Once or twice, he asked the receptionist whether there was a problem, but was reassured that Mr. Bragg knew he was there.

Lunchtime came and went. Suarez asked for another cup of coffee. Two o'clock went by. Suarez read Fortune *magazine for the third time, cover to cover. He was extremely hungry, having left home in the very early hours of the morning, but didn't dare leave the office in case he missed Bragg and angered him.*

Finally, at a quarter past five o'clock in the afternoon, Bragg's secretary came out of the elevator and approached Suarez. Suarez stood up, expectantly.

"Mr. Suarez?" asked the smartly-dressed woman.

"That's me," he replied, smiling.

"Mr. Bragg has asked me to tell you that you're fired. Good afternoon."

Barking up the Wrong Tree?

Poor Mr. Suarez. But spare a thought too for the agency, because life isn't always a bed of roses for them. On international accounts, agencies are often caught uncomfortably between the agenda of their client at Head Office and the agenda of their "local" client in each country. In cases where the two simply fail to agree, it's actually far more common for the agency to get the chop than Suarez and his brethren.

Half of an agency's life is spent frantically trying to hang on to existing business, and the other half is spent frantically trying to replace it.

Just like any other highly competitive, talent-based industry, the advertising business revolves around the constant search for innovation: it's often the only way that individual agencies can achieve any kind of standout. Hardly a month goes by when we don't read of some agency "totally re-thinking" the way advertising is created: some months it's the dawn of the "media-neutral integrated communications consultancy"; other months it's hot-desking and mobile telephones, client-friendly workspaces, and payment by results.

As one "creative-only ideas shop" crows about the death of account management, a "virtual communications resource" is banging on about the replaceability of creative teams, and farming out all its briefs to freelancers. Planning, media, and production are separated from and reintegrated back into the agency with bewildering rapidity. As I write, the hot issue in London is the threat to the advertising business from management consultants (largely imaginary in this country, as far as I can see, even if it is true that the agencies are rightly afraid of losing their strategic edge)—so everybody is frantically chasing deals with the consultancies.

Now, if you talk to clients about the issues which most concern them, an increasing proportion will confirm that building their brands abroad is somewhere around the top of the list: a recent survey of senior marketing staff in 11,000 U.S. companies[1] shows that increased competitiveness created by globalization is their "overall most significant concern." Most are reasonably indulgent about the cavorting of the advertising agencies and their frantic attempts to appear innovative: clients appear to see this as a necessary ritual dance which helps them to distinguish a little more easily between otherwise rather similar businesses.

But when it comes to talking about new ways of operating internationally, the advertising industry, despite reinventing itself with tiresome regularity, has absolutely nothing new to offer. It's still flogging the same basic, distributed network concept which J. Walter Thompson invented exactly 100 years ago: a full-service, fully-staffed advertising agency in as many countries as you can possibly think of—and then a few more, just for good measure.

A friend of mine who works in a large agency network called me the other day to say he was leaving for Kazakhstan, where he is to set up the network's newest office. Kazakhstan, for heaven's sake! There aren't any *consumers* in Kazakhstan!

But for many years, the network game has been simply one of pinning flags on maps—indeed, many big agencies openly admit that they consider their creative credentials to be of distinctly secondary importance. What seems to count (at least, when you're chasing the really big global accounts) is a kind of bullish imperialism which has precious little to do with "executional" details.

The truth is almost painfully obvious. What more and more clients now desperately need is smaller, faster, strategically-minded, business-aware, creative, responsive, cost-effective, culturally sensitive *international brand communications agencies,* and that's the one thing that this mighty industry seems least interested in developing.

Globalization is creating a tidal wave of businesses which require the hunger, dynamism, flexibility, and creativity of the domestic hotshop, combined with the maturity, geographical reach, and local sensitivity of the traditional networks. Clients want to deal with principals, not with junior account executives, and many of them don't want to pay for great swathes of "added value": what they want from ad agencies is strategically informed creativity, and what they want from international agencies is strategically informed *international* creativity.

158

Networks were, quite simply, never designed for international advertising: they were designed for *multi-local* advertising. The need is now acute for a new kind of resource which is purpose-built for developing regional and global campaigns.

And it's not just the globalization of client companies which is creating this accelerating demand for internationl competence: it's also driven by the globalization of media. International space is *available:* in print, television, cinema, radio, outdoor, instore, direct marketing, editorial, sponsorship, on the tailplanes of airplanes and the sides of space rockets — and, most significantly, online.

The internet is a fundamental part of the picture: for the first time in history, we have a medium which is *international by default:* what you say and what you show on the internet is *everywhere,* instantly. An often-repeated point, but worth mentioning: it costs no more time, money, or effort for a consumer in Ethiopia to access the menu of a sandwich bar in Alberta than it does for an investor in New Zealand to view the prospectus of a mutual fund in Norway. That fund, and that sandwich bar, are global businesses now, whether they like it or not.

So the tidal wave is gathering pace, and in the absence of any satisfactory alternative, the big agency networks are still carrying out more than 80% of all the international work that's going — despite the fact that by no means all their clients actually *need* a geographically-distributed solution, or such a heavily-resourced one either.

The remaining 20% mainly consists of those valiant and conscientious businesses which are prepared to bear the extra financial and administrative cost of hiring a different domestic shop in each one of their overseas markets, and themselves take on the considerable burden of creating brand synergies, encouraging message consistency, maintaining common standards, sharing best practice, and coordinating the efforts of all those fiercely independent players.

WHEN NETWORKS WORK

So what are the big networks good for? They are certainly great repositories of talent: apart from anything else, they have most of the really bright people in advertising working for them.

Well, they're ideal for servicing the communications needs of the larger, more complex, more mature multinational corporations. These are companies with well-established marketing functions in many countries, and significant domestic budgets to go with them. In such cases, promotional needs are often largely market-driven and market-funded, and a local, full-service agency to service the local client is a necessity. The benefits of a network in such cases are numerous.

Firstly, and although this is by no means a priority for all clients, it's a bulk buy for the corporation: by aligning all of their global or regional advertising into a single network, they can often do deals which are highly advantageous.

Secondly, the co-ordination provided by the "lead" office of the network, at least in theory, ensures conformity to brand in all of the company's communications, however different the needs they may be addressing from country to country. A network should be able to take off your desk at least part of the mammoth task of coordinating your messages and ensuring trueness to brand in dozens or scores of countries: it will certainly save you the bother of doing it "manually" with large numbers of independent shops.

Thirdly, hiring a single network, again at least in theory, provides a certain guarantee of consistent quality across all markets—presumably this was high up on the list of reasons why Mr. Bragg, the global Brand supremo in our disaster story, hired a network agency in the first place. (Some would argue that this is precisely the area in which networks fail: after all, if you hire the network, you're obliged to subscribe to *their* idea of which is the best shop in town, not yours; and in any case a chain is only as strong as its weakest link. They may be No. 1 in a couple of countries, but further down the list in other markets you consider equally important.)

Fourthly, networks provide excellent geographical coverage, and the larger ones probably have more offices than you do. Again, this is something of a double-edged sword: their distribution may well not match yours—they may have seven offices in Germany when you only need one, and none at all in Lithuania, which might be your biggest growth market. (Of course, they also have one in Kazakhstan, which is the last country on earth you'd ever consider selling your product!)

Conventional wisdom has it that you always need a network to advertise packaged goods internationally—especially the lower-priced commodities like soap powder and toothpaste—because consumption patterns and consumer behavior are so diverse from country to country.

Conventional wisdom is talking through its hat, as usual. When are consumption patterns and consumer behavior *not* different from country to country, may one ask? It's true that many people speak about the convergence of culture, the global teen market, the international homogeneity of the so-called MTV generation, the identical need sets surrounding IT-related purchases, but as I described in Chapter 2, this is only true in a very superficial sense: here, we're not talking about national culture changing, because by and large it doesn't change. What's changing here is taste and fashion, but taste and fashion aren't reliable, durable, predictable, deep-down motivators of behavior.

The reality is that however similar such audiences may appear to be on the surface, they have spent their lives growing up in different places, and that makes them respond to brands and messages in *fundamentally* different ways. International advertising is as much about understanding and celebrating difference as it is about spotting and exploiting similarities, and from this point of view selling trainers to teenagers is no different from selling soap powder to housewives.

161

They may consume the same products, but they consume them in different ways and for different reasons: the classic examples, often quoted, are the fact that going to McDonald's is a cheap and fast refueling stop if you live in New York, but a high-status evening out if you live in Moscow; and that young people buy Walkmen in America so that they can listen to music without *being disturbed* by others, whilst young people in Japan buy Walkmen so they can listen to music without *disturbing others*. *This* is culture.

To help you get inside the skin of those consumers, of course you need people *from* that country. I just don't happen to think you need people *in* that country.

As a colleague once put it: "If you need your people serviced, hire a network; if you need your *brand* serviced, hire an independent agency." But how, you might well ask, can an independent agency do international advertising?

We'll answer that question in the next two chapters, but first, a little more about the way things have *always* been done.

A LITTLE TALE OF NETWORKS

When I started out in advertising, I joined the London office of a major international advertising agency as a junior copywriter. The agency will remain nameless, to protect the innocent—suffice to say that it could have been any one of 20 big network agencies in town.

I was so very junior, they put me by myself in a tiny, windowless room in the basement, somewhere between the boiler room and the staff canteen, and set me to work writing small-space, black-and-white trade ads for sheep dip. I wasn't even senior enough to have my own art director.

But the reason I'd joined this particular agency rather than one of the more glamorous creative shops was because, perversely, I was actually interested in the international side of the business. I'd studied modern languages at Oxford, and had a definite *penchant* for foreigners. But in those days (this was 1985: international advertising certainly existed, but was still in its infancy) anybody who actually *wanted* to work on international business—especially a *creative* who wanted to work on international business—was clearly out of their mind.

Soon after I joined, a stray account manager wandered down my corridor (an unusual event, this: I assumed he'd got lost while looking for the canteen), waving a TV script and wailing pitifully, "does anybody here speak French?" Fool that I was, I dashed from my room to volunteer, and was instantly demoted to the hitherto non-existent position of International Coordinator To The Creative Director.

This completely fictitious post basically meant that they drove me out to Heathrow Airport and put me on the first plane bound for The Rest Of The World, and it may be my imagination, but I seem to remember the Creative Director pushing me through to Departures rather quickly, as if he feared I might change my mind.

For what seemed like a very long time, I flitted like an unwelcome ghost between the offices of the network—in South and East Asia, the Americas and Europe—and was vaguely expected to kind of monitor and report on international creative "issues" (whatever those might be). I wasn't really expected to do anything about them, though: just report.

It was a truly fascinating experience, and little by little, a picture began to emerge.

The first thing I noticed was that we seemed to be *extremely bad* at doing international work. For some reason, the moment two or more offices were asked to collaborate on any project, things sort of fell apart. People stopped talking to each other, everybody became extremely critical of everybody else's ideas and exceedingly protective of their own, and I began to hear a certain phrase, which was destined to become painfully familiar to me in the years which followed: *This will never work in my market.*

My agency, in common with nearly all of the large networks, had perpetual difficulty in maintaining high creative standards—a problem which persists today. We've seen in earlier chapters why this is no accident: creative and international are two substances which very, very rarely mix, and many clients have reconciled themselves to the belief that the best you can hope for is a kind of streaky emulsion.

It rapidly became apparent to me that a psychopath in his worst nightmares could not have invented a worse way to do international advertising campaigns than an international advertising agency network.

About Motivation

It's actually quite obvious, once you start to think about it. The reason why people in advertising agencies bother to get up in the morning is because they love to create ads. Their *raisons d'être* are, in no particular order: coming up with great creative ideas, casting glamorous models, going on location to Tahiti, winning awards, and getting rich and famous.

Who can blame them?

But what happens on an international campaign is that only one agency—the so-called "lead" agency—actually gets to do all that exciting strategic, creative, and production stuff, while the rest of the network is expected to sit obediently at home, waiting for the fun to be over, so that they can get to work diligently crafting translations or "adaptations" of the TV scripts or print copy for use in their own market.

Hardly surprising, then, that our overseas offices often became obstructive and intractable. More often than not, they'd give it to a junior account executive to translate, or even palm it off onto the local client (who in one case regularly passed the ads on to his nine-year-old daughter to translate for her homework).

At the time, we laughed about this problem and called it "not invented here syndrome." But this didn't begin to do justice to the sheer scale and the utterly crippling effect of the problem; or, indeed, to calculate how damaging it was to the already fragile relationships which existed between the offices of the network, and to the quality of our end product.

I don't think it's an exaggeration to say that what we were asking these people to do was utterly humiliating to them. After all, copywriters and art directors don't get paid what they get paid because they can write or draw nicely: they get paid because they can come up with astonishing new concepts to galvanize the performance of their clients' brands. Out of thin air. When you actually let them do it, and when they're good at it, it's almost like magic.

And we were going to them, time after time, and saying things like, "Hey, chaps, here's a new global brief." And of course they'd get all excited and say, "We've got a wonderful idea for that." And we'd reply, "Er, actually, we've *had* the idea. We're *London,* you see." So, a little crestfallen, the people in Frankfurt or Rio or Hong Kong would say, "Well, can we do some writing and drawing, then?"

And we'd reply, "Well, we've done the drawing. But we'd love you to do some writing. At least, not actually *writing,* because we've already done that too—could you just sort of translate it for us? But not a *literal* translation, please, we need something really good. . . ."

And then we acted all surprised and frustrated when they gave it to the receptionist to translate, and we took our meager comfort in complaining bitterly about the obstinacy of foreigners.

After a few tries, I discovered that it wasn't much fun being lead agency either. I remember that the first time an international brief landed on my desk, I was wildly excited about it. I pictured my creative work running in dozens of countries around the world. I may even have called my mother.

But after the second or third time I'd been practically reduced to tears by a grim voice on the phone, somewhere in the network, muttering—

Zis vill not vork in my market!

—I found that all the pleasure had vanished. The malignant presence of the network was like a gray cloud, hovering just over our heads. "Sod this," we all said, "let's stick to local work. At least we'll only be arguing with the client."

And the most agonizing thing about the network was that it was *slow:* every request for support or advice from another office seemed to take an age, and as often as not, that was the real reason we often ended up inventing "international" solutions ourselves.

If you talk to managers in network agencies these days, many will claim that the speed problem has now been fixed as a result of major investments in communications technology, but frankly I'm skeptical. Speed of service in a network is not governed by the rate at which instructions or requests are carried between offices, but by the *delay* incurred before the request is met.

Network agencies have been able to communicate instructions between one office and another at the same speed since the big American agencies like McCann-Erickson began to develop their global networks in the early decades of this century: they had telephones then, and an e-mail is somewhat slower than a phone call, without the additional benefit of real-time interactivity.

Yes, it's true that if the request is more than verbal, and involves showing people materials, then the fax was the *really* significant development, in around 1980: the internet has merely continued the same developmental path, simply enhancing the quantity and quality of materials which can be shared between offices at more or less fax speed.

But believing that technology can resolve the speed problem is missing the point. The reason there are delays is nothing to do with how fast the request travels down the wire or up to a satellite or between two baked-bean tins and a piece of string, but (1) how *important* that request is to the person who receives it, and (2) the ability of the person making the request to *monitor* and physically *chase* the person until they come up with the result.

What happens as a result of physical distance (combined with the extra irritation — and the perfect excuse — caused by

166

working in different time zones) is that people simply *take longer to do things.*

Once again, the problem is not a simply resolved technical hitch, but a deep psychological mystery connected with the elusive nature of teamwork, the absence of clear motivations to work together, and the lack of clearly perceived *common aims.* In other words, it's not that people *lack the equipment* to collaborate: they *lack the will* to collaborate, and nobody's invented a machine yet that can fix that.

OF LOVE, AND IN-TRAYS

The reality, of course, is that an advertising agency is basically an out-tray: its particular skill lies in creating new messages and sending them out into the world. When it is expected to act as an in-tray for other people's concepts and other people's projects, it won't do it well and it won't do it willingly.

And advertising is just like anything else in this world: it's good when it's done with love. But the network seems purpose-built to ensure that as many people as possible treat every part of the process with as much hatred and irritation as possible.

In a network, what ought to be a creative process, for all these reasons, ends up as a destructive process. Somebody somewhere starts off with a good creative idea, which is interesting, striking, spiky, and looks like this:

Then they ask people around the network to check it out for use in their markets, as of course they must. And those people, naturally somewhat piqued at not being invited to actually contribute to the creative process, are more inclined to propose massive, utterly damning objections than helpful minor modifications, so they immediately set about thinking of all the reasons why it's no good for their country—because it's not their idea and because they won't get the credit if it works (although they'll most certainly get the blame if it doesn't).

So the French creatives knock off one point from the star because it might just be considered offensive in their market. And the woman from the German office says that somebody else did something a bit like it last year: off goes another point. The Italians can't live with the humor in the headline, so that goes too. Fairly soon, that interesting, striking, spiky idea starts to look something like this:

By this stage, the honor of the natives being satisfied and the energy of the "lead" creatives exhausted, time has usually run out, and the network thus arrives at the chosen creative idea for its international advertising campaign.

Let's be honest: extracting any kind of agreement on any subject from a large group of brilliant, determined, excitable, creative people from around the world is not a task for the faint-hearted. Those who prosper in and relish such roles are the politicians and the diplomats, not the creatives or the perfectionists.

And that's why all those honest attempts to find the idea that everybody loves invariably end up in a desperate, eleventh-hour struggle to find the idea that nobody minds.

In consequence, most of the international advertising campaigns in the world are desperately dull and boring and bland and soulless, because *it's the stuff that nobody minds.*

CAN NETWORKS WORK?

Well, I soon saw that we had two choices in the matter. Either we made an honest attempt to create genuinely international work, involving all our offices at the start of the process and actually *using* their local knowledge and creativity, or else we should stop pretending, and simply create everything from London without referring to anybody else at all.

Fortunately, we were just about humble enough to accept that the second option would never result in proper international ads.

Obviously, if the first option was going to work properly, it couldn't be done over the telephone: we needed to sit down together and brainstorm properly, and we were advised that the group wouldn't carry the necessary decision-making power unless we brought in the creative director of each office to join the session. So we set to work organizing our first global brainfest, and soon found ourselves faced with a completely different problem: This time it was pure politics.

As a general rule, creative directors are expected to be spoilt, opinionated, fussy, neurotic and paranoid individuals. That's what makes them good at their job. They won't travel unless you book them six months in advance, and pay for their family, bodyguard, hairdresser, poodle, camera, makeup, and lighting to come along too. (No, most of them weren't at all effeminate. They were just incredibly vain.) The sheer administrative struggle involved in getting all of those geniuses into one place at the same time proved too much for our poor creative secretary: she left after a week.

In the end, the only creative directors who actually showed up to our first session were the pragmatists and the schemers (the Germans, the Dutch, the Norwegians, and the French, as it happens), and it soon became clear that the real reason they'd shown up was not to contribute but to *fight*. Each wanted to be the one who came up with the "winning" idea, in order to return home victorious with the lion's share of the budget, the lead agencyship, and the right to cast glamorous models, go on location to Tahiti, win yet more creative awards, and get still more rich and famous.

Perhaps I shouldn't have been surprised. After all, each of these men (and of course they *were* men: I often wonder whether things might have been different if some of them had been women) all represented competing companies. The fact that all those companies had the same name over the door was the merest cosmetic detail.

I began to suspect that the truth of the matter was rather simple and rather bleak: if a client company wants an advertising campaign to run in sixteen countries, it needs sixteen advertising agencies like it needs a hole in the head.

Because, quite apart from the difficulty of getting any good work out of such an organization, it was slow, it was expensive, and most of all it was supremely, gothically, cataclysmically wasteful. Our poor clients, somewhere along the line, were footing the bill for the maintenance of an abominably inefficient business. That endless repetition of function (a full-service agency in every one of over 200 cities, with account management, creative, production, media, real estate, tea-lady, and 11 Porsches in the parking lot) was the kind of over-resourcing of the manufacturing function which, if we could only have seen the analogy, most of our clients had eliminated from their businesses decades before. It was all admirably suited to serving domestic clients in each individual country, but woefully inappropriate as a distribution channel for international work.

Unsurprisingly, it is often difficult for network agencies to make much money on international accounts. If you are Ogilvy & Mather, and your client is IBM, spending the best part of a billion dollars a year on global advertising, then there's still money sloshing around even after you've turned that figure into agency fees and split it up between 274 hungry offices. But the vast majority of new international clients are spending $50 million or less on their campaigns,[2] and the simple fact is that on an average fee, this turns a decent-sized global win for the network into a large number of rather small accounts for the individual businesses within that network. You can massage the figures any way you like, but there's no escaping the fact that the big international accounts are often little more than loss-leaders.

BEHAVING INDEPENDENTLY

Almost the only way a network agency can attempt to make the smaller global and regional accounts run faster, more smoothly, and more profitably is by pretending it's not a network at all, and handling them out of a single office.

The trouble is that the individual offices of networks often have no particular international competence: individually, they are simply domestic agencies, and their experience of participating in the major global accounts has usually taught them very little about advertising or consumers in other countries, and a great deal about ignoring, over-ruling, evading, and outmaneuvering one's colleagues in those countries in order to get "proper" creative work through the network.

Running an account out of a single office is usually presented to the client as a marvelous compromise: you get the international experience, insight, and maturity of a top-twenty agency for barely more than the price of a domestic shop, *and* (it is implied) have the mighty resource of a global network available at all times to advise and support the business, without actually having to pay for it except when you need it—perhaps by the hour.

The first part is certainly true: as I have said before, the top 20 agencies often have some of the smartest people, and there's little question that the quality of the strategic thinking may well be better, on average, than you would get from most small shops. But the implication that each office of a network, simply because it carries the same name as 100 or more other agencies around the world, is in some way a microcosm of the entire system—that you can get international advertising from one office as you can clone a parkful of dinosaurs from one drop of their blood—is pure fantasy.

In my experience, it's also somewhat misleading to imply that the other offices of the network will give their full support to the "lead" agency if it's not a proper network account— heaven knows it's hard enough to get their help even when they *are* being paid to service it full-time. If they're only spending a few hours a week on the business, their involvement is likely to be fragmented, their concentration poor, their input nugatory.

After all, even to do an hour's work on a piece of advertising business, you still need a day's briefing in order to understand the issues deeply enough to make your hour's work worthwhile; and advertising agencies simply aren't cut out to be pay-by-the-hour consultancies. It's not in their nature, it's not in their culture, and it's not the reason why each one of their employees fought for years to get a job in one of the most competitive businesses in the world. These are *creative businesses*, and if they are any good at all as advertising agencies in their own right, they are in business to create, not to supply services to other agencies.

Every self-respecting ad agency in the world exists in order to lead, not to follow, and although self-interest and sheer survival means that this culture must be modified or repressed in a network environment, it is a dichotomy which is implicit in the very structure of multinational agencies, and I have seldom seen it satisfactorily resolved.

A Sorry Tale

A friend of mine who runs a translation agency recently told me a rather chilling tale. One day, he had a call from a secretary at a pre-press company—a business which makes films and color separations for ad agencies—asking him "how much is French?"

Resisting the temptation to put down the phone and report the caller to the police for propositioning him, my friend asked a lot of questions and finally discovered the source of this cryptic enquiry. It turned out that the ultimate client was none other than one of the world's top five cosmetics companies, which had recently appointed one of the world's top five advertising agencies to handle its multi-million dollar global creative and media account.

Now, since the agency had offered the client a very substantial discount in order to win the business, and since the work was to run in a very similar form worldwide, there was actually very little money left for creative and production fees. So the agency had proposed to "centralize" the account out of London. "Centralize" was really just a neater way of saying "under-service so we can make more money."

(It has to be said that this kind of agreement is quite often the product of a perfectly willing collusion between agency and client: the client wants to avoid interference and obstruction from its overseas offices just as much as the agency does from its own, so they cook up the deal together "to improve efficiency," without ever really admitting to each other that they're both doing it for a rather different reason.)

My friend from the translation agency, guessing that this was the tip of a substantial iceberg, asked me to speak to some people at the agency in question and see if I could help him get to the real source of the business. So I asked around, and after some assiduous detective work, eventually managed to piece together what had happened.

When the agency's first campaign was approved by the client, the Head of Client Services had asked the Account Director to organize producing the creative work for the 15 markets where media had been booked. The Account Director, naturally, gave the task to his Account Manager, who passed it on to the Account Executive, who had never worked on an international account before, having just joined the agency from a small sales promotion agency in Leeds.

This young man was too ashamed to ask his superiors how this kind of thing was normally done, so he sent an e-mail down to the Head of Creative Services, ordering translations of the copy into 15 languages (the Head of Creative Services was too polite to point out that only 12 were needed, since some of the languages on his list were things like "Belgian," "Swiss," and "Austrian"). The Head of Creative Services passed on the note to his secretary, who bundled it in with the request for a production proposal from the pre-press company: they were asked to quote for "setting the English text in 12 foreign languages."

Since the pre-press house had never done any foreign work before, the Account Manager there had asked *his* secretary to get out the Yellow Pages, call three or four translation companies, and get the cheapest quote, so that they could mark it up and include this in their quote to the advertising agency.

She found one company that "did" all the other 11 languages more cheaply than the rest, but they wanted to charge more for French and German because they were busy that week and needed to bring in extra translators. It turned out that someone in the secretary's own office spoke a little German, which meant they could save money by doing that one in-house, but she still needed one final supplier who could match the other company's best price on French.

Hence the call to my friend.

I wonder how the Senior Vice-President of Marketing at this global top-five cosmetics giant would have felt if he knew that this was how one of the world's most experienced international advertising agencies was proposing to manage the localization of his creative work.

Alas, the chances are he wouldn't have thought there was anything particularly unusual in any of this. After all, ignorance about language and culture is not the exclusive province of international advertising agencies, and if all the marketing people with "international" in their job titles were any smarter than their opposite numbers on the agency side, they would have made damn sure that their agencies had *gotten* smart by now, and I would probably be writing a book about cookery or gardening at this point.

AN OBSERVATION ABOUT ASPARAGUS

Anyway, after I'd been round the world two or three times, internationally co-ordinating, it became clear to me that it all added up to a disastrous recipe: precious little financial motivation to treat international accounts with any dedication or enthusiasm, combined with the low personal motivation which most individuals in the network feel about finishing off a job that someone else has started. On project after project, the lead agency was biting the tips off the asparagus, then shoving the plate over to the rest of the network with a satisfied burp, and expecting gratitude.

If only there had been some chance of the lead agency-ship rotating a little, so that everybody would at least get the first bite once in a while, then things might have been bet-

THE FIRST ASPARAGUS OF THE SEASON.

Farmer (at Market Dinner). "WULL, GEN'ELMEN, I DUNNO WOT BE THE C'RECT WAY O' SERVIN' THESE 'ERE, BUT I GEN'ELLY EATS JUST THE ENDS OF 'EM MYSELF!"

[*Helps himself to the tops!*

Another global campaign is served up.

ter—we did try to organize "internal pitches" for work, and occasionally proposed campaigns from other offices, but time after time, the client (invariably English-speaking) would find it more convenient to hand the master brief to London or New York.

Every agency boss in the network spoke perfect English, of course—indeed, many of them were British or American—but it wasn't much to do with language, and it was a lot to do with culture. The ideas which London and New York produced, and the way they spoke about those ideas, were 20 times more accessible to the vast majority of our clients, and to everybody except the rest of the world, they simply looked like the best work.

When the client was British or American, the U.K. or U.S. agency's work was *a priori* the only work they felt they didn't have to look down on; and on the rare occasions when the client *wasn't* from Britain or America, then the U.K. or U.S. work was the only work they looked up to. The expectation of superior work from those countries, driven merely by the brand power of our countries of origin, was enough to prejudice everybody in our favor. And we weren't complaining.

So if an agency is getting no money, no glory, no satisfaction, no applause, no fun, and no responsibility out of an account, small wonder if that account tends to drift towards the bottom of the pile on people's desks. The work which will tend to drift towards the top is the *real* reason those people are there: the domestic work, which is what pays the bills, drives and motivates the individual businesses which actually make up the network, and keeps people happy.

NOT-QUITE NETWORKS

To be fair, it isn't quite true that nobody has ever tried to do things differently. For example, there has been a bit of a vogue in recent years for independent agencies around the world to attempt to provide an alternative to these conventional groups by forming themselves into loose alliances, "independent networks" and other perversions on the theme of low-commitment affiliation.

These not-quite networks, which often have neat-sounding brand names, are best described (usually by people working at the agencies which make them up, actually) as *defensive networks:* in other words, they're not really there to actually manage international accounts, but rather as a means by which their component agencies can get onto the serious pitch lists—because the big accounts invariably require candidate agencies to tick the box marked *international capability,* even if it's not required for the job in hand.

"International capability" represents a kind of glass ceiling which prevents many a promising local or regional agency from growing beyond the medium size, and joining an independent network may seem like a heaven-sent opportunity to keep moving forward without selling out.

But independent networks, in my experience, unite in one atrocious muddle almost all of the drawbacks of the conventional network and almost none of the advantages of the truly independent agency. On the rare occasions when a stray international client actually calls the not-quite network's bluff, things quickly fall apart: *not invented here* syndrome in these networks is elevated to levels of bloody-mindedness which are simply staggering, and you can quite see why.

After all, if you're part of a traditional network—say, Leo Burnett in London—and you need the team at Leo Burnett in Milan to translate one of your ads into Italian, or review the local competitors, or set up a focus group, at least you can get on the phone and *tell* them to—after all, your client is their client too, and there's a respectable element of self-interest and plain common sense in the transaction.

Chances are you share quite a lot of corporate culture and working systems too. At least the agencies which have been part of a network for some years have had the opportunity to find ways of collaborating, and merely in order to survive and continue to win international business, have managed to resolve or patch over the fundamental dichotomy I described earlier: that if they are good agencies, they can't be good network partners, and if they're good network partners, they can't be good agencies.

In a network, there is also money for creating network solutions, and top-level managers whose job it is to make sure they work: if you need to set up a separate international department, for example, in order to resolve the dilemma between in-tray and out-tray, the group may even help to fund it, because the group lives or dies according to its ability to win and retain big international accounts.

But agencies which exist primarily to service a domestic market, and live or die according to their ability to produce striking and original creative work within the culture of that market, and may only spend a few days a year on international business, are almost comically ill-equipped to support each other in this way. It's a bit like paying Domenico Scarlatti $20 to play the ukulele at your six-year-old daughter's birthday party. He'll only agree to do it if he's *really* desperate, and there's a fair chance he won't do it with much feeling.

So if you're Katzenbauer and Murphy Advertising in San Francisco, and you need your friends at Bianchi, Rossi & Verdi in Milan to translate one of your ads into Italian, or review the local competitors, or set up a focus group, then God help you. They will, naturally, be knee-deep in some crucial pitch on which the future of their own agency depends, and your business will get pretty short shrift. Actually, you'd better pray they're not interested in it enough to do a proper job, because if they are, that means they're also interested enough to try and steal the business from you.

In short, independent networks are the Idea from Hell, and I don't know a single agency that enjoys being part of one, or a single client who's happy with the work she gets from one.

One-Stop Shops and "Gnatworks"

And, finally, there are a few independent or partly independent creative shops which manage to win and handle international accounts from a single office, or via a small number of wholly-owned subsidiaries or "hubs."

Personally, I have my doubts about hubs and spokes and centers of excellence and all the other euphemisms which people use for networks. My feeling is that the moment you acquire or build offices in other countries, however small they may be, you become a network by definition, and the fact that it's a very tiny network merely means that it offers much less of the not very good thing which much bigger networks offer.

You are instantly and irreversibly in competition with Ogilvy & Mather and their ilk: you have joined that species. The only difference is that you've lost, because Ogilvy & Mather have 274 offices and you have 2.

One of the real benefits you get from a mature global network is sheer, brute *coverage:* wherever you go, they'll be there. But to have only a handful of regional offices in, say, North America, Europe, and Asia, raises something of a quandary: if it's meant to be a network, then having two or three offices is scarcely any better than having one—indeed, it spreads out your people in a way which *diminishes* efficiency rather than enhancing it, and simply makes it harder for those people to work together. It puts them all in different time-zones, and puts them in different teams, with the inevitable effect that collaborating between offices is never done quite as willingly or productively as collaborating within the same office.

And if it's not meant to be a network, then what is it?

Most of the "new-style" international agencies I speak to claim that they're using their overseas offices in a different way from the old networks: some claim that their function is not to receive finished work from the lead agency and adapt it for their region or country, but for each one to be a lead agency in its own right, servicing clients from that region. So, effectively, these offices are not a distribution system, but a

179

kind of wholly-owned but independently operating franchise of the original business, set up in a new market to expand the agency's brand and try its luck in virgin territory.

Now, this would be absolutely fine and totally credible if each one of these shops were creating solely *domestic* work in the country where it's located, but the fact is that they all advertise the same degree of *international capability* that the lead shop offers. Which leaves two possibilities: either they are using the other offices as a network (and, as I have said, an extremely slender network it is), or they are doing *pretend* international: planned, created and executed in a "lead" market, and linguistically retrofitted for the rest of the world.

Others of these "gnatworks"—usually the ones with small offices throughout one region, rather than a few hubs scattered around the world—claim exactly the opposite, and say that the function of their overseas offices is *purely* as a delivery system for international work created by the "lead" agency. These offices are not meant to be creative advertising agencies in their own right, but "postboxes" whose sole function is to service the international needs of the main office.

This raises a different but equally serious objection: who on earth would want to work in an agency like that? No self-respecting creative, that's for sure: perhaps very junior creatives, just starting out, who are lured by the promise of doing *anything at all* for a major brand, so they can get some impressive-looking creative work in their books, even if all they did was translate the copy.

And the trouble with that is, however demeaning senior people may find it to "adapt" other people's creative work, it still isn't something which inexperienced copywriters can do well: for the work to stand any chance at all of surviving the passage from one language to another, the copywriter who adapts or rewrites the copy has to be as good and experienced as the one who wrote the ad in the first place—otherwise, there will be a drop in quality. So unless you can promise self-respecting creatives a reasonable quantity of original assignments, they simply won't work for you.

And if there aren't any creatives in these satellite offices, and translation is carried out in the "lead" country, that leaves account handlers, who, being based in the same country as the local clients, will very soon start to feel lonely and isolated from the main agency. I've seen this happen on several occasions: because the only people they see during the hours of daylight are their local clients, whose culture and language they share (not those of the lead agency which hired them, because, quite correctly, the agency hired them *from* that country), they will soon feel much more like the client's employee than the agency's. They will tend to have more sympathy with the client's opinion too, and gradually cease to operate as a useful representative of the agency. The consequence is that within a year the agency will find it's effectively paying the salary and occupancy costs of a brand new advertising manager for its client.

My contention is that, despite the many efforts to make some of these solutions look different, there really are only two types of ad agency doing international work:

1. *Networks.* A collection of geographically-dispersed ad agencies attempting to collaborate on international business
2. *Domestic shops.* Which generate domestic work, superficially modified during the executional phase to resemble international work

Sorry, but in my book, you're either one or the other.

INTRODUCING SMART CENTRALIZATION

The longer I spent working in a big multinational agency, the more I understood how misconceived the whole idea of the network was, and the more undistinguished twaddle I helped us pump out into the ether on behalf of our global clients, the more I became convinced that this was a shamefully wasted opportunity.

So, in 1989, I left the network with an absolute conviction that international advertising ought to be so much *better* than the best domestic work. I still have this conviction today. The challenge is of a far higher order—you know that if you've created a message that really does work at a deeper level than popular culture or language, it must be pretty good.

Indeed, even when I'm advising clients who don't actually have any plans to market their brands abroad, I sometimes recommend that they go through the international exercise anyway, simply because it sharpens the mind so beautifully, and forces you to concentrate on what's *really* true about your brand and your products.

If only you can learn to relax, and listen to them speaking to you, and enjoy the chaotic music they make, then all those different cultures and languages quite literally *cancel each other out*, leaving the purer, deeper, simpler, and truer concepts untarnished. It's like some mysterious smelting process—all the dust and rock and impurities are burned up in the flames, leaving a thread of pure gold running out of the crucible.

Deep down inside all of us, if we only know how to look, there is a common culture which is sharper and more relevant than the ephemera of local culture: this is the area where we talk about what it's like to be a human being. The messages to be found at this level are truly funny, because they're profound; they're truly persuasive because they're profoundly true; and they are *international by default*, because they touch us as a species, not as nations.

But none of this powerful stuff was getting through at the multinational agency where I worked. The reason was simply that the network was *structurally incapable* of listening to the other markets: it only knew how to impose, and the energy only flowed in one direction.

For me, the challenge was to create a structure in which the flux of cultural richness, creativity, market knowledge and strategic insight *from the markets* could be efficiently and generously directed back onto the strategic and creative processes, and ultimately onto the brand itself.

This structure had to be much, much smaller, and it had to be infinitely more simple. So, rather as a dwarf star is created when a large, complex, diffuse system can no longer hold together and implodes in on itself, forming a smaller mass of incredibly dense substance, so a drastic centralization of the entire international process seemed to be the only route.

Physically centralizing the strategic, creative and production processes of a global campaign into a single agency is, however, only part of the answer. For the client, it's convenient and it's cheap, but it's not sufficient: if that central agency is not *itself* international, then it is merely, according to my previous distinction, a "domestic shop generating domestic work, super-ficially modified during the executional phase to resemble international work." In other words, retrofitting.

The fundamental challenge of international marketing communications is about preserving the perfect balance between *sensitivity to the culture of the brand* and *sensitivity to the culture of its consumers* around the world. If you abandon or relax your grip on the first sensitivity, you end up with fragmentation, loss of identity, and loss of control. Abandon or relax your grip on the second, and you fail to communicate effectively, and fail to build a global brand.

The traditional domestic agency model looks like this:

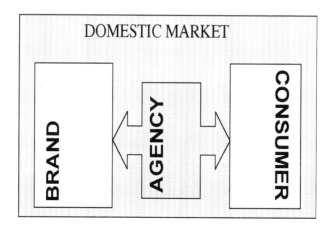

The traditional international model, using a network agency, looks like this:

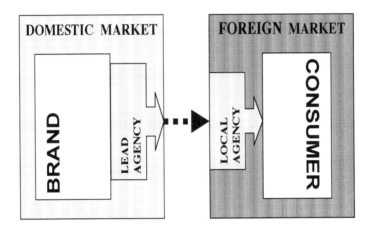

The *smart centralization* model eliminates the "lead agency–local agency" split, and simply takes agency-trained individuals from each foreign market and relocates them to a single, central agency, which is in one office, sometimes but not necessarily located in the lead market. Here, they are able to "cluster around" the brand, and inform its actions and behaviors at source, rather than modifying them at target.

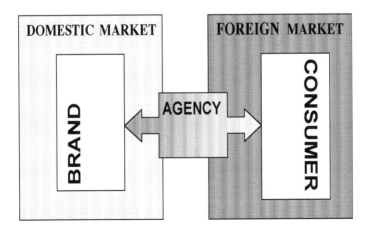

This, in a nutshell, is *smart centralization,* and I believe that it has a significant part to play in the future of international communications.

The superior shortness and directness of the route between consumer and brand significantly enhances the ability of information and creativity to flow in *both* directions: market feedback is instinctive and virtually instantaneous.

As long as there are still some small and medium-sized agencies *left* over the next few years (it seems that any shop with any clients or any competence gets sucked into one of the big groups almost as a matter of course these days), smart centralization is a way for them to become extraordinary.

If they can make it work, they can do better than sell out to the big groups for huge sums of money: they can *take them on,* and win.

My belief is that really quite small agencies (by which I mean 20 or 30 full-time staff) can plan, execute and deliver global communications strategies and multimedia campaigns which are truly sensitive to local market conditions, fast, creative, effective, economical, and true to brand.

And they can even have fun doing it. What more could anyone desire?

In the next three chapters, I'll explain in more detail how agencies and client companies can adopt the principles of smart centralization, and *get global.*

6

The New International Line-Up

At the Olympics a few years back, a fast-food company decided to celebrate the international spirit of the games by printing special editions of its wrappers and takeout boxes, bearing the flags of all the nations taking part that year.

Nobody especially noticed the promotion except the Saudi team, who accused the company of sacrilege. Feelings ran high; letters of protest were dispatched in all directions, and there were murmurings of a fatwah *against the perpetrators of the outrage. The company had little choice but to bin the entire packaging run.*

What they had failed to realize is that flags just don't mean the same thing everywhere. Unlike the flags of Western nations which are usually bland symbols of unity, sovereignty, or long-forgotten territorial ambitions, the Saudi flag bears a verse from the Koran ("there is no God but Allah, and Mohammed is his prophet on Earth"), and is a sacred and very present emblem of the nation's devotion to Islam.

Hardly surprising, then, that seeing it reproduced on fast-food wrappers (hamburgers, what's more, which of course no good Muslim would touch) was seen as a pretty insulting gesture.

The company lost a great deal of money and dignity, the sales promotion agency lost the account, the director of marketing lost his job, and the Saudi team won the 400-meter relay. Perhaps there's justice in Heaven after all.

TOWARDS WORLD ADVERTISING

The moral of this story is also the theme of this chapter.

People from different countries look at familiar objects from different angles, and although this can all too easily give rise to appalling misunderstandings, it can also become a creative force of breathtaking potency if we only learn how to harness it properly.

This fact is the basic premise of *smart centralization.*

The reason for putting the complete global team into one office isn't because it's a whole lot cheaper than a network—although it is.

The reason isn't because it makes the whole thing so much more *controllable* than a network—although it does.

The reason isn't because it's so much *faster* than a network—although it most certainly is.

No, the real reason is because this team makes *better creative work* than a network, and this is why:

Creativity, as I mentioned in Chapter 4, is now pretty much the key challenge in advertising. Other people, of course, have realized this, and all around the world at this precise moment, thousands of highly imaginative, highly motivated, highly paid, *monocultural* creative teams are sitting down together, all trying to come up with the most staggeringly original creative idea ever invented.

And that's just their problem. Your cultural background defines, to a degree which is quite scary, the way you think, the way you dream, the way you invent. Your culture dictates the way you tell stories, the landscapes you create, the characters you populate them with, and the ways they behave.

Consequently, in a monocultural group, people are basically rearranging the same sets of cultural icons, over and over again. Even though we are all exposed to the influence of other cultures much more than we used to be, the creative working practices of most companies are still basically a closed loop. Re-deploying elements from a single culture may occasionally and briefly create the illusion of newness, but it is fundamentally an illusion: everybody in the group is working, more or less, between the same cultural tramlines.

Ultimately, such a group becomes sterile because it's culturally too pure: richness and inventiveness derive from diversity. The Nazis believed that purity of race (of which purity of culture was just one aspect) would eventually lead to the creation of a master-race: but as every schoolchild now knows, this is simply not good biology. If you get a bunch of blue-eyed, blond-haired people to have sex together, within three generations you'll have spawned a race of slant-eyed goofs who can't count up to three. But if, on the other hand, you stir up the gene pool as much as possible, your children get progressively brighter and more beautiful. (I speak, of course, from personal experience.)

The parallel may seem far-fetched, but the process works. Throw open the brief to a wider group of cultures, and you throw open the windows of the creative department in a way which is simply staggering. The way a Japanese thinks is *utterly different* from the way a Belgian or a Bulgarian thinks, and the interference patterns you set up when such people work together are astonishingly productive.

I like to call this *world advertising*, because it works just like world music. If you get a Polish string band to jam together with a Bolivian rap artist, the music they make together will be, by definition, new music. Nobody in the world will ever have made those combinations of sounds before, for the simple reason that nobody has ever done anything as odd as this before—bringing such an unusual group of people to play together.

Now you may not like it, and it may not be easily or obviously marketable: but there will be chords, perhaps scraps of melodies, which are absolutely new, and the art of the thing lies in taking those new elements and weaving them into something relevant, something commercially viable, and which people around the world will genuinely want to hear.

At World Writers, where the World Advertising model comes from, the people we use in the group don't necessarily correspond exactly to the markets where the work will eventually run. We recently ran a creative session for a client of ours who was planning a campaign to run in France and Germany, and I had one of our Chinese creatives in the team alongside our French and German creatives, and the English team from the client's domestic agency. After a very productive hour, the client said to me how much she'd enjoyed the session, and, rather embarrassed, said, "And that Chinese man was awfully good too, but you *do* know, don't you, that this work is only running in Europe?"

"Yes," I replied.

"So, er, why was he there?"

"Because he thinks differently from the French and the Germans!"

This is absolutely *not* the same thing as political correctness: the kind of school-mistress fairness which says that you shouldn't leave anybody out of things in case you hurt their feelings: here, it's purely practical.

Unless you have a native on the creative team, you can't build the needs of his or her compatriots into the advertising early enough for it to be an integral part of the idea; and unless the team is fairly mixed, its thinking is likely to be monodimensional.

It's also pure self-interest, because mixed groups simply have *more fun*.

BUILDING THE MULTICULTURAL TEAM

The basic requirement of smart centralization is to have a permanent *international creative team*. Without this, and the consequent ability to build in the needs of consumers around the world at the very roots of the advertising process, an agency cannot claim to be international.

At World Writers, we have done this pretty thoroughly, and built a team of agency creatives from all over the world: we physically relocate as many of them as we can afford over

190

to London and have them working full-time as part of the core team. The more the merrier; and the more cultural diversity there is, the more exciting the results, and the more fun we have as a group.

We call our team members "creatives" because we've pretty much abandoned the old-fashioned distinction between copywriter and art director. I have to admit too, speaking as a copywriter, that I never really liked the implication that the copywriter was simply an executional specialist (a mere *writer* of *copy*—and *copy*, in any case, is a term which strongly implies that your work isn't original!) whilst the art director was a leader and a genius (a *director* of *art*) who didn't need any executional ability at all, because there were minions to look after that detail stuff.

Personally, I've never met a good copywriter who didn't think visually as well as verbally, and half of the best headlines I ever wrote when I worked in agencies were actually dreamed up by my art director. Sure, somebody has to do the copywriting, and we tend to have at least one creative from each country who can do that, but the artistic talent is spread out pretty randomly throughout the team.

Unusually for an advertising company, we also have a Director of Music in our creative team: the importance of music and sound design in all broadcast and internet work is so fundamental (and it's so critical to get it right in international work), it seems quite strange that this aspect of advertising is traditionally left until the last stages of creative execution, and very seldom carried out by anyone with any specialist musical knowledge, let alone an understanding of the international music scene. As the music business finds that its big "international" acts, the money-spinners of the 1970s, 1980s and 1990s, are losing more and more ground to better-loved (and perhaps less cynically "commercial") national performers, these skills become ever more crucial.

Something very important also goes on at the level of creative direction: both East and West are represented.

This bilateral left brain/right brain arrangement is, we feel, absolutely fundamental, in order to ensure that both hemispheres (geographically and cerebrally speaking) are fully represented in all our thinking.

You could claim that the ideal global creative team would have a Creative Director from every single country in the world, but this would be unwieldy as well as expensive, and would defeat the purpose of maintaining a small, purposeful team in one location: the very notion of a single Creative Director, who imposes his or her creative "vision" (and consequently his or her cultural values) on the rest of the team, is fundamentally incompatible with the model of smart centralization and cultural sensitivity. It risks undermining the carefully bias-free structure of a genuinely international creative team, and for this reason I favor a system with *two cultural directors*, working closely with a creative praesidium (which is composed of senior creative people from six or seven regions: say, South America, North America, Eastern Europe, South Asia, South-East Asia, Southern Europe, and Northern Europe).

The reason why it's possible to have just two cultural directors is a key part of the smart centralization concept: although the permutations of cultural difference around the world are unmeasurably vast, there is a very pronounced and very fundamental divide between East and West.

This divide is mirrored in the split between the world's major religions: the Judaeic, Christian, and Islamic traditions in the West, and Hinduism, Buddhism, Shintoism, and Taoism in the East. Broadly speaking—and this is *very* broad—Western cultures and religions are characterized by the notion that there is a single truth which is accessible to true believers, and what is not the Truth must be falsehood; in the East, one seeks Virtue rather than Truth, and within this framework, opposites may co-exist without logical objection, within the essential and harmonious duality of *yin* and *yang*.[1]

This profound and deeply-rooted difference in the Eastern and Western approach to life lies at the heart of many more obvious differences in the different ways our societies are structured, our companies are managed, our consumers behave, our languages have developed and our brands are built.

The Chinese were right all along, of course: this apparently conflicting duality more or less happily co-existing within the same species and on the same planet, pretty much proves the superior robustness of the belief (to put it in particularly Western terms!), that there is no absolute or universal truth, and that balance is everything. (Actually, if you take the philosophy to its logical conclusion—again, a peculiarly Western habit—then *both* systems must be equally valid, and it is equally true to say that there is an ultimate truth as it is to say that there is *not* an ultimate truth, and the acceptance of duality is no more right than its rejection.) But that is starting to sound like a circular argument, and we risk ending up like the robot in *Star Trek* which destroyed itself because Mr. Spock rather cleverly told it that everything he said was a lie.

The simple *yin/yang* symbol may well be as revealing and truthful a representation of our planet, after all, as the complex and beautiful photographs of the Earth from our satellites, and that's why we find it indispensable to share creative direction equally between East and West.

KEEPING THE PEACE

One interesting difference that results from a multicultural lineup is that the quality of the creative work you produce no longer depends on having "star" creatives on the team—for the simple reason that the team itself is the star. Its multicultural diversity is the "secret weapon." In fact, I recommend actively avoid hiring creative stars, because they often want to take the creative lead, and this might bias the thinking in favor of their particular country.

Bear in mind that the cultures which some of our team come from—particularly the Eastern cultures—don't prize aggression and visible self-confidence as qualities, and faced with a dominant, outspoken Westerner, they may refrain from contributing altogether, rather like the American and the Japanese I talked about in Chapter 2.

Maintaining a productive and friendly balance between all these very different individuals requires a certain amount of careful orchestration and a great deal of wisdom, tolerance, and understanding: but keeping a happy multicultural company isn't nearly as difficult as people sometimes imagine. The reality is that if you bring together a group of young people from widely different countries but the same industry and set them to work together, they will tend to get on together. They'll have just the right balance of professional experience and interests in common, and education, viewpoint, and beliefs that are interestingly different.

Time and again, I've found that many of the worst misunderstandings and tensions caused by people's different cultures can be avoided simply by rendering those differences *explicit:* the mere fact of acknowledging the existence of culture, and discussing its role in our behavior, can serve to help people get on better together, and realize that their differences are not "personal" but "societal." This immediately lifts the level of the argument out of the danger area, and into a zone where it becomes not merely harmless, but actively interesting and engaging.

Talking about cultural difference as *science* (using, for example, Hofstede's dimensions), is a wonderful defuser of difficult situations. When the Americans are cursing the Italians' laziness and the Italians are sneering that it's time the Americans got themselves a life, you can simply point out that these different views of life and work are simply the result of two very different scores on individualism and power-distance, and suddenly it's nobody's fault any more.

People find culture fascinating: every culture on earth has its own equivalents of those old, old jokes which start "There was an Englishman, an Irishman, and a Scotsman. . . ." These jokes, although they are often discarded as racist, are actually evidence of the abiding fascination of culture, and confirm that a point of difference can easily become a point of contact. As I mentioned in Chapter 2, it's interesting to note that a common feature of politically correct behavior is the careful *avoidance* of all reference to cultural differences: the only possible reason for rendering such references taboo is that they are believed to be insults, and only a racist believes that it's insulting to call people what they are.

Naturally, there are management issues which need to be considered in any multicultural workplace: depending on where you come from, your expectations of the company you work for, and the way it manages you, tend to vary quite widely. In some countries, people expect to be managed very loosely, and are happiest when left pretty much to their own devices; in other countries, even the "self-starters" expect to be managed very closely indeed, with fixed and regular reviews, formal assessments and pay discussions, written job descriptions. The British management style, especially in smaller creative companies, tends towards the laid-back, and people from some more "disciplined" countries find this disconcerting: it can make them feel vulnerable and demotivated.

The only possible solution to this problem is the kind of creative approach to reconciling different expectations which Trompenaars describes—avoiding the "happy medium" which is so often a unsatisfactory compromise for both parties, and aiming for an entirely new solution which is created out of the confluence of two conflicting requirements.

In reality, such differences are not so very far removed from the kind you'll always find between individuals within the same culture—in a multicultural environment, they are simply a little more pronounced. In either case, it's a bit of give and take on either side: they have to make some allowance for the fact that they're working abroad, and we have to make allowances for the fact that they come from abroad.

I have always found creative people to be, on the whole, naturally tolerant, and the constant stimulus provided by all that difference, the sense that we are all working in a unique international environment, and the fact that the vast majority of us are sharing for the first time in our lives the daily adventure of living in a foreign city, all conspire to create a team spirit which most of us have never experienced before in any company. You can feel this most clearly on Friday lunchtimes when we all eat together (an almost unbroken weekly tradition since the company was founded in 1989) and talk about anything at all but work in progress.

At one end of the table, our Brazilian creative is engaged in a passionate argument about something — probably football — with a Korean bridger and our German direct marketing expert, whilst at the other end, a Pole, a Finn, and two Italians are having an impromptu and chaotic Italian lesson. (Did you know that Finns pronounce Italian almost better than anyone else in Europe — and vice-versa? — if you want to prove this, next time you're in a room with a Finn and an Italian together, ask the Finn to say, "Look and listen to the sea," in Finnish, and watch the Italian's face whilst he's saying it.)

Looking down the table, you really get the feeling that these people are actually *happy* to be there, doing what they're doing. And that's more than you can say for many offices.

Actually, although I would rather not test this theory out, I believe that although multicultural workplaces certainly create many opportunities for misunderstanding and disagreement, they fortunately don't provide a very fertile breeding-ground for office politics: on the rare occasions in the past when an individual has attempted to create factions or divisions within the team, it simply hasn't got very far. I can only liken this to the way that certain hi-tech fabrics are constructed in order to be tearproof: instead of having all their fibers aligned, which creates natural faults and encourages tearing, rip-stop fabrics have their fibers intentionally

196

mis-aligned, so that a tear can't accelerate and its energy is quickly absorbed. The intentional mis-alignment of culture found in an international team may possibly have the same effect, but perhaps I'm letting my advanced fabric metaphors run away with me. (That's what comes of working for Du Pont, probably.)

Maintaining the Difference

It is clearly important to celebrate and enjoy our cultural diversity wherever possible, and to learn from it. For this reason, we encourage any kind of cultural exchange: whenever we have somebody from an interesting country working with us for a short period — on a work placement or just visiting for a couple of weeks — we set them the task of preparing a seminar, or a whole series of them, about their home country: its culture, its advertising industry, and what it's like to live there. This seminar is delivered to the whole company, so we all end up with a little more understanding of the places the rest of the team come from. It's all influence, and helps to broaden our horizons, as well as understanding each other a little better.

A while ago, we started turning these seminars into something more formal and permanent: we call them our *Postcards from the World*. The postcards are simply a 10-minute amateur video, scripted and shot by our creatives when they're at home in their native country. It's just a quick (and usually fairly quirky) portrait of what it's like to be 25, or whatever, and living in Sweden, or Latvia, or Brazil, or wherever, today. Sometimes they wander around the shops in their home town, commenting on the products they like and the ones they don't, or looking at the posters around town and explaining what they mean. Sometimes it's more personal, with interviews on serious subjects with friends and family; sometimes it's more like a piece of vox-pop research in the street. Each postcard is designed to help bring alive something of the country which our client is exporting to—just to help them, and us, see beyond the demographics, and catch a glimpse of the places our advertising will actually run, and the people who will actually get to see it.

I ought to mention that we also love having students on the team. I can't understand why more companies don't see the value of students: they're young, enthusiastic, cheap and motivated. They're as yet uncorrupted and unprejudiced by experience in establishment companies, and their thinking is still wide open—not yet narrowed down by conventional agency practice. (Now, we're beginning to experiment with hiring retired or semi-retired people, for a similar reason: during a lifetime of work, they should have seen sufficient varieties of prejudice to be able to abandon it, and they are also, in theory, sure enough of themselves to be less selfish and self-serving than younger people. We'll see!)

So we're never without a few bright foreign marketing and advertising students around the place: and one of their most useful functions is to act as cultural Bridgers, helping to bridge the gap between our regional group heads in London and our freelancers around the world.

This means that even though it's difficult for us to justify having a full-time creative team for a country like, say, Vietnam, where we're unlikely to be handling more than a project or two per year, at least we have a mechanism for ensuring that somebody in our office can talk to the freelance creative teams in Vietnam in their own language, understand what they've created when it comes back to us, supervise the typesetting and proofread the print work, speak to the local client in his or her own language and get approval on the work, and make minor changes to the copy if necessary.

Of course, with all these people from around the world based full-time in London, we run the risk that they will quickly become acculturated by living in Britain—inevitably, they learn the language (this is often one part of the reason that they're attracted to the job in the first place), and start to acquire as much (or more) sympathy for the British advertising which surrounds them than for the type they were raised on back home.

They also start to lose touch with what's going on in their own country, and this is a particular worry for creative people. It's scary how quickly this happens: when you move abroad, and start to live and work in another language, within a matter of months or even weeks, you begin to lose a little certainty, a little of your grip on your own popular culture. All this is stuff that we've learned by instinct, unthinkingly, by osmosis, and consequently we don't really know how to hold onto it when different influences are trying to crowd in and replace it.

So to maintain the real value of our overseas creatives, we have to put them through a fairly elaborate program of *constant cultural refreshment*. This involves exposing them as continuously as possible to the cultural influence of their native country—fortunately, cable and satellite TV means that they can watch the same things in London that they would be watching back home, and TV is an extremely important source of popular culture. We subscribe to literally hundreds of magazines in dozens of interest areas, and the creatives are encouraged not simply to flick through these, but to read them intensively, to clip the ads, and maintain a database of current advertising from each country.

Whenever possible, we also send our creatives home for a month's paid "sabbatical" each year, and insist that they go and stay with their parents. If they don't want to stay with their own parents, we loan them somebody else's. The important thing is that they remind their brains deep down what it's really like to be Swedish or Greek or Korean: to walk the dog, buy the newspaper, and argue with your kid sister. And while they're there, we try to organize a temporary work placement for them in a local ad agency that we're on friendly terms with.

In the end, though, people generally gravitate homewards, and although the prospect of a couple of years' intensive international experience in London working on great accounts is a real draw, sooner or later they'll often want to go back to their own countries. And that's not such a bad thing for the agency either, as it enables us to recruit new talent fresh from each country on a reasonably regular basis, and this in turn helps us to stay properly in touch with current thinking and trends in each region of the world.

And the ones who don't want to go and we don't want to lose can always learn a new specialism and move to a different function within the agency.

Clearly, keeping a permanent creative team from at least the core global markets, and keeping them fresh whilst they're in London, isn't a cheap process by any means, and the fact has not escaped me that if we'd used only freelance creatives over the last 10 years I'd probably have retired by now, knee-deep in expensive German sportscars. The problem is that without the *permanent* multicultural team, the small miracle of cultural cross-fertilization simply won't take place—there'd be no world advertising.

Without the permanent team, you simply become a broker of freelance talent, which is just an inferior kind of network. And as in all networks, there's no sense of ownership of the creative idea, so little love is expended on its execution; little loyalty to the "lead" agency, so little motivation to do the best work possible; and no direct contact with the senior client, so a very limited feeling for the brand, the company, and where they're trying to get to.

It's extremely hard to organize a structure in which freelancers can do the work as well as permanent team members. A creative needs to ask, on average, 8,034,746 little questions about each brief in order to execute it relevantly: if you're a freelancer, you simply can't call up the office 8,034,746 times, so you may end up taking a safe, simple route. We get around this problem by retaining as many of our freelancers as possible; by bringing them in at least at the start of every major project; and "inculturating" them into the team several times each year.

Presumably with these kinds of issues in mind, people often say to me that new communications technology must be a blessing to my company, but to be honest it's difficult to see it as anything much more than incremental improvements on the telephone, and it certainly doesn't remove the need for a permanent team. Yes, e-mail has definitely become one of our key communications tools, and it's difficult to imagine how we ever managed without it. (Lest I be accused of technophobia, I'm proud to say that we had e-mail in 1989, when it was virtually pointless, because there was nobody to communicate with except the service provider and your own mailbox.) Yes, the internet is a wonderful thing, and it has certainly made the way we manage international creative approval a great deal simpler—by posting up images of our proposed work on the intranet, clients around the world can view roughs, add comments on sticky notes, and participate in discussion forums. Yes, electronic delivery systems mean we can deliver completed communications around the world in a flash with no need for physical branch offices to help us out. Yes, really affordable, really fast, really high-definition videoconferencing, when it finally happens, will be a great improvement on the telephone, and a wonderful way of cutting down on unnecessary traveling, but the real creative magic happens when creative people work together, phsyically, every day of their lives, as members of a real team.

In addition to all the complexities of getting on with people from different cultures, learning how to work with other people, especially as part of a creative team, is a long process even when you spend every working day together on shared projects. When collaboration is sporadic, and the collaborative projects are secondary to your main business, it's quite likely never to happen at all.

THE MYTH OF CONSENSUS

Now, one of the aspects of managing this team which it has taken us longest to understand is the whole business of reaching consensus. I used to make the mistake, as I expect most people would, of imagining that once you had this wonderful polycultural team, finding the ultimate global creative idea was simply a matter of sitting them all down together and waiting for them to agree on something.

But, oddly, they seemed unable to reach it. I suppose I was failing to spot that attempting to achieve consensus by a simple majority vote is a kind of congenital democratic tic we all suffer from in the Western world—the almost unchallenged assumption that the stuff *most people like* is what we should go with.

Trouble is, democracy isn't an awfully good principle for creating global advertising. Supposing you're planning a campaign to run worldwide, and everybody likes it except the Hungarians, who have perfectly valid reasons for defining it as unsuitable for their market. What do you do? Run it in Hungary anyway, with a little note on the bottom of each ad saying, "We know that you won't like this ad very much, but we promise it's going down a storm in Germany, France, and Britain."?

More to the point, do you force the Hungarian marketing department to spend their precious advertising budget on running it for the sake of global consistency and neatness, even though everybody knows it's a waste of money?

This isn't democracy. This is fascism.

Well, I soon began to discover that the most valuable ideas *weren't* usually the ones which most people more or less liked. The really exciting ideas tended to polarize the group—some people absolutely loved them and some absolutely hated them—and we had often rejected these ideas because of the vehemence of certain team members' veto.

We probably wasted a lot of good ideas. In reality, what we have found to be important is the *strength of the reaction*, rather than the *level of acceptance* of the idea. The best thing to do is leave the room altogether and not come back in until the noise level has reached a certain pitch—the "clapometer" principle, if you will—then, when you come in and find that half the team are standing on their chairs saying they'd rather sell their grandmothers than run with this idea, and the other half are standing on the table swearing they'd rather slash their own wrists than *not* run with this idea, you know you're onto something interesting.

Why? Because it's far easier to turn a strong negative into a strong positive than it is to turn nothing into anything. And advertising has to be strong stuff or it just won't register.

Having all those different cultures and different perspectives within a single creative team certainly does create a richer stock of initial ideas. But what they also do, as I mentioned before, is *cancel each other out:* the multicultural group effectively eliminates the superficial. Anything that is too local for another group member to grasp or appreciate tends to get rejected; consequently, what we end up with is stuff which is garnered, by default, from a much deeper layer.

What we are looking for is not harmony, but chaos — even conflict. Ideas which don't ruffle the surface of our consciousness are ideas which don't count, and the beauty of the multicultural team is that chaos, interference patterns, and commotion get enhanced and accelerated, rather than smoothed away. It's rather like the way that space probes use the opposing gravitational fields of planetary bodies to "slingshot" themselves into deep space: as the idea passes around the multicultural team, it gathers pace. This is the complete opposite of the distributed international model, where the addition of each new cultural viewpoint tends to create a gradual deceleration of creative ideas until they finally stop altogether.

Getting a Handle on the World

In recent years, we've begun to find that the conventional geo-political groupings of countries aren't always terribly helpful when it comes to planning international advertising campaigns. So we've done away with those monstrous

clumps of territory beloved of multinational corporations—
EFIGS (England, France, Italy, Germany and Spain),
EMEA (Europe, Middle East and Africa), and, for all I
know, Entire Northern European and Mediterranean Area
(that's ENEMA)—and replaced them with sociocultural
groupings, based primarily on religion.

This is not because we're particularly pious, but simply
because the sacred traditions of a people are often a far more
reliable guide to their present-day cultural inclinations than
the random borderlines invented and squabbled over by
politicians and generals.

And in case anybody should find grouping consumers by
religion a little too wishy-washy, a little too pretentious, and
not quite hard enough data for their tastes or marketing
needs, they might like to ponder on Table 6.1,[2] showing average worldwide income per capita for four religious groups.

So on our cultural map of the world, Turkey is in the
Middle East, but Israel is an island off the coast of New
England. Belgium is sometimes two countries, and so is
Italy, but Ecuador and Venezuela are almost always one.
Lithuania is part of Russia, but neighboring Estonia is joined
to Finland. I was about to add that we don't recognize some
of the current divisions within the CIS or Yugoslavia, but I'd
better stop this before I cause a diplomatic incident.

Obviously, these are gross approximations, as they need
to be. There's no doubt that perfectly valid cultural divisions
can be observed to an almost infinite degree of specificity—
many would claim that Germany or Spain are very far from

Table 6.1   Average Worldwide Income Per Capita for Four Religious
Groups

RELIGIOUS GROUP	INCOME PER CAPITA
Cadoaism	$245
Jains	$368
Buddhist	$6,742
Shinto	$26,912

single entities, and I've heard convincing arguments in favor of distinguishing the different cultures of different *villages* in Sicily. Ultimately, in fact, each one of us has his or her own *personal* culture, and in a limited way that's what direct marketing attempts to cater for.

PREPARING THE INTERNATIONAL CREATIVE BRIEF

Creating a brief which accommodates at least the fundamental requirements of each overseas markets is, of course, an indispensable part of the international planning process, and yet many client companies and agencies with little experience in developing international work may frequently overlook this need altogether.

But even agencies which habitually develop international campaigns often do little more than pay lip-service to the needs of other markets, and the recognition that they may have differing needs tends to be more the grudging result of an acceptance that if ignored, the local clients will create more trouble later, rather than an actual interest in discovering the differences and similarities within their markets, and finding out what challenges and opportunities these can offer the brand and its advertising.

It normally goes something like this: the planners and strategists in the "lead" agency start thinking as soon as they are briefed by their client. This is a quite understandable tendency which they can't really help—it's the way we're all made. But often, they'll also spend quite a bit of time refining this initial approach with the domestic client (the one they already have the strongest relationship with in any case) before setting off on a tour of the country managers, and this is where the hierarchical approach starts to become somewhat pernicious.

When they reach the first country manager (let's say in France), the overseas envoys of the international agency are commendably open-minded: their approach is normally along the lines of "tell us about your market," whilst in their minds they are already, inevitably, beginning to explore ways in which their approach can be merged with the requirements of the French market.

Next stop is Germany, and the meeting now tends to start off with the chief envoy saying, "We were thinking of adopting an approach something like this, which appears to have international potential. Please tell us all about your market, and we can discuss whether this approach can be made to work in Germany."

More or less irrespective of what the German client now says, the conversation in the next country (we'll call it Italy) tends to run something like this: "Here's our proposed European strategy. Do you have any serious objections to it?"

By the time they've reached Spain, the fact-finding mission has become a strategy presentation, and the envoys' opening gambit runs: "Here is the European strategy. It's been a pleasure meeting you."

The end result of this imperfectly objective process is a piece of strategy which has been sufficiently distorted by the influence of the one market they've *allowed* to influence it, that it works less well than a purely domestic strategy might have done, yet at the same time manages to ignore every single basic requirement of every other market.

The only trouble is, by visiting all those people and pretending to listen to them, the agency has effectively promised them a say in the matter, and should not be in the least surprised that when the country managers find their opinions and needs totally ignored in the final document, they become extremely angry and obstructive.

In my view, a more intelligent approach to the process works in almost exactly the opposite way. For a start, instead of going around looking for commonalities, I believe that our envoys should look for differences, and indeed actively *encourage* difference. They should positively applaud eccentricity and local-minded tactical issues. If they come across a country manager who appears reluctant to tell them something different or incompatible about his or her country, the envoys should actually *force* them to think of something. If the Portuguese say, "We're the same as Spain, now go away and let us get on with our work in peace," we should bully them until they've told us something concretely different about their country.

Incidentally, I don't see any reason why the envoys shouldn't be the creative people who will ultimately develop the advertising campaign: after all, the shorter the loop between input and output, the more likelihood there is of market requirements being faithfully reflected in the creative work.

Having the creative teams meet their opposite numbers on the client side and do their own market evaluation is an extremely effective way of bringing them face-to-face with the strategic and tactical realities which their executions will ultimately have to address. It also gives them an additional opportunity to observe and talk to the consumers they are targeting.

I refuse to believe that just because an individual is lucky enough to possess a creative talent, he or she is automatically incapable of dealing with clients, or contributing to the thinking which defines the creative brief. Not having too many dedicated non-creative people also makes the team smaller, faster, and cheaper to run. It's simply a question of always taking care to hire people who can do both, and I have to say that this is only really a problem in Britain, where there is a kind of convention that creative people take pride in being as unlike the "suits" as possible. Yet again, it's partly a class thing: the idea is that you need an Oxbridge-educated lady or gentleman to be polite to the client, but a Cockney barrow-boy to act radical and dangerous and make the adverts.

When I first started in advertising, it took me over a year to get my first job in a London agency as a creative, and I was constantly rebutted on the grounds that I "ought to be a suit."

(I speak English with the accent technically known as *received pronunciation*—in other words, it doesn't come from a region but from a class, and is supposedly "received" from institutions such as private schools, Oxford and Cambridge Universities, the BBC, and so forth. Actually, I rather thought I'd received it from my parents, but I suppose the experts know better.)

Eventually, I threw self-respect to the winds, falsified my résumé (deleting all references to Oxford and private schools and replacing them with carefully-crafted episodes like dropping out of art school after six months, and working as a cleaner in a bus station: it was the first real piece of copy I wrote in my life); I assumed a pantomime Cockney accent, dressed in torn jeans, and was instantly rewarded with my first job.

The British cliché (promoted mainly by the creatives themselves) is that creatives are aggressive, touchy, inarticulate, diehard, and single-minded "visionaries" who simply aren't interested in the opinions of the person who's paying for the work. They are so in tune with the cutting edge of popular culture that it's almost impossible for ordinary people to have an ordinary conversation with them, and they have an ingrained disgust for strategic and financial considerations. This all means that you can't take them to client meetings—which is no doubt part of the intention—and the account handlers often bask in the reflected glory of being the only people who can communicate with and control these mad dogs. It's all part of the process of mystifying the creative product as much as possible, the result of agencies' deep-seated fear of being "found out" by the client as tricksters or frauds, a paranoia they never really seem to lose.

In most other countries, it's much easier to find creative people who are experienced in taking their own briefs and presenting and debating their own work with the client. They are perfectly happy about being their own advocates (I once had great difficulty persuading one of our creatives from Finland that he didn't need to wear a tie in the office). Yes, there is often some truth in the argument that creatives get very emotionally attached to their own work—as they should—and consequently find it quite difficult, even painful, to discuss its merits and demerits in an entirely objective way.

But I also believe that presenting and arguing the case for creative work is a creative task, best done by the people who understand creativity best: the teams themselves. It also helps them to learn quickly and directly how to produce work which is relevant to their clients' real needs. So the dilemma is easily resolved by having one member of the creative team create the work, and another present it.

I'm not saying that dedicated account handlers are unnecessary: but in a centralized international team, you certainly don't need one for each country. I also think that creativity is vital for the dedicated account directors who lead the account, and nobody understands creative work better than people who are able to do it themselves—my favorite kind of "suit" is always someone who wasn't born wearing one.

MEANWHILE, BACK AT THE RANCH . . .

The agency should staunchly resist the temptation to begin planning until its envoys (creative or otherwise) have reached the end of their trip, and it certainly shouldn't start thinking about the domestic market until it has first heard from everybody else. The envoys' opening sentence should be the same in every single country: "please tell me exactly how and why your country is different from everybody else's."

When the envoys get back home, a team is convened with one native representative from each country (usually a member of the creative team) and the whole group discusses all the issues raised in each market, and from a culture-mapping study which has been carried out simultaneously with the field trip, and any other data which the client or agency may have supplied. Ideally, the regional or global marketing director with ultimate responsibility for strategy is also a member of this team.

At this stage, the individual specialist (or external consultancy) who is charged with preparing the culture-mapping analysis will present their initial findings to the team. Their input at this stage is likely to be a series of fairly general observations, as there is no *proposition* or *message* yet to be tested against country profiles. It may well be little more than a proposed clustering of the markets, for example: "We may be able to treat Scandinavia and the Netherlands as one cultural group since they are all feminine societies, unless our creative treatment ends up being relevant to the issue of uncertainty avoidance, in which case we might need to consider Finland as belonging to the same group as some of our Asia-Pacific markets."

This kind of general cultural context is an extremely valuable supplement to the tactical marketing issues returned by our envoys, and helps to guide the group towards creating useful "blocks" of meaning or insight. The "harder" value of culture mapping occurs later on, when actual propositions or messages have been developed, and these can be tested for likely appeal and relevance against the cultural profile of each country. (It goes without saying that if the timing or budget on a particular assignment don't stretch to in-market testing of concepts, the *cultural* testing of concepts is a piece of desk research which can be carried out relatively quickly and with relatively little impact on the overall cost of the project.)

Here's an important point that's easily overlooked: people get better at doing things the more they do them. For example, after the international strategic team has heard the ethnopsychologists' general market observations a few times, they will begin to internalize and become familiar with the broad cultural characteristics of key markets, and this familiarity will, in turn, condition their thinking on each subsequent assignment, and gradually make it more instinctively international, and turn them into better internationalists. It will also help the envoys to better understand the various different country managers and their markets on subsequent fact-finding missions, and make better use of their input.

This extraordinarily valuable learning curve is a far cry indeed from the almost opposite process of "negative learning" which can so often occur in traditional network agencies. Because each office of a network has a vested commercial and emotional interest in *not* collaborating with the "lead" agency and *not* contributing their market knowledge, insights, and experience to the thinking (usually because they have learned that it will either be ignored or rejected as "not invented here syndrome"), the members of the lead agency team will gradually become more and more expert at working on international campaigns without the benefit of their foreign colleagues' input. And on the occasions when input *is* given by overseas offices, the lead team becomes extremely adept at *excluding* it from their thinking, because it is almost guaranteed to be tailored at sabotaging their efforts to come up with a common international creative strategy: the "utterly damning objections rather than helpful minor modifications" which I mentioned in the last chapter.

I mentioned that the team we put together in order to discuss strategy should contain a creative from each country. It is crucial that somebody from *each* country is part of the team, and on equal terms, because it's here that the real needs of each country are most at risk from becoming steamrollered by group dynamics and the need to reach some kind of consensus. Each team member has to act as the ambassador of their country and their local client, and ensure that nothing genuinely fundamental gets overlooked (in fact, there's no reason why the local client can't act for himself or herself in this part of the process, if they prefer).

Now, the only reason why this principle ever needs to be modified is when the campaign needs to run in so many different countries that the size of the team becomes unmanageable. Actually, we work in exactly the same way when producing the creative work later on in the process, and once people have gotten over the ingrained notion that cre-

211

atives can only work effectively in pairs, they are often surprised just how nimble and purposeful a large team can be.

But it's certainly true that if you have more than about 10 people in a room, it can slow things down a bit, and nobody really gets to say everything they would like to say. Some rules are also useful, too—no interruptions, no side conversations, no criticism of other people's ideas, etc. Edward de Bono describes a miraculously effective technique involving a series of colored hats,[3] each one of which stands for a particular type of discussion. (The black hat is the only one which permits analysis or criticism of anyone's ideas.) This way, everybody collaborates and moves together in the same direction. We find that, apart from making seemingly difficult issues very quick and simple to resolve, it also reduces needlessly destructive or antagonistic conversation, and serves to protect the less assertive members of the team from the more assertive ones.

In cases where the team does get too large, it's important to be completely flexible with the individuals' preferred way of working: some people naturally team up together, and sometimes they prefer to work on a problem in smaller groups, or even alone. All this means in practice is that you need several planning sessions of different sizes: there can be an initial briefing and free-for-all, then breakouts of whatever size or permutation of team people feel happiest with (and this phase can go on for several days or even weeks), then a full-team feedback and update session with general discussion and filtering of what's on the table. The filtering can also be done "offline" if there are a lot of proposals to be reviewed or if the brief has to fit 20 or more markets.

Obviously, some sacrifices have to be made by all in order to reach a useable theme or thought which is internationally applicable because it is profound rather than because it is shallow: the important thing is that no factors are overridden or overlooked at this stage which might jeopardize the *basic effectiveness* of the campaign in any individual market. Personal preference, likes and dislikes, can be put aside for the time being: in any case, the ultimate question of the (not yet existent) creative work's probable effectiveness in each market needn't (and almost certainly can't) be decided at this stage.

Both "hard" and "soft" issues may become important at this stage, and are generally concerned with irreducible or incontrovertible factors about individual markets — promotional legislation, competitive situation, market maturity, or special conditions relating to the core target demographics or ethnopsychology. Whether such issues actually have a bearing on the underlying strategic route (which is all we are attempting to define at this point) or purely on its creative execution, is a key part of the agenda at this stage of the process.

It shouldn't be forgotten that what we are doing here is no less a creative process than the development of the creative idea: without a similar leap of the imagination at this point, there is every chance that the campaign we finally end up with will be executionally rather than conceptually creative — a distinction which I outlined in Chapter 4.

For this reason, assuming that one has creative teams which are accustomed to thinking strategically and in pure brand terms, and are able to resist the temptation to proceed too quickly into executional detail, it is a phase which should not, in my view, be restricted to planners, strategists, account people, and clients.

Having said this, the temptation to think executionally should never be resisted *too* vigorously. There is something of a convention in marketing circles that the disciplines of brand strategy and planning are in some way *intellectually superior* to the creation of messages, and should never be distracted or polluted by mere executional considerations.

Actually, I think that the forced separation of theory and practice is an extremely risky habit when devising advertising and marketing communications. After all, the only way in which the consumer will ever come into contact with the brand is via *executions* of strategy, rather than the strategy itself, so unless the strategy is to some degree informed by its likely or feasible executions, or at least measured against them at regular intervals, it runs the risk of moving into a theoretical stratosphere which will render it useless as a framework, guide, or set of instructions for those executions. I've seen many examples of brand positioning work which is so successfully removed from the ambit of creative executions that it's entirely worthless: you could give it to six agencies and end up with six campaigns pursuing six totally different directions.

Apart from anything else, I freely admit that some of the best planning I've ever come across has happened backwards: somebody has made a premature creative suggestion, and its reverse deconstruction has resulted in a key strategic insight. I wouldn't ever subscribe to a system which was designed to prevent this kind of serendipity from occurring.

GETTING DOWN TO BUSINESS

The purpose of the planning meeting, informed by the market intelligence and local client requirements reported by our envoys, and by the observations of our culture experts, is simply to see whether any common theme can be drawn out of all this difference. But it's important that the whole exercise is carried out in full understanding of the fact that a successful outcome is by no means guaranteed. It is *never* a foregone conclusion that a coherent yet meaningful international communications strategy is possible, and only at this stage, with the information now available from market and from our cross-cultural analysis, can we begin to decide exactly where, along the continuum of multidomestic to "monoglobal," is it possible for us to create a competitive, effective, and distinctive communications campaign.

Even if the desire to create a single global campaign is deeply enshrined in the policy of the corporation, and even if this requirement forms a part of the client's brief to the agency, it should never be taken as granted that it is either feasible or desirable, and an agency is simply failing in its duty as paid advisor to the company if it accepts this policy despite clear indications that it cannot be as effective as a multidomestic approach.

For this reason, I would advocate that companies consider global or regional campaigns as a tactical instrument rather than a corporate strategy: the viability of such campaigns is not a constant condition, and will depend on the choice of markets, the nature of the product or brand, and the conditions it encounters in each market at each point in time, and a host of other changing considerations (not least, the ability of its agency to succeed in reconciling a mass of often apparently conflicting market data into a valid and distinctive single strategy).

On the other hand, when an international campaign *can* be made to work, it can be tremendously powerful, for the reasons I outlined at the end of the last chapter: if we do manage to strike a seam of common truth, a *self-justifying* reason to speak to consumers around the world or throughout a region with the same message, then the campaign will be worth running by definition, because it will be more unusual, more striking, and more effective than a domestic campaign.

There is one further important issue to be borne in mind at this stage of the strategic development process: that all thinking is *media-neutral* as well as *culture-neutral.* The vehicle which we ultimately use to convey our international message is an extremely important facet of our ability to tailor it to the individual features of each market—probably more significant, for example, than the other important country-defined "variable" in the process, the copy on each execution.

For example, the niche characteristics of our target group within one particular market might be more effectively catered for by using direct marketing to fine-tune the audience, rather than by using different copy alone to fine-tune the message itself in a mass-media vehicle, such as television or outdoor. The recipe for success is, of course, a combination of the two, but unless we are bearing our message delivery system in mind at this early stage, there is a chance we could fail to spot the usability of an apparently invalid international proposition — or, indeed, the invalidity of an apparently useable one (because of the unavailability or shortcomings of a particular medium in certain countries). The classic example of this is a TV idea *specifically designed* for a 90-second slot, which ends up working very poorly because such spot lengths are simply not available in most European countries, and it has to be squeezed into a 30- or even 20-second version.

Then we make our brief. Page One of the brief is the common ground, including that leap of the imagination, the central motivational insight which holds good for all of our cultures and all of our markets — a distinct possibility when you're dealing with a region such as Western Europe or Latin America, but less likely for a global campaign. Cultural differences and market differences — especially connected with different usage patterns or a different state of market maturity — will usually mean two or three variants on the common brief for the whole world: as I have indicated before, the most sensible way to divide the planet for the purposes of communications strategy may *not* be according to how the company itself is organized, or by geography, but by market maturity or some major cultural axes.

Page Two is different for each market, and derives directly from our envoys' conversations about market differences with each Country Manager. Page One leads to the core creative idea, and the pictures. Page Two leads to the words and the choice of media, and is used to build vital market-specific and culture-specific targeting into the advertising. And that's really all there is to it.

First you find the common ground (or, ideally, the *un*common ground). Then you *dance* on it.

216

WHERE THE IDEAS COME FROM

At World Writers, internal meetings generally take place in English, which is inevitable. Since at any given moment several of our staff tend to be teaching each other new languages, it does sometimes happen that the members of a particular group all share another language—French and Spanish are common alternatives, and our Scandinavians always perform that slightly unnerving trick of carrying on a perfectly fluid conversation in Swedish, Danish, and Norwegian all at the same time.

But since much of our work involves partnering the client's existing domestic agency in the United States or United Kingdom, even if we were happy to have our meetings entirely in Urdu or Serbo-Croat, this would be rather inconvenient for our partners.

Naturally, everybody's command of English varies enormously, and relatively few people speak it perfectly.

Yet the fact that we are obliged to use English in order to communicate with each other sometimes provides its own creative stimulus. You must have had that experience where you hear a song performed in a language which you only know slightly, or perhaps just inaudibly in your own language, and the words you can pick out make you think it's saying something incredibly profound and beautiful—until, years later, you find out what the lyrics actually were, and are shocked to discover that it's the most trivial moon/June stuff. Something similar happens in our groups—either there's something weird about the way people are expressing themselves in English, or there's something weird about the way other people understand them, or both—but people are constantly misunderstanding each other, and with endlessly fascinating results.

I've heard partially deaf people say how much they enjoy keeping their hearing aids switched off because of the extraordinary things they imagine people are saying when they can't quite hear them properly. The point is, these are more interference patterns, more chaos, and it helps to keep us from thinking along predictable lines.

Sometimes sayings and clichés can be an extremely valuable area to explore. A manner of speech is, after all, a highly artful, highly polished, often very vivid way of summarizing a common experience in a few choice words — so it's good language. But interestingly, there's not all that much crossover of manners of speech, set phrases, proverbs, and clichés between one language and the next — so what might seem an unacceptably hackneyed phrase in one language could appear amazingly inventive and totally new when transferred to another language. For example, where in British English we might say that a stupid person is "as thick as two short planks," the Dutch would say "dumb as a pig's ass" — and both of those sayings work rather well when transposed into the "wrong" language. If we loan each other our sayings, we suddenly find that our language has become much enriched, more unexpected, more graphic, more surprising.

In the course of an English conversation, one of our Spanish copywriters once used a saying he was rather fond of in his own language — "you're stupid enough to give a bald man a perm" — and everybody else found it so graphic and comical that it has practically passed into the language. Similarly, I remember once spending around half an hour trying to explain to a Swede who worked for me the meaning of the English expression "to get your knickers in a twist" (to get upset) and when he finally got it he hardly stopped laughing for three days. In the end, he used it in an ad which a lot of other Swedes found equally amusing.

Incidentally, dear reader, if you've only carried on reading this far because you were so puzzled by the title of this book, and you happened to miss the clue in the Introduction, I'm about to release you. Every language has its own cute euphemisms for death: in English, we bite the dust; the French push up the cabbages, the Italians pull their leathers, and the Germans bite the grass. (Actually, they *eat* the grass, but if I hadn't used some poetic license, then the title of the

218

book would have slipped beyond "intriguing" and into the realms of "weird.")

The great thing about these figures of speech is that they are, literally, *figures:* much more than tricks for playing with words, they are often so imaginatively and strikingly visual, that they only really achieve their full potential when illustrated.

One of the things we try very hard to do in all of our creative sessions is to put off until the last possible moment talking about *advertising*—because, as I've said, advertising carries its own culture, which to an extent is international, and as soon as you start thinking in terms of headlines or visuals, you're already limiting your thinking and starting to tramline yourself.

When I was working for a big agency, I spent some time working in the Tokyo office, and was surprised to see that when a new brief came in to the creative department, the team would often go out to look for inspiration before they started writing or drawing—and amongst their favorite haunts were museums and art galleries. I thought this was amazingly mature behavior, and in striking contrast to London practice, which usually involved us going to the pub and getting plastered.

Story Time

All over the world, at this very moment, people are telling stories to each other. Whether it's around the campfire in the plains of Mongolia or in a seatback movie in a plane over Manhattan, our ability to reproduce and enhance experience or fantasy through stories is one of the most fascinating and enduring qualities of this curious species we belong to.

Much of world culture is founded on stories: they are how wisdom is preserved, how we teach our children, how we remember our past, how we anticipate the future. People never tire of hearing stories, because however short they are,

Inspiration: Japanese style . . .

stories almost always have a beginning, a middle, and an end, so they have their own movement, their own force, and they *take you with them.*

Stories can give morals, prove points, or merely entertain. They can be as elevated as parables, or as trivial as jokes.

Here's one I rather like (and it's only fifty words):

The Midday Sun Burns Brightest
But the Midnight Sun Burns Longest
"One glance from your Nordic eye," he said angrily, "and hailstones batter my mimosa."
So she exiled her memories of icebergs and pleased him by raising their children in Provençal sunshine.
Dying, she said, "Toss my ashes to the northern lights, to drift among birches and be buried by snow."[4]

Stories make advertising. If you look carefully, it's remarkable how many advertisements, at heart, are simply stories, or fragments of stories.

They don't have to be silly stories, of course. Some of the most powerful tales I can think of are much more *aha!* than *ha-ha*. What about a man who got lost and found his way again by marking his path? That's Theseus in the labyrinth in Greek mythology, but it's also Hansel and Gretel, and maybe it's an ad for an internet service provider or candy or a gardening magazine.

What about a man who just popped out on an errand and was *never seen again?* You can read that story in any newspaper, any day, anywhere in the world, but it's also the beginning of a thousand adventure stories, and maybe it's a story about a new car, life insurance, or a newspaper. It's absolutely breathtaking in its power, because it finishes on a note of infinite possibility.

The problem—and the danger—is that being simple and being a simpleton are awfully similar: and even while you're successfully exploiting the highest common factor, you're never more than a hair's breadth away from the lowest common denominator.

I once read a story in a newspaper which I've never forgotten: a young man's fiancée died of a mysterious illness the day before they were due to be married, so he ended up going to her funeral instead of their wedding. The story is very simple, almost classically so (probably not, it goes without saying, suitable material for an advertising campaign, unless it were to be a public service campaign of some kind). It's very sad, not tragic in the proper sense (actually this is pathos, not tragedy)—but is it profoundly relevant to all of us?

As we delve down into our psyches to find what lies beneath culture, to find the true core of common experience, it may seem at first sight that these deep layers offer the advertiser little of real value: a couple of childish jokes, a man getting lost and then finding his way again, a sad, sad story from a tabloid newspaper.

But the reality is that the core theme of our creativity could well be something quite simple, quite childish: it's what we *do* with this stuff that makes the difference.

221

What made that story about the wedding and the funeral different for me, and what made it stick in my memory for ever afterwards, was a chance quote of the bridegroom's: he said, "I should have been leading her down the aisle today, but instead I'm following her coffin." By chance, or perhaps by design, he had encapsulated the stark symmetry of his tale of woe in a single, lapidary utterance; he had also given the visual imagery of the event a metaphorical value; and he had injected some intensely powerful irony into the depiction of his wretchedness. He had taken a rough stone and deftly cut and polished it into a jewel, whose brilliance might never fade. In short, he was a poet, perhaps just for that one instant in his life.

Performing the equivalent of this trick in advertising is a lot to do with having the courage to let go of the executional details at the start of the creative process, and devoting one's energies instead to finding the *idea* which is robust enough to mean something to anybody who's ever lived.

These stories, which need never be more than a sentence long, can be minuscule parables, or just beginnings of stories, or ends of stories. They can be condensed epics, or descriptions of almost nothing happening. The Japanese are very good at these—there was the tale of the prince who fell asleep and dreamed he was a butterfly; and when he awoke he could no longer be certain that he wasn't a butterfly dreaming he was a prince.

SOMETHING OLD, SOMETHING NEW

One useful trick is to look at other people's stories, and mentally step back from them, half close your mind's eye, and see their pure structure—the storyline itself, in its purest form. It's good to do this with great stories from great literature or great folk traditions—the Norse sagas, Shakespeare and Dante, Jewish folk stories, the tales of Nasreddin Hodja, the Bible, the Thousand and One Nights, the Upanishads, and

all the rest of them. Once you've picked out the pure structure, you can re-dress the story with surface detail which is
appropriate to your culture, and to the task in hand. Or you
can change the plot, or stick the ending of one story onto the
beginning of another, like that children's game where you
swap around the body parts of animals.

It's very interesting that the stories of antiquity preserve
their fascination so well across the centuries, and it is probably the same qualities which enable them to travel so well
across time that also enable them to travel successfully
across geographical and cultural space too. A Shakespeare
plot keeps much of its relevance and impact in the very different culture of British society 300 years later; it also keeps
it across 3,000 miles, and works a charm on Indian audiences today. This is the stuff that means things to human
beings—this is the stuff that talks about what it's like to be
alive on this planet.

These stories aren't ads until they are somehow pressed
into the service of a brand, it goes without saying. They are
little glimpses of how different life can be if looked at
through another person's eyes, or from another perspective.
They are stimuli, scraps of structure, starting-points which
may lead to unexpected destinations. But the point is that if
you *start* somewhere different, your journey is far more
likely to lead you somewhere different too.

Another technique which I've found extremely useful is
martianism, something I borrowed from a group of English
poets, especially Craig Raine, writing in the 1970s.[5] Martianism is when you pretend you've just arrived from Mars and
are looking at everything for the very first time. You can only
guess what people are doing and what things are for. You end
up speaking about familiar objects in an extremely unfamiliar
way: what *are* those metal boxes on wheels that eat people
and then carry them away in long lines? The tone of voice
becomes naïf, childish, almost magical. Such a tone of voice
never fails to be striking and unusual, and in advertising, it
cuts majestically through the surrounding media babble.

Often, we try to imagine we're far in the future or far in the past. This tends to lessen the sense of distance between each member of the multicultural team, and reduces the distraction caused by the high level of cultural difference. For example, if the brief is to sell a car, we might start off by pretending that we're selling it three days before the first ever passenger car appeared on the market; or we might decide that it won't actually be available until another 30 or 40 years from now.

Sometimes a similar and equally interesting effect can be obtained by describing the product as you would to a five-year-old — although I've found this only really works properly if you actually get a real five-year-old in front of you. The other advantage of doing this for real is that the response you get from the child is usually more unexpected and illuminating than the stuff you're saying yourself.

Here's another 50-word mini-saga to prove my point, this time written by an eight-year-old:

The Conquering Alien
One year ago on Venus there was an alien who wanted to conquer the Univurse. When he got to Earth he landed on a school, he went through the air duct and though some of the holes, he saw a class called 4P, they were so ugly he went home.[6]

But when you get back to earth after your flights of multicultural fantasy, don't forget to answer the brief: you still have to do that, but you might just find it looks a bit more inviting than it did first time round.

In the next chapter, I'd like to concentrate on some more of the practical issues connected with Smart Centralization, and show the types of structures which can cope with the demands of servicing big global accounts out of a very small agency.

7

Going It Alone

Not really a disaster story, this time, more a legal comedy:

Ferrero, the Italian confectionery company, once produced a TV commercial for their flagship product, Ferrero Rocher, which was known as The Ambassador's Reception.

This slightly primitive spot showed a group of extremely upscale (and evidently cosmopolitan) guests at a cocktail reception in an ostentatiously luxurious house. A liveried butler offers the guests Ferrero Rocher chocolates from a silver salver, and the punchline is rather self-consciously delivered by a glamorous woman in a very shiny evening-dress to her host, "Ambassador, you spoil us."

It's an extremely basic aspirational scenario which would hardly be noticed at all in Italy if Ferrero didn't spend such colossal sums of money putting it on air every 15 minutes or so throughout the evening, but which achieved almost cult status when it was aired in the United Kingdom.

British audiences were shocked to the core by the bluntness of the ad's appeal to their snobbery, the lack of wit or charm, the absence of any creative devices whatsoever, and the crass 1970s-style upmarket imagery. They could only interpret this unwarranted, vulgar, and evidently foreign intrusion into the cozy club of their highly sophisticated domestic advertising environment as an extremely subtle piece of irony. The ad was endlessly discussed and debated in the media, and in the end it was painstakingly and expensively remade for Ferrero UK by a British director, and the bothersome subtlety of its "irony" was replaced with something a little more reassuring—a style which was unmistakably high camp, and clearly intended not to be taken seriously.

Needless to say, throughout the entire run of both the original ad and the remake, sales of the offending article rocketed.

Well, Ferrero decided that they'd like to use this ad in France too, but they quickly ran foul of the national broadcast regulator, the BVP (Bureau pour la Vérification de la Publicité), which will not allow scenes showing the consumption of alcohol on TV—in the ad, all the ambassador's guests are sipping champagne. So the production company put the film back into post-production and recolored all of the guests' champagne so that it looked like orange juice, and re-submitted it to the BVP.

After a while, the BVP came back saying that the orange color was rather faint, and viewers might think that the guests were drinking mimosas. So the film was treated again, and this time the drinks were colored with an unequivocal, almost fluorescent orange.

The BVP considered the new edit, but was still uneasy. The real problem, they decided, was not the color of the liquid itself, but the fact that it was being drunk out of champagne glasses—after all, cocktails come in all kinds of colors. By now, the production company were thoroughly fed up with the whole business, but they post-produced the film a third time, this time painstakingly editing out the long stems of each guest's champagne glass, and finally the BVP approved the ad for broadcast.

So, if you're ever lucky enough to catch the French cut of the Ambassador's reception, watch very carefully, and you'll see that the ambassador's guests appear to be drinking day-glo orange nuclear effluent, and each time they put their glasses down, they float, mysteriously suspended, a couple of inches above the tabletop.

MAKING SMART CENTRALIZATION WORK

And the first moral of this story is, as you would expect by now, a cultural one: be careful how you communicate class. It's yet another of those episodes which illustrate how *differ-*

ent people's perceptions and symbols can be, even when they're relatively close neighbors.

But there's a much more practical moral to the story too, and this chapter aims to be, above all, a practical one. Doing successful international advertising is, as well as a mighty cultural and creative challenge, a *gigantic* technical and logistical challenge. This is just one example of these technical challenges: the wide variety of promotional legislation which your brand will encounter is bewildering, but like all of the practical stuff, it *can be learned.*

In this case, for example, the solution is quite a simple one: it's probably better to get your scripts run past the broadcast authorities in each of your export markets *before* you make the film, not after.

Smart centralization can turn a local agency into a global agency, and there seems little question that a single agency which can *genuinely* provide the same or better service than a large group of companies has an outstanding competitive edge in today's rapidly globalizing world.

But as we've seen, smart centralization means addressing a whole series of very tough challenges, some of which are decidedly counter-cultural for the vast proportion of small, independent, domestic ad agencies.

Many advertising agencies developing international campaigns for the first time fall foul of the kind of technical hitches which the Ferrero story shows—as do many agencies which have been doing it for decades and ought to know better, but persistently promote anybody with real international experience way beyond the level where they can actually achieve anything, and replace them with junior executives who have no international experience whatsoever.

It all appears to derive from a perception that international work is not a specialist skill-set, and requires no special training or experience. Knowledge of a second language, for example, is only now beginning to get a mention in recruitment ads as an asset for graduate trainees in international advertising agencies in the United Kingdom; the United States lags even further behind. In no case that I have ever observed is a second language stated to be a requirement. In many other countries, it has been commonplace for years—but once again, this is conditioned by the fact that there is far less pressure on native speakers of English to acquire a second language than there is on non-native speakers to acquire English.

Agencies which are new to international work often misjudge or ignore the need to modify their domestic workflow patterns: the default assumption about creating a campaign for international use appears to be that this is basically a domestic campaign with an extra production phase towards the end ("translation," of course, and some extra dubbing in the case of TV, or extra sets of film in the case of print work). Quite apart from the often disastrous cultural consequences of such an approach, of which I have already spoken at enormous length in earlier chapters, it can cause huge administrative problems too.

Executing an international campaign is a more complex exercise than executing a domestic campaign: it often appears to be so to a degree which is quite disproportionate to the number of markets involved. This extra complexity is driven by seven main factors:

1. As we've seen in the previous chapter, *developing a brief* which covers off more than one country can be a huge and often intellectually demanding task, and this implies much extra research, planning and local-plus-international client liaison.
2. The *creative* phase of the process has also been described in Chapter 6: suffice to say that a lengthier creative process is inevitable, because of the extra number of different executions which need to be reviewed internally, and because of the larger creative team.
3. A far more complex *approval phase,* since each execution needs to be seen and reviewed by the in-market client as well as approved by the international client

(this is almost certainly going to be a requirement, despite the fact that the work is usually written in a language which he or she cannot read).

4. If deemed necessary, and if it's possible within the timeframe and budget, in-market *testing* of creative concepts or executions may take place, and this is clearly a very much more complicated and expensive process than its domestic equivalent. It also generates far more information which needs to be subsequently processed back into the creative strategy.

5. Internal administration of the *pre-production phase* of the campaign (typesetting of multiple language versions, casting voiceover talent in different languages, negotiating fees and buyouts in various languages and legislatures, proofreading and quality control, etc.).

6. Management of the *production phase* (creating color separations and, often, many hundreds of different resizes for a variety of overseas print media, as well as post-production, dubbing, subtitling, etc in multiple language versions for TV work).

7. *Trafficking* of multiple executions in multiple country versions, legal approvals, distribution to (and liaison with) the media in each country.

Compared to a simple one-country campaign, which is a relatively agile and maneuverable craft, an international campaign is like a supertanker: once it gets moving, it can take 5 miles to slow down, 10 miles to change direction, and 15 miles to come to a complete stop.

In a domestic campaign, because of its simplicity, there is a fair degree of flexibility allowable within process and timings: for example, if a last-minute change needs to be made to the ad just prior to production (either because the client requests it, or because of a change in product specification, or because of a sudden change of heart in the creative team), this is still possible. In an international campaign, it can cause a tremendous knock-on effect which risks derailing the entire process.

It has to be said, however, that adopting a policy of "simultaneous origination" of copy in all the required languages does, (in addition to making the different versions read like advertisements rather than translations of advertisements) serve also to protect the process from one of the worst effects of this kind of change. If all the country versions of the copy have been translated or adapted from a finished "master text" in English, then any change to that text, even a tiny stylistic tweak, pretty much automatically implies making a similar change to each language version, and this can cause chaos during the last stages of a multi-country project. If each country version, on the other hand, is written independently from a country-specific brief, then unless the change is a fundamental regional or global re-brief, the chances are good that it won't actually have any effect on the other versions.

Incidentally, the other irritation that simultaneous origination eliminates is the often-quoted problem about different languages occupying different amounts of space on the page. Although it's true that most Indo-European languages are less concise than English, received wisdom like "German is 25% longer than English" is pretty meaningless unless you're translating from one into the other. If you're not, then it's a relatively straightforward matter to write to a given length: if you tell an English and a German copywriter that they both have to answer the same brief in not more than 100 words, then of course they can both do it. But be careful if the layout is very tight, because German *words* are often longer than English ones, so 100 German words might well take up more space than 100 English words.

The possibility of changes occurring late in the creative development process must always be anticipated. There are really only two ways of dealing with it: either copywriters have to lose the habit of sitting down with the typographer and making last-minute tweaks to their copy in order to make it sit better on the page, or, preferably, this event has to be legitimized, written into the process, and organized in such a way that *each* copywriter in each language has the opportunity to direct the typesetting of their own version. The fact that this becomes very much simpler with a single international team is a further illustration of its innate superiority over geographical distribution.

A similar system needs to be enshrined in the process for producing international TV work, so that essential minor changes to the script during shooting or recording of voice tracks are possible, but that this freedom is made available to *each individual country team,* and no global changes to art direction, photography or footage are made without reference to each team as well.

An important philosophical change underlies these practical considerations: agencies managing international assignments need to accept and embrace the notion that the consistent elements of the creative work (and this includes soundtracks as well as the visual elements) are the *common property* of the complete international team, and not merely of the lead market, and must always be treated as such: *nobody* has the right to decide anything without reference to the other owners. A tiny change to a prop in a photograph, for example, might create a slightly better link between the picture and the headline in one language, and otherwise seem like an insignificant detail: but that detail might render another country version completely meaningless, simply because its headline works with the visual in an entirely different way.

In other words, advertising becomes significantly more of a *team effort* on international campaigns, and recognizing this fact is essential to the proper working of the international agency.

MANAGING THE APPROVAL PROCESS

The creative approval phase is one moment where it's all too easy for an independent agency with an international account to reveal serious shortcomings, and make its client rue the

231

day he ever turned his back on the multinational or multi-local agency solution. This is the moment when a lack of intimate local knowledge really begins to show, and where all the pent-up resentment of those disenfranchised country managers is turned full force onto the hapless independent international shop.

It all starts when the agency's account handler turns up on the doorstep of the overseas clients to show the long-awaited creative work.

Whether the agency presents one creative proposal or many is partly a matter of taste and partly a matter of culture: yes, you've guessed it, in some countries (such as France, Italy, Germany, and most of the Asia-Pacific countries) agencies are always expected to present a range of options, and in others (such as Britain, Spain, and Brazil) it's okay to make a single recommendation. And of course there is much variation within this pattern: some agencies have strong feelings on the matter, and make a policy and a virtue of doing the opposite of what's normally expected by clients in their country. This is something which an international agency, based in another country, should be extremely careful about doing: if a local agency breaks the rules of client service etiquette, this may be tolerated and even appreciated as a mark of their strong convictions, whereas it will be assumed that a foreign agency simply doesn't know the rules.

It's a fact which agencies new to international business often overlook: their client service techniques need to be culturally adapted along with everything else. I've often seen excellent and appropriate creative work from an agency in one country rejected by clients in another simply because the agency has failed to take the precaution of figuring out the right way of presenting work in that country.

A common example of the problem frequently occurs when a U.K. agency is given a pan-European assignment, and attempts to persuade a country manager in, say, France or Germany, that the work they have created is perfect for those markets too. Now, account handlers in the United Kingdom behave towards their clients rather differently than is the custom in continental Europe. In the United Kingdom, some agencies treat their clients with a confidence and even arrogance which agencies in other countries can only gasp at: the understanding is that the agency are the experts on advertising, and the client's subjective opinion on creative issues is of limited interest. That's because, over the years, an understanding has been established between U.K. marketers and agencies that ad agencies know more about advertising than marketers do, and consequently it's foolish to hire an agency and then tell them how to do advertising. There is an acceptance, won (it has to be said) over many decades of excellent service given by U.K. agencies to their clients, that you don't buy a dog and bark yourself.

Now in many other countries, agencies are not considered to be consultants or partners, with almost equal status to their clients: they are vendors, pure and simple. (I hardly need add that one thing *all* agency and client relationships have in common, no matter which country we're talking about, is the fact that relationships between individuals are invariably more significant drivers of practice than such general rules.)

One of the reasons why Italian advertising is so dreadful is because this service relationship has never really changed, and although Italian creatives are perfectly capable of coming up with wonderful ideas for campaigns, they almost never actually get made. What we see on TV is the dismal, 1950s Procter and Gamble–style *grocer in white coat recommends new product to actress pretending to be grateful housewife (both voices badly dubbed)*, or another perennial favorite, *two photographic models pretending to be ordinary couple offer expensive liquor to two other photographic models pretending to be their friends during carefully stage-managed party in a designer apartment; delight ensues (all voices badly dubbed)*.

Yet compare this dross, which the Italian advertising industry still churns out every day, with the extraordinarily daring and creative output of the Italian industrial and graphic design studios, architectural practices, publishing companies, and fashion houses, and it's hard to believe that both come from the same culture.

Italian advertising agencies have never really managed to convince their clients that they perform a quite respectable, skilled, and specialized task: the result is that most Italian clients think they can do advertising themselves, and if they weren't so busy being clients, they would. An ad agency, therefore, is a company staffed by professional layabouts who can afford to spend their time performing this very simple trick, but which can't be relied on to do it without constant and massive interference from the *real* marketing expert, the client himself. The consequence is that almost all Italian advertising is developed by committees, and invariably ends up taking the least daring and least contentious route.

So imagine how a typical Italian Marketing Director must feel when some monolingual English account man in a bad suit turns up and announces that *this* is the advertising that is going to be running in his market.

In reality, it's difficult to see how anyone can successfully present creative work to a client unless they both come from the same country. Apart from anything else, even though that country manager almost certainly speaks excellent English, part of such a conversation invariably involves talking, in detail, about the advertising which is to run in that manager's country: and there can be nothing more frustrating for him or her to have to discuss the intricacies of, say, Danish copy, *in English,* with somebody who doesn't know a single word of Danish. It's just not a sensible conversation to be having, and all the English "account handler" can really do in such situations is obediently take notes and report the comments back to somebody who actually understands their application to the advertisement in question. Talk about Chinese whispers.

"Not Invented There" Syndrome

Quite aside from such practical considerations, it's important to remember that there are all kinds of reasons why country-based clients aren't very happy about receiving advertising for their market from an agency which is based in a different country. For a start, the whole idea is simply counter-intuitive, and whilst it may be clearly in the interests of the corporation to do things this way, it's in the nature of country-based marketing managers that they are more concerned about the country that they are responsible for than the happiness or wellbeing of corporate HQ.

"How can a foreign agency possibly understand the intricacies of my market?" they may (quite understandably) ask. This sense of disbelief is liable to be particularly acute in cases where a company has changed from a multidomestic to a global or regional model: in such cases, the local client is also having to cope with the sudden loss of influence, responsibility, and quite probably budgetary control, as well as a direct relationship with a trusted local agency.

These are very unhappy clients, who instinctively see the new, central agency as the symbol of their unhappiness. They may have spent years building a relationship with a local agency, only to see the relationship summarily terminated by their bosses in the name of "globalization." (This relationship may even have involved the manager receiving a percentage of his advertising budget back from the agency in return for giving them the business. This is known as a *kickback,* and many people would be surprised to learn that it happens in all kinds of perfectly respectable countries.)

In short, these are managers who used to have money and power.

The first stage of centralization means that they have their budgets, and responsibility for the brand campaigns, taken away from them. There is sometimes a second stage where their control over national advertising is taken away.

At the third stage, their agency is fired. At the fourth stage, even the direct marketing, sales promotion, PR, and sponsorship are centralized.

The fifth stage is often imminent and has a lot to do with the fact that a local marketing, advertising, or brand manager is no longer really needed any more, and sales becomes the key discipline. No wonder these are unhappy men and women.

Now, a manager from Peru or South Africa or Norway is liable to be very upset indeed if she or he is hardly consulted before being sent finished advertising. After all, years of hard experience in selling a particular product in a particular market are not to be lightly dismissed, and the fact that this advertising probably comes from America or Britain, of all places, where we are justly famous for our lack of interest and understanding of other cultures and languages, is guaranteed to create skepticism.

If you were the U.S. country manager of a Greek-owned multinational, and some agency in Athens sent you your next American advertising campaign, "adapted" from the Greek, and instructed you to run it on national TV, you would be surprised to say the least. You would probably say something like, "What the hell do these people know about my market and my language?" And, in all likelihood, you would say this before you even read the script.

Approval Techniques

It is traditional practice in international advertising to use an English-language "master" ad or concept in order to get advance approval and buy-in from overseas subsidiaries. Based on the assumption that all these people speak pretty good English, it's felt that there is not a lot of point in going to the trouble and expense of getting the new campaign translated until you're sure that all the countries want to take it. Perhaps there's also a sneaking feeling that this is a safer moment to get buy-in, because people always complain so much later on about the translations.

This may well be true. Things written in a foreign language, as I've said before, are always seen through that misty, glamorizing veil of partial comprehension, and English looks *particularly* good: the language of Hollywood, American presidents, and the Beatles, the authentic language of all the great advertising in past years, that snappy, instant, *modern* language that everybody who's anybody speaks: how can they not like the work you show them in English?

Anyway, the new international campaigns tend to be shown to market managers in large groups (usually when they're all together for the marketing managers' conference), and group dynamics dictate that even if they do have some reservations about the work, it takes an awfully brave or awfully determined country manager to speak out at this stage.

Deep down inside, they may be frightened and they may be outraged, but they're uncomfortably aware of two things:

- This is the famous British/American creative advertising. It's supposed to be the best in the world. If I admit I don't quite understand it, I will look like a fool.
- It was prepared by the advertising agency which has been hired by my bosses. I'd better be careful what I say about it.

Privately, our Country Manager resolves that he'll wait until he gets the work in his own language, and then if he still doesn't like the ads he can always blame the translation — after all, nobody can deny that at least he speaks his own language better than some Brit in London.

And even if he does like it at first read, our local manager may not fully understand what the ad is actually saying, and how it's saying it, until he finally *does* receive it, translated into his own boring, familiar, decidedly unglamorous language, and then he notices that it's quite wrong for his market, and digs in his heels.

ABOUT DIMINISHED RESPONSIBILITY

People often assume that these managers are mainly upset by their loss of responsibility when the account is centralized. Actually, what they often find far more worrying is their sudden *increase* in responsibility in an area most people don't feel very secure about at the best of times: the creative work.

When they had their own local agency, at least the agency *sold* them the copy, and reassured them that it would work in their market. Now, when it comes from a foreign agency in a foreign market, they are expected, on their own, to "sign it off" and declare their faith that it will sell the product. Couple this with the fact that it's advertising which by definition they will not understand well or feel much sympathy for because it comes from an alien advertising culture, and you'll see why it's almost inevitable they'll try to tear it to shreds. The least they will do is show it to everyone in their office, their family, their street, their home town. They will sleep with it under their pillow for as long as it takes until the number of their objections outnumbers the words in the copy.

Job satisfaction has a great deal to do with the balance of *influence* and *responsibility* which people feel they have in their jobs.

A "real" marketing director with total, autonomous control over advertising spend and development in his or her own country, has both the influence to determine the nature and quality of the communications used, and responsibility for its success or failure in the marketplace. This is a comfortable balance for most ambitious and competent people.

A "dependent" marketing department which receives standardized work from headquarters and merely has to ensure that it runs in the right place at the right moment has neither influence nor responsibility: again, for certain personality types, this is a comfortable balance (a sinecure, in fact).

But a country manager who receives centrally-produced work, yet is asked to vouch for its suitability in his or her market, is being given responsibility without influence: a very uncomfortable combination indeed, and we shouldn't be too surprised when people react very strongly against such arrangements.

It seems clear that the traditional system of producing a concept in English and getting international "approval" in this way is deeply flawed, and highly likely to create all kinds of tension and disagreement within the client company, not to mention mistrust of the agency.

I had a client once who, after years of grappling fruitlessly with this problem, decided that toughness was the only solution. So he used a London agency to produce all his European advertising, and when their work was sent out to his country managers, he informed them that they were allowed to do *nothing* but sign off the work. No comments, discussions, or criticisms would be accepted, but in case of an absolute disaster (such as factual errors in the copy) they were each given a power of veto: in the last resort, they were allowed simply to refuse to run the campaign.

Surprise, surprise: every one of them vetoed everything that was sent to them. As John F. Kennedy once observed, "Those who make peaceful revolution impossible make violent revolution inevitable."

One of the key advantages of using a single, multicultural creative team is that it's relatively fast and simple for international concepts to be developed (1) simultaneously for approval in all the relevant languages of the campaign, and (2) as a direct response to direct input from each market. Consequently, the system effectively eliminates the "disappointment factor" which is endemic in the traditional system; it also makes each country marketing team feel that they share ownership of the campaign — because they do — and although the creative team is clearly answering primarily to the needs of "brand central," nonetheless they have continuous and direct influence, at least in detail if not in broad scope, over the content of the work which will eventually run in their market.

Over time, the clients in each market will register that the person who is producing work for their country is:

- A native of that country
- Qualified to be creating advertising for that country
- Ensuring that the special needs of that country are incorporated upfront into the strategic and creative process
- Developing a dedicated media plan and producing freely-written original copy to a country-specific copy brief defined in partnership with the country manager
- Dedicated to producing the most effective and original work for that country, within the strictures of an international campaign, even if they are physically located in another country

Once this realization has been established, it will also provide reassurance to the central client, because his or her country marketing people will gradually stop raising objections to the basic principles of international campaigns, and get more and more involved in the specific task of ensuring that those campaigns are doing their job properly.

And a central client who is reassured that this is occurring is a client who no longer suffers from *not invented there* syndrome: and the principle of smart centralization starts to become vindicated.

TESTING THE WORK

I mentioned before that international advertising will invariably be judged alongside domestic work by consumers, and by the same standards, and since they neither know nor care

240

whether it is appearing simultaneously in other countries too, they will make no special allowances for it. Indeed, if they did know this, it is perhaps more likely to prejudice them *against* the communication than for it, because nobody likes to think that they're not getting special treatment.

I also mentioned that the primary criterion for judging whether a piece of marketing communication should run or not is how effective, distinctive and competitive it is *in the context of the market where it appears,* and not how faithfully it adheres to global communications standards. For these reasons, I have always advocated incorporating an effectiveness "safety net" of some kind into the international advertising process, which kicks in before the campaign is actually committed to the media.

One system which is particularly effective, although expensive and somewhat tortuous, is the "beat it or buy it" system: basically, any country has a right to create and run its own, locally-produced work, as long as it conforms to overall brand guidelines—with one condition. It must allow its own campaign to be tested against the international or regional work which the central marketing department and its global agency have produced (by an objective and previously-agreed testing method). Unless there are strong indications that the international work is likely to be *as effective or more effective in that market* than the market's own work, then the domestic work will run.

(The common practice of encouraging the countries to accept the international work by paying for it out of a central budget, yet insisting that if they produce their own they must pay for it themselves, is not incompatible with this model, but it will obviously skew the response in favor of the international work.)

What I like about the system is its inherent—and very internationally-minded—assumption that the onus is on the *multi-country* work to prove its validity in the context of each market, rather than vice-versa. Obviously, it depends entirely on the company having the time and leisure to double-test everything it runs, and also on there being a sufficiently mature and capable marketing function in market, with its own agency and its own budget to pay that agency, in order for such a system to work: I believe that Colgate-Palmolive used to operate a system of this kind in Europe, and probably only an advertiser of this scale could really justify the use of such tools.

For the emerging international company which has no wholly-owned marketing resource abroad and no local agencies, and may be selling direct to market through distribution deals, franchise operations or other third party agents, such thoroughness is pure fantasy.

However, it is possible for a company with a single, central international agency to mimic this system to some degree: rather than develop and test its own domestic work in-market against the international campaign, it can still be extremely revealing to test domestically-produced advertising from its *competitors* against the proposed international campaign. Simply by substituting the competitors' logo with its own, the company can see whether consumers notice the difference between local and international work, and whether they appear to prefer one or the other. It's also very worthwhile having a culture-mapping expert to compare the two campaigns, and comment on the different ways in which their style of discourse is targeted (or not) at the culture of the consumer.

BUT WILL IT WORK?

It's certainly true that a great deal of money can easily get wasted on testing concepts and ads for international campaigns. One of the most common reasons why agencies in a centralized situation (and their clients) like to test their concepts in overseas markets is simply to find out whether the concept has resonance and meaning in other countries.

Personally, I think that this is a little like banging your head against a brick wall until you're cross-eyed and then paying somebody else to tell you if the wall is still there.

I frequently get calls from clients and agencies asking whether their ideas are going to "work" in another market or not—perhaps predictably, their first and principal concern is whether the *executions* of those ideas, usually in English, are translatable into the language of the markets they are destined to appear in.

I'm always glad when they ask, because I have a simple answer, which is free. The ones that don't ask me are often running expensive research groups all over the planet to ask exactly the same question, and they may not get a simple answer at all.

Actually, without wishing to over-complicate the issue, I have *two* answers: one is yes, and the other is no. It depends on what they mean by the question.

If the question is "Is it possible to execute this concept in French?" then the answer is yes, and it's the same answer whether the question is about Macedonian, Zulu, or Welsh. If you can do it in English, you can do it in any other language in the known universe: it just may not look or read quite the same. And I don't need to see the ad or know anything about it at all in order to answer that question.

If, on the other hand, the meaning of the question is "Is it possible to say *precisely* the same thing as this in French, yet without this in any way altering the style, meaning, relevance, creativity, wit, and originality of the English?," then the answer is no. And once again, the ad itself is immaterial to this question. Indeed, it's almost certainly impossible to say precisely the same thing as this in *English* (for another English-speaking market) without needing to modify the message in some way.

There's a third possibility. If the meaning of the question is "Will this core concept have resonance in France?," then the answer could be yes *or* no, but it depends on (1) whether they actually *have* a core concept—whether their creative thinking is conceptual or executional—and (2) assuming that they do, how they eventually express it in French. If their messaging is properly mapped onto the French culture, and takes due account of the laws, the market situation, the competitive set and all the rest of it, then it may well work, and if it doesn't, then it probably won't. And I don't think you need a focus group to tell you that.

The *main* point is not the suitability of the raw materials, but the skill of the craftspeople who are to work with them: perhaps the most appropriate answer to all these questions is another question: "Do you have someone who can *make* it work?"

The important point behind all this is that there is *very little point indeed* in taking advertisements created in one market and testing them in another, unless you can show them in their final, market-specific form. Simply taking a U.S. or U.K. ad, getting the copy translated, and testing this abroad, is an illogical, expensive, and haphazard way of creating advertising for that market.

Some agencies don't even bother with the translation, and leave the work in English, relying on the group's moderator to translate and present at the same time. Slapdash though this approach may sound, it can actually produce truer results, because the moderator may turn out to be a better interpreter of the work than a written translation: My experience of international research companies is that their understanding of international issues is, on the whole, far superior to that of their agency counterparts. This is partly because they spend their lives meeting real consumers in a wide range of markets, and observing their reactions to messages from other cultures—which is extremely good training for enhancing one's cultural sensitivity—and it's partly because they spend their time *listening* (being service companies). Furthermore, they are more often multilingual than people on the agency side (it's a job requirement for most international moderator jobs), and this tends to go hand-in-hand with cultural sensitivity.

So despite the fact that performing a live, ad-hoc translation of a piece of difficult advertising copy is probably one of the hardest things you can do with your brain, a smart bilingual moderator may well be able to give the group a fuller picture of what the advertising is actually trying to achieve than the mediocre translations which the ad agency buys back home at $50 per 1,000 words, and done overnight by overworked, underbriefed literary or technical freelance translators.

PRODUCTION AND PRE-PRODUCTION

Historically, one of the areas where conventional agency networks have been almost indispensable to their clients was in the technical side of producing and trafficking large and complex campaigns in various media between different countries, on time, and to a high standard.

They were able to do this because each of their offices had its own production department, and it was a relatively simple matter for them to work together and shift the stuff around.

Technology, of course, has changed all this. It's now the easiest thing in the world for an agency to create finished work onscreen for almost any medium, and send it directly to the media, anywhere in the world, in real time. You can post up concepts for approval on a private intranet for clients in any country to comment on. You can record voiceovers for TV work by ISDN link between recording studios, and direct the session by video link from anywhere in the world, so you don't need to fly your foreign voiceover talent around the world any more. You can e-mail a broadcast-quality radio or TV commercial from Sri Lanka to Guatemala in minutes. Marketing departments around the world can download ads or templates from an online library of marketing materials. You can view a print ad on-screen from the other side of the world and make changes to the copy just before it goes to press.

I could go on. But it seems to me that I just heard the distant rumbling of one of the last concrete advantages of the geographically-distributed network collapsing.

A WORD ABOUT AGENCY TYPES

There are basically two kinds of ad agency in the world: *Type A* are those which are primarily interested in doing good work, and *Type B* are those which are primarily interested in making money. All other things being equal, Type A agencies *invariably* end up making more money than Type B.

And there's a second distinction, which is even more important: let's call them *Type 1* and *Type 2*.

Type 1 agencies are by nature and by habit *executional* agencies. They are craft shops, and they like to make ads, which is absolutely fine. You give them a brief, and they make an ad, and their work is often extremely good work, especially if they are also a Type A agency.

Type 2 agencies are, by instinct and by habit, *cussed*. They will not take simple instructions and simply execute them. They insist on questioning every damn thing their client tells them. They get a brief, and immediately start rewriting it. They are asked to make an ad, and they start asking difficult questions about what the company is actually *about* and where the company is actually *going*. They use annoying words like "brand" and "strategy" all the time, instead of "photography" and "artwork."

Now, if—and it's a very big if—they are also extremely good at creativity; and if they end up with a client who is prepared to answer, or find out the answer to their questions, and not lose patience when they challenge every single assumption he makes; and if they are also a type A agency, then, Mr. or Ms. Client, you have an authentic gem in your hands, and would do well to keep extremely quiet about them, because the moment the world finds out, all the other clients in the world will beat a path to their door.

A Word about Service

Ad agencies, however high-level and valuable the strategic advice they are giving to their clients, are service businesses, and they shouldn't forget it. I am tempted to say that this is a universal rule, and if you follow it closely, you can't go far wrong. After all, when you become an international agency, your style of service needs to adapt itself to every one of your overseas clients, not just to the senior client in the international marketing department.

I am, of course, talking about *style* here, and not content. As far as I am concerned, accepting that one is in a service business does not in any sense affect the quality or rigor of one's advice: it merely conditions the spirit in which it is offered. You can still be a Type A1 agency, and not lose your service ethic one jot.

It is far more risky to default to the equal-partnership-style relationship which is sometimes found in the United States and the United Kingdom and practically never anywhere else, than it is to default to a more service-oriented model, which is far more likely to match client expectations everywhere else on the planet. After all, you can easily make an exception when dealing with the Anglos.

An international agency could do far worse than pursue a *multicultural* approach to service style, and consciously adopt the best service practices from the cultures where the best examples are found.

Thus, one could aim to combine the informality and self-confidence of the English with the efficiency and reliability of the Germans, the warmth and flexibility of the Italians, the dedication of the Koreans, the courtesy of the Indians, the creativity of the Brazilians, and the precision of the Swiss.

Informality means knowing that, as human beings, you are your clients' equals, so you will not put on an elaborate show of humility, but that since you are in a supporting role, you are there to support them. In other words, this role does not in any way affect your *identity*, so you don't become a

craven vassal, but it does express your *values* and condition
your *behavior.*

Excessive formality too often masks a lack of real
involvement in your client's business. If you really care
about something, you don't waste your efforts on meaningless ceremony—but beware: what passes for simple respect
in one culture might seem like shocking rudeness in another.
Yet another reason why multicultural account management
is essential.

And self-confidence means knowing your capabilities
and your right to trade without making a song and dance
about it. It's service, not servility.

Efficiency and reliability means exactly what it says.
Only promise to do what you really can do, and deliver it
with no fuss. It can take years before clients realize you've
never made a mistake, and about .03 of a second to realize
when you just did.

Warmth and flexibility means a human service: it's the
necessary counterpart to the Swiss/German/Korean side.
Don't stick to silly inflexible rules, and don't refuse to help a
client just because something is their fault and not yours.
Within the bounds of what is culturally acceptable, you will
probably want to become friends (in the business rather
than the social sense) with your clients, so that they look forward to dealing with you.

Dedication means understanding that you're there to
help, and even if it sometimes means taking on some extra
pressure to keep a client happy, you'll do it in the name of
relationship building. The one thing you should never do, of
course, is compromise the quality of your work—no matter
how desperate the need, nor how hard they push you, if
you're sure you can't do the job properly in the time, it's a
million times better to politely refuse than to do it and screw
up. Because after you've screwed up, suddenly nobody will
remember or care about the impossible deadline.

If you really are a single, international agency offering a
valid alternative to giant networks, you might think you're

already doing the world a big favor simply by existing. But in business, it's always a good idea to offer more than you have to, and more than people expect. Then, instead of being merely satisfied, they will be absolutely delighted. Satisfied customers don't say bad things about your company to other people, but delighted customers say good things about you. A nice aim is to *astonish* people with the quality of your service.

It is easy to overstate the importance of the vocabulary we use to describe the way we do business, but I have to say that I've always been slightly bothered by the use of the word "account" in English-speaking advertising agencies. (Yes, I know, I've used it simply *dozens* of times in this book, but old habits die hard.) People in agencies these days talk a great deal about their desire to be considered as true "strategic partners" to their clients (often referring to a somewhat mythical age when this came naturally to both parties), but then they go about their daily business in the usual way, appointing *account handlers* to *account manage* their *key accounts*. Now, say what you will, but I have an account with my grocer, and part of the subtext with which that peculiarly old-fashioned term is replete is the understanding that if he doesn't give me proper service, I will *take my account elsewhere*. "Account" is a forelock-tugging sort of word which seems to imply formality, servility, distance, a consciously unemotional relationship, contingent purely upon mutual commercial interest. Personally, I think it might be giving clients the wrong signals.

I may be giving quite unwanted lessons about how to run an advertising agency, but whilst we're on the subject of service I would like to tell you about a tiny nightmare I occasionally have.

Sometimes it's very tempting, when you're putting through a call from an exasperating moaner of a client, to say to the poor soul who has to speak to them, "Bad luck, that dwork from Allied Global Technologies wants to speak to you again." We've all done it, and sometimes we shout it across the office.

Just don't do it! It's not that I mistrust technology or any-thing, but you can be absolutely certain that the one time you do say something like that, it will be precisely the same moment when a freak short-circuit occurs deep within the main processor chip of the phone system, and your voice, instead of being conveniently cut off when you press Hold, will sail clearly down the line to the dwork from Allied Global Technologies, and *he will hear you.*

The chances against this actually happening may be 879,904,866,403,000,000,000 to 1, but I bet you it still will. And if you shout it across the room, that will be the exact moment that the dwork's mum comes in to ask for a job cleaning the office.

If your staff want to let off steam about clients, which is a perfectly natural thing to want to do, encourage them gently to do it outside the office, and preferably not in crowded restaurants. Bonneville Flats, late on a January evening, is ideal.

I've often noticed that in the well-run agencies, the account handlers never speak ill of their clients, even in their absence. I used to think this was just toadying hypocrisy, but now I think I understand. It's practice. Unless you make a *habit* of respecting your clients, you'll be found out.

Poor people. Just like us, they're sensitive to the point of neurosis.

ON ACCURACY

One of the greatest risks which a single-office international agency runs is making typographical mistakes in foreign lan-guage copy: one of the real advantages of the network system is that in each office, you have hundreds of mother-tongue employees, all of whom are potential proofreaders, so the chances of an error slipping through are vastly reduced. Now when a single agency is processing large amounts of material, and there may be no more than one person in the company who actually speaks each language, the risk is serious, and needs to be reduced as far as possible.

It's all about precision, and precision means doing routine work according to simple, failsafe systems. You need the best available error-checking software in every language you deal with—but you also need to bear in mind that you need a human being from the right country to use it, because the best software in the world can't qualify anybody to proofread in a language that is not their own mother tongue.

Software can't cope with the creative use of language; it can't advise you on whether an error in the Turkish copywriter's ad was truly accidental, or intentionally informal usage, or maybe an alternative spelling that's more recent than the software. It can't warn you if the Greek word for "poison" (which happens to occur once in the body copy for perfectly innocent reasons) happens to end up sitting right over your client's logo, and your client happens to make food products. It can't tell you whether it's right for the Japanese copy to run from top to bottom, and not from right to left. It can't tell you whether that tiny squiggle underneath the second letter in the Vietnamese headline is a piece of dirt, or a diacritical mark. Or is that the second-to-last letter?

So, in addition to software, you need native proofreaders. Lots of them, and smart, wide-awake, literate ones. This is one thing which freelance translators are often very good at. And you need a failsafe system to ensure that every piece of copy you send out is checked, and double-checked, and that somebody else double-checks the double-checker. Because nothing could be better calculated to undermine your claim to be a genuine, viable alternative to local ad agencies than if you can't produce 100% error-free work, 100% of the time.

For the same reason, your "native creatives" must be the people who cast and direct the actors and voiceover talents you use in all your broadcast and video work—never trust international casting agencies to do this for you. Are they qualified to point out that the beautiful, mellifluous tones of that handsome Italian actor are actually gutter-Sicilian of the first water? Can they tell you that the Israeli woman who seems so perfect for your fruit juice commercial was famous throughout Israel 10 years ago as the face of your client's number one competitor? If the answer to all of these questions is most definitely yes, buy the company. If it's no, then you need to find somebody who *does* know.

ON CREATIVE INTEGRITY

This section sounds as if it's going to be boring and pious, but I promise it's not. It's not especially about international work, though, so I crave your indulgence, but I do think it's quite important. It's about *admitting when you're wrong*.

One thing used to really bug me when I worked in other people's agencies. We would get a brief to write an ad and, say, eight weeks to do it, so I and my art director would sit around playing darts for seven weeks and four-and-a-half days, and then frantically scribble down some old rubbish just before the account handler left to go and see the client.

Suddenly, this piece of ill-conceived drivel became our life's work, the most important piece of creativity ever devised in the history of commercial communications, and if anybody dared criticize it, we would explode with rage, without, of course forgetting to express our bottomless contempt for their petty-minded inability to recognize pure genius when they saw it.

We may have overdone things a tiny bit.

And then the account handler, who was under strict instructions not to return to the agency unless it was to report that he'd successfully sold the work to the client, would waste hours of his and the client's time trying to persuade her that it was brilliant, even though it was quite patently not answering the brief (which we hadn't read).

And the client (who was far from stupid) would point out that it was failing to answer the brief, and she wanted something else. But the account handler would carry on fruitlessly and infuriatingly trying to persuade her that, despite all appearances to the contrary, it really was nearly okay, and only needed a couple of small tweaks to make it perfect. (Who'd want to be an account handler?)

And I wondered for many years about this behavior, and eventually came to this conclusion: creativity is a bit of a mystery. A very few people can do it, and most people can't. The ones who can find it quite easy; the ones who can't, just can't. The trouble is, the ones who can do it, because they find it quite easy, and because everybody else seems to think it's so difficult, live their lives in a constant state of terror of being *found out*. Which is why they defend their work so hotly when challenged.

But there's more. Every time they *do* manage to have an idea, it's a minor miracle, and they are also terrified that it might be the *last idea they ever have*. So if anybody ever asks them to bin one idea and come up with another, they will go to almost any lengths to avoid having to take that risk again, and fail, and be *found out*.

So my advice to creatives is simply this: if you've had more than one idea in your life, it's quite likely that you'll have some more. Indeed, as Dave Trott used to say: "The brain is not a well, it's a muscle. The more you exercise it, the stronger it gets." I'm certain he was right. You *will* have another idea, believe me, and although ideas are certainly precious, that doesn't mean you need to be stingy with them.

We also had a funny policy of refusing 9 out of 10 client requests. The policy wasn't exactly written down anywhere, but I swear the ratio never altered in all the years I worked in agencies. Most of the requests, it goes without saying, were perfectly reasonable, courteously made, and quite simple. But we refused to comply with 9 out of 10 of them, on principle.

The reason for this was something to do with proving who were the experts around here, and also, I think, a little bit more of that old fear of being found out again: we were afraid that if we made it look too easy to comply with a mere layperson's requests, and treated them as reasonable, we might demystify our arcane processes, and the client would find us out, and stop paying the very high fees we were asking.

The reality was really rather different. For a start, the client invariably knew exactly what we were doing, and how we did it, and saw it as a perfectly respectable set of skills. Secondly, she didn't think we were charging too much for it, otherwise she wouldn't have agreed to pay. Thirdly, and most importantly, she found our behavior mildly exasperating, because we always behaved as if advertising, or the executional part of advertising which we performed for her, was the most important thing in the universe, and for her it just wasn't. It was a relatively minor part of her week, and she just wanted things to be friendly and straightforward, and we, apparently, didn't.

We charged our clients in devious and roundabout ways: media commission, production markups, dodgy deals with suppliers. The only thing we didn't charge for was creative work and the odd bits of quite decent strategic thinking which we occasionally produced—and, of course, those were the only things we did which were actually of any value.

RELATIONSHIPS AND COMMUNITIES

I am convinced that there is much value in the idea of agencies taking stakes in their clients' businesses in part lieu of fees, whenever this is appropriate and possible. It is a practice which immediately creates a series of very healthy dynamics in the relationship.

- First of all, it guarantees that the agency will be absolutely focused on contributing, in everything it does, to the long-term success of its clients' business.
- Secondly, it virtually eliminates the client/vendor mindset, and creates a partnership—or, as Jason Ollander-Krane of the Ceres consultancy in San Francisco puts it, a *community*.
- Thirdly, it encourages agencies to seek out promising new talent for their client list as well as clients seeking

out promising new agencies. This creates a healthy and dynamic marketplace, and more suitable matches.

- Fourthly, it provides marketing help at low cost just when startup companies most need it, and when it's most crucial.
- Fifthly, it is payment by results, but without the complexity of measurement which such scenarios normally involve.

Ollander-Krane's theory of communities[1] carries a secondary relevance in this context: in addition to helping agencies form more equable partnerships with their clients, payment by stakeholding also implies a role for the agency as forum, enabler, focal point, or "town square" for all its clients. The same principles which help an agency to identify client companies with mutually appropriate needs and aims, also tends to encourage a natural grouping of client companies around the agency: they may not be in competing businesses, but they will have much in common.

According to Ollander-Krane, all commercial relationships, whether they are between client and agency or corporation and consumer, are essentially community development projects: you begin by looking at where to locate the town square. Then, you assess which kinds of client companies you will be trying to attract to the town square, and what an agency brand needs to stand for in order to attract and keep them there.

The agency, occupying the central position of communications enabler for all these companies, can also create a community of best practice, experience sharing, and idea-swapping which is to every community member's benefit.

DEFINITIONS OF INTEGRATION

Agencies can only really enter into this kind of relationship with their clients when they practice full, *vertical integration:* in other words, when they share responsibility with their clients for marketing or even corporate strategy as well as its consumer-facing execution. If they are merely executing a strategy devised by others, their responsibility for the effectiveness of the approach is so reduced as to make payment by results extremely unfair and extremely difficult to calculate.

What I call vertical integration is an essential part of smart centralization for agencies: it's having the ability to inhabit—intellectually as well as practically—every region of the brand development process, from new product development through to consumer-facing execution and subsequent tracking.

In this sense, it's a rather different concept from the horizontal integration which agencies often preach but seldom practice: horizontal integration is simply about recognizing that having a complete palette of brand communication tools is an essential prerequisite of marketing in the twenty-first century.

As I mentioned before, this kind of integration is a no-brainer, a hygiene factor: an ad agency using horizontal integration as its point of difference is like a travel agency with the positioning, "When we sell you a vacation, we don't just offer you airline tickets: if we think that boats, trains, hotels, and car hire are right for you, we promise we'll tell you!"

I confess that I'm completely unable to grasp what the *alternative* to such a positioning could possibly be—"We're the agency which doesn't give its clients objective advice."? "Unlike other agencies, we don't believe in offering our clients a full range of solutions."? This would be rather like an investment broker saying, "We *only* advise our clients to invest in treasury bonds."

I'll talk about the practice of horizontal integration in more detail in Chapter 8—"More than Just Ads."

When I worked in big agencies, the lack of vertical integration was a real problem. As I discovered much later, our clients were often perplexed that no matter how long we worked on their account, we staunchly refused ever to learn anything about their business beyond the purchasing end of the marketing department. We, the creative teams, never really had the first inkling about the business realities of the client's operations, and I don't believe that our planners and client service people really did, either.

This split between advertising and marketing is almost a tradition. The client spends months and years learning his business in minute detail: what makes it work, its threats, its opportunities, its vision, its operations. Then he hires an advertising agency to communicate the very soul of that enterprise to its consumers, and spends perhaps a couple of days passing on all of that learning to a bunch of people who know a lot about advertising, but may not know very much at all about the client's industry sector at all.

Then, typically, the advertising agency will retire for a couple of weeks to think about advertising. And they will produce a campaign, which they will assess for suitability based primarily on whether it's good, original, creative advertising or not. And then they'll show it to the client, and unless they're psychic, there's a good chance it won't very accurately reflect the realities of the business it's meant to be selling.

Personally, I believe that if advertising agencies want to be considered as more than performing fleas, they need to resolve this issue first. There are three very simple ways in which an agency can bridge the gap between marketing and advertising:

One is to have a member of the client's staff as permanently as possible on the team throughout the planning and creative process. Obviously it isn't going to be very easy to get a senior executive (these people do have jobs to do), but even a trainee brand manager on the agency's team is useful to inject some of the culture of the client's organization into their thinking, and a million times better than nobody. It's important to do this because the essence of a good relationship is collaboration, not surprises.

The second way is to employ an independent business strategist from the client's own industry to advise the agency on everything it recommends. At World Writers, we usually hire a freelance management consultant to perform this function, and we pay them out of our own fee to sit in on all of our planning and creative sessions. They are *not* creative, marketing, or branding people, and they often don't have much to say about our creative ideas—they might sit there for hours without saying anything, and then say something like, "Well, if you tell me that's a great ad, I believe you, but I have to say that you're talking about a part of this company's business on which they make no margin at all." Or else they might say, "That's a neat idea, but you're talking about a competitive situation which in six months' time won't exist any more." And those couple of sentences make them worth their weight in gold.

Sometimes, we even get our consultant to present the creative work to the client: we consider that (1) if a business consultant, whose only concern is to contribute to the bottom line, or to shareholder value, is able to present a piece of communications with a straight face, then it's probably worth presenting, and (2) we know he'll do it in a language which not just the marketers but the other people in the client company will understand.

The third way is probably the simplest and smartest of all: for the agency to hire strategists, planners, creative and client service people from the client side as well as from its own industry, as we have always done. It is *strangely* anomalous for a company to consider itself capable of advising others unless it has direct experience of doing what they do.

And, of course, the best recipe for true vertical integration is a combination of all three techniques. This is how we know that every communications proposal we make has the bottom line (and not just the Clios) built into its rationale.

In the next chapter, I'll talk more about horizontal integration, and how it combines with the principles of Smart Centralization to create *true* global brand communications.

8

More than Just Ads

———

Now here's an interesting tale, told to me recently by an Australian art director. Not, I'm afraid, a disaster story this time: but it's certainly a thought-provoking cross-cultural encounter.

My friend's agency in Melbourne were developing a campaign for a brand of sunglasses, and the press executions were simply photographs of people from around the world, wearing the product. The pictures were taken by a well-known Australian photographer, who travelled around the Pacific Rim, picking out the most interesting and incongruous faces as his models.

One of the most interesting ads in the campaign shows a Buddhist monk in Thailand wearing a wacky pair of mirrorized women's shades, and the nicest thing about the picture is the expression of clearly unfeigned delight and happiness on the face of this elderly monk.

Here's how it happened.

The photographer (who, incidentally, is a very striking-looking fellow—immensely tall, with craggy features and long blond hair tied up in a pigtail) told his interpreter that he would like to visit a famous Buddhist monastery. But when the pair reached the inner courtyard, the interpreter saw that a funeral was taking place, and suggested that they'd better come back some other time.

The photographer was having none of this, and insisted on approaching one of the monks as he prayed. The interpreter was horrified, and begged him to leave, but he simply said that if she wouldn't

259

help him, he'd just have to do his best without her. So, very reluctantly, she made the necessary introductions.

To the surprise of both photographer and interpreter, the elderly monk appeared delighted and completely unshaken by the arrival of this huge man in his outlandish costume at the funeral of one of his brother monks: when the interpreter explained the purpose of their visit, the monk insisted on changing into his best saffron robes, and posed patiently, even eagerly, trying on several different pairs of the sunglasses when asked, and without once losing his blissful smile.

With dozens of great shots in the can, the interpreter and the monk got chatting.

It turned out that the monk was completely convinced that the photographer was none other than the returning soul of the monastery's first abbot who had died several centuries before, and who they had been expecting to join them for the funeral that day. The Australian, at least in their eyes, perfectly matched the figure they were expecting to see, and consequently the monk was more than happy to fall in with his requests, no matter how strange the rituals he required them to perform.

Now the interesting thing about this story is the moral you decide to draw. Is it:

1. *The monks were right, and the Australian photographer really was the latest incarnation of the long-dead abbot: of course, he didn't know this, but all of his previous life had been leading him up to this point, where he finally appeared again before his brother monks in the guise of an Australian photographer.*
2. *The monk's belief that this photographer from Australia was the reincarnation of a long-dead abbot was, of course, superstitious nonsense, but this clash of cynical, intrusive Western commercialism and innocent, credulous Eastern spirituality is yet another tragic precursor of the spread of capitalism and the death of culture.*
3. *They were both wrong. Weird stuff happens.*
4. *The interpreter and her brother, the monk, rigged the whole thing in order to provide their client (the manufacturer of sun-*

glasses) with an amazing PR story to go with the advertising campaign.

ADS AREN'T EVERYTHING

It's certainly an interesting question: which piece of communication contributes more equity to the brand: the photograph of the Buddhist monk, or the story about how it came to be?

Or maybe neither of them really make much difference at all: maybe the one thing which has really contributed most to the runaway success of the brand is just the lovely color of those little tags hanging on the sunglasses in the store.

Part of the rise of integrated marketing can be explained by the fact that client companies, in recent decades, have started wondering just *which* half of the marketing spend is going to waste, and demanding that marketing departments justify their enormous expenditures in the same way as every other department of the company has always done.

A friend of mine tells me that in the multinational company where she is marketing director, a manager wishing to buy a new photocopier for $5,000 has to produce a written report justifying his choice of machine, whereas she only sent a brief memo to the CEO, informing him *after* the event that she had just committed her entire annual budget of nearly $80,000,000 on advertising and media.

That's one aspect: another is the fact that "mass" markets have almost entirely disappeared, and the mantra one hears repeated over and over again is that companies are no longer competing for share of market, but for share of consumer. Unless you can track down your consumer with a full range of media and targeting tools, and be wherever he or she is, and wherever your competitors *aren't*, then you're simply not giving your brand a chance of survival and success.

A further aspect is the need for consistency. I've questioned the notion of consistency in the context of international messages, but in the context of pan-media consistency of voice, it's indispensable. The brand *must* be clearly recognizable in every form and at every appearance, otherwise, at best, it will take far longer for the consumer to "learn" its personality; at worst, it will create confusion and prevent loyalization. And the simplest way to achieve absolute consistency of voice throughout all media is by ensuring that the same group of people are responsible for developing or at least planning all those executions.

Hence the rocket-like growth of direct marketing and all its attendant disciplines. But old prejudices die hard, especially in the United Kingdom, where specialization by media has long been the order of the day, and there are some very ancient snobberies indeed about which kind of work you do.

As I said in the last chapter, horizontal integration is very much a "no-brainer," yet still there are more resolutely specialist above-the-line shops in existence than I believe the industry will be able to support in the immediate future. The only reason I can think of for this anomaly is connected with the way in which many agencies still view themselves: they think they are still in a manufacturing business, not in the knowledge business.

If you see marketing communications primarily as a production service, then there are obviously significant financial implications involved in delivering a full range of media solutions. Just as a factory must make a considerable investment in plant and labor in order to add a new product to its line, so a traditional "output-based" ad agency feels that it can't credibly claim to be media-neutral unless it can provide "full-service," physical delivery of materials in all media, and that means much expensive hiring and acquiring.

For me, advertising at its best is a knowledge business: we are in the business of strategic brand communications consultancy, creative idea generation, and creative execution (or "art"). It really doesn't reflect badly on an advertising agency if it can offer this rare and highly valuable expertise, but not possess the mechanical and technical resources to follow through to manufacturing, delivery, and fulfillment. That seems to me to be a very different kind of business to be in: it's commodity service stuff, and very substantially price-driven. And there are lots of places you can outsource it.

So if you take this view, then the "acquisition" of a pluri-media capability is really about acquiring knowledge and understanding: it's an intellectual acquisition, and like many intellectual acquisitions, the return on investment is pretty much as good as you want to make it (depending on the quality of the people you hire, of course).

UPSTAIRS, DOWNSTAIRS

But despite the strength of these arguments the snobbery still persists, as is evidenced by the fact that in Britain we still refer to media advertising as "above the line" and direct marketing as "below the line." (The all-important question of corporate reputation and public relations appears to be out of the picture altogether—perhaps it's considered to be a secretarial job.)

This line, which used to divide the exciting and glamorous world of advertising from the sordid industry of mere promotion, has become the front line of a pitched battle. The direct marketers, tired of staying below their line like obedient limbo dancers, now argue their superiority over "indirect marketing," saying that their own methods are *accountable* and *demonstrably cost-effective.*

The fat cats of the advertising industry have lost a good deal of self-assurance, as well as weight, in recent years. They have noticed that several large, traditional media advertisers, most notably and scarily Heinz, have started spending big money below the line.

The reactions have varied from complacency ("It'll never catch on, you can't sell products without proper advertising") to some pretty frantic bandwagon jumping.

In the last year or two, a number of the grooviest London creative advertising boutiques, previously so far above the line you could hardly see them, have started rebranding themselves as "integrated marketing consultants," "total communications specialists," and worse. They preach loud and long about the necessity of through-the-line marketing, rightly saying how no communications program is complete without *consistent* branding across point of sale, packaging, direct mail, web pages, promotions, shelf wobblers, key fobs, and oh, maybe a spot of prime-time TV too.

Frankly, I don't believe they really mean it all that deeply: I suspect most clients who approach these agencies for a direct marketing campaign will only get lunch with the managing director if they decide to throw in a few TV commercials for good measure.

The sad fact is I can only think of five or six creatives who work in direct marketing because they actually want to—most would be writing TV scripts in ad agencies if only they could get the job. And we should not be too surprised: after all, it's hard to start off a mailshot with those magic words, "We open on a deserted beach in the Maldives. . . ."

But direct marketing is definitely booming: it's currently reported to be growing at twice the rate of the advertising industry, and agencies are now discovering that it is, potentially at least, a far more profitable business to be in than media advertising, so it hardly matters what anybody says about it.

Right now, the best place to observe the direct marketers celebrate their new status is at the annual forum of the European Direct Marketing Association in Brussels: here, they too can dress up in tuxedos and cocktail dresses and murmur "Loves, darlings, you're too kind" into a microphone as they hand each other trophies. And they don't even have to lose that *frisson* which hard response data always gives to the true direct marketer, for these awards are as much about *effectiveness* as they are about *creativity*.

I always thought that a couple of percent response was something to be proud of in a mail campaign, but these people don't seem to get out of bed in the morning for anything under 70 percent. In the darkened hall, loud rock music greets yet another emotional team as they troop up on stage to collect their prize. "This campaign," intones the host, "generated an *eighty-four percent* response!" The audience murmur approvingly. The next winner "created an uptake *over one hundred and fifty percent* greater than expectations": obliging gasps from the audience.

I suspect there's been some massaging of reality here: we all know that extremely low expectations are often well rewarded in this life; and the 84% response of the first campaign may have something to do with the fact that the 100 left-handed Swiss factory workers whom the agency mailed were being offered free left-handed silver cutlery for life. The 16 who didn't reply were presumably away on holiday when their letters came.

I don't think it's wrong for the direct marketing industry to pat itself on the back: after all, it is doing extremely well in an extremely competitive climate.

But what I do find depressing, as the business becomes more and more international, is the sight of so many U.K. and U.S. direct marketing agencies making exactly the same mistakes which their advertising colleagues made 10 years ago when media advertising started going truly global.

They are failing to take cultural differences adequately into account, they are approaching foreign markets in exactly the same way and using exactly the same methods they have used in their domestic market, and they are relying heavily on language to solve all of their international marketing, branding, and strategic problems for them.

But practitioners of international direct marketing have a greater responsibility to their clients than briefly generating octogenarian response figures. In this respect, the integrated marketing gurus are right: expressions like "above the line" and "below the line" no longer mean much.

Here, the proper structures for creating culturally-sensitive international campaigns are even more painfully lacking than they are "above the line": there are fewer competent networks specializing in integrated marketing than in

265

mass-media work, and consequently the need for agencies to figure out how to use smart centralization is even more urgent. Just as the big agencies tend to prefer big brands and big consumer markets, so they prefer to deal in big-budget media campaigns: and this is partly because getting creatives in branch offices to adapt the generally longer and more difficult copy of direct marketing is even harder work than persuading them to apply their minds to a 30-second TV script.

Direct marketing is a branding instrument as much as TV or press advertising. It, too, plays a crucial part in building the immensely complex personality of an international brand, and that is an area of marketing where the sterile mathematics of effectiveness are just not enough: as we discovered long ago when first figuring out how to do indirect marketing for global companies, we must also learn to harness the mystery of *culturally relevant creativity.*

WRITE ME LIKE YOU KNOW ME

A while ago, I received a mailing from an American company:

> Dear Mr Anholt,
>   NOW! A $50 value on your next purchase of . . .

I binned it. Not because I didn't understand it, or because I didn't want the product. I didn't even want to find out what the product was: that tone of voice simply bothered me, because I'm British. Its direct, no-nonsense approach struck me as intrusive and aggressive.

Later, I retrieved the mailer from the bin and tried to rewrite it in a way which would have worked on me. It ran something like this:

> Dear Mr. Anholt, have you ever noticed how *tricky* it can be to find a company which really understands. . . .

266

and so on. The $50 value, duly converted into pounds sterling, appeared in the postscript.

Now if this is the kind of difference which we can expect to find between two countries where we are widely reported to speak the same language, imagine what the differences must be between, say, America and Japan. Or Brazil and Turkey. Or Korea and Italy. Or anywhere at all and anywhere at all.

For a variety of reasons, these differences tend show up more dramatically in direct marketing than in print or broadcast advertising. It's partly because, as I mentioned before, media advertising broadly stems from a single, Anglo-American tradition, and although the medium has been much adapted and developed in each country where it has taken root during the last century or so, it is still, to a degree, an international culture in its own right. Direct marketing and especially direct mail, on the other hand, can trace their heritage directly back to the arts of business letter writing and face-to-face selling, and are consequently far more deeply rooted in the conventions of commerce and etiquette in each country.

One only has to look at the classic French business letter to see how different these conventions can be, even in neighboring countries: the ending of a letter can run into several lines of elaborate and highly formal circumlocution, whilst in most other European countries, the equivalent of "Yours sincerely" is considered perfectly adequate.

And we shouldn't forget either that promotional law varies quite dramatically from country to country. This is especially significant when we're dealing with sales promotion—despite the continued efforts of the direct marketing industry, there is very little consistency between the rules and regulations governing marketing even in a relatively united region like Europe. Thus tiny details can become crucial, such as the fact that you're not allowed to give anything away for free in Germany, so the free books you give away in the United States may need to cost one mark each in Germany.

Don't Think What to Write, Think of a *Reason* to Write

Direct mail, as soon as it's easily recognizable as direct mail, usually becomes junk mail almost by definition. But attempting to disguise the fact that you're selling something, through euphemism and prevarication, tends to make things worse, and greatly increases the recipient's irritation at being disturbed on such a trivial matter.

The reality is that no matter how important you believe your product or offer to be, there's not a lot of point in writing a letter to a stranger simply in order to say, "Please buy this, I think it's really good." The emptiness of this communication is somehow worsened if the company comes from abroad—at least if it's the equivalent of the corner shop asking you to buy stuff, then you can deal with it, but if the request comes from the other side of the world, you tend to feel doubly invaded.

In order to write to a stranger, you need something to say.

Some of the best and most effective direct marketing campaigns I've seen have been those which are centered around some kind of marketing *event:* the company has actually caused something to happen in the real world, something intimately connected with their main activity or product range.

In these cases, the direct marketing letter becomes the *necessary means of communication* for announcing that event, inviting people to participate at every level, nationally or internationally, providing detailed information about participation, and following up after the event. Writing to customers under such circumstances is self-justifying: no longer an unwelcome intrusion into their lives, the letter is the bearer of genuinely useful or interesting news.

The agency doesn't have to cudgel its brains to think of something new to write about, or new and more palatable ways of selling the product; the consumer doesn't have to switch on his emotional defenses; the letter has a simple communicative function, and practically writes itself.

Consumers will soon pick up on this behavior, if it's adhered to with absolute consistency, and will always read the letters they get from you, because they've learned that you never write unless you have something to say.

A real marketing event is primarily a public relations exercise: it could be the sponsorship of an award or show which is relevant to the target market, the announcement of an important conference, or the publication of a major piece of industry research. It could be something a little more adventurous: a fashion house hiring Christo to wrap up the Eiffel Tower in its latest fabric, or dressing up the London Symphony Orchestra in pink spandex tuxedoes for one evening. Whatever it is, it must be more than a purely commercial exercise, like a new product launch or a store opening: it must show the company actively contributing to the industry or market sector in which it operates. The company must be seen to be *giving* (and that certainly doesn't mean that it can't also be making money out of the event), rather than simply selling or merely making a noise about carrying on its normal business.

The more complex and engaging the marketing event becomes, the more opportunities for direct marketing are spawned by it. An international competition can generate a long-term loyalty program; the launching of an industry award can be fleshed out with prizes at college, professional and amateur level, across all target countries or regions, with each level requiring its own database, ongoing mailing program, telesales opportunities, follow-up research, and so forth.

The trick is simply to harness the creativity of the team at a somewhat higher level than direct mail usually does: instead of having those powerful creative minds puzzling over what to write in the next mailshot, far more interesting and far-reaching results can usually be achieved by setting them to work on the question "Let's think of a *reason* to write to people."

It goes without saying that if the company's brandbook has been properly and carefully written, there should be no hesitation or difficulty in choosing the kind of event which best matches the brand's character and aspirations: of course, much damage can be done to the brand by creating an event which sits uneasily with the consumer's existing perceptions of that brand.

Marketing through events is, at heart, a way of making the marketing budget go further as much as it is a way of making communications more welcome to the consumer. A successful event can generate many times its own cost in PR value, and thus becomes almost automatically a multimedia, interactive communication with the target market—so instead of merely creeping apologetically into the consumer's home through the mailbox, the brand comes pouring out of every medium—the phone, the newspaper, the internet, the TV, and the mail—with a message that is much closer to editorial than advertisement.

WHY GOD IS IN THE DETAILS OF INTERNATIONAL MARKETING

The glamorous parts of any marketing campaign—which is to say, the print and broadcast work—are perceived to be glamorous because they have big media budgets behind them, and large numbers of people spend large amounts of time and effort making sure they're done as well as possible. Getting the consumer's attention and raising the basic threshold of brand awareness is known to be an expensive, important, and difficult process.

But what happens "below the line" plays an equally vital role in turning potential trialers into regular consumers, in building loyalty out of mere awareness, and generally in reassuring the consumer that the realities of purchasing and using the product and interacting with the company live up to the expectations generated by the brand.

I know, as a consumer, that if I am attracted to a brand by media advertising, my expectations of product experience are high, and if they are followed by inadequate collateral, my esteem for the brand may well sink to a lower point than before I saw the TV ad, simply because I have been encouraged and then disappointed. It would be interesting to draw the disappointment curve of an average consumer in this circumstance: the higher the peak of initial interest is, the more steeply it drops towards irritation and rejection. The topography of goodwill is simply this: the higher you climb, the further you fall.

This is especially the case in international communications, where betraying ignorance or insensitivity towards the consumer's cultural environment can seriously damage brand confidence.

It's easy to justify taking infinite pains over making a TV commercial truly relevant to each of its target markets: but somehow the same attention to detail, quality, love, craft, local knowledge, and brand understanding must be expended on every word of every instruction manual, point-of-sale display, pack copy, follow-up mailing, brochure, annual report, web site, exhibition stand, customer magazine, and all the rest. The same principle is equally important for internal communications, since employee disappointment in the brand can be even more damaging than customer disappointment.

However impossible a task this may sound, we cannot escape from the fact that if a brand is to speak at all, it must speak well—otherwise it had better stay silent. The challenge for exporting companies is to find their own way to achieve this end, perhaps by building their own internal briefing, creative, and quality control structures, and bringing the task of creating below-the-line international materials in-house—an issue which I will discuss in more detail in the next section.

More often than not, the main reason why a company's international communications are so problematic is because the importance of the issue is underestimated, and unqualified or inexperienced people are put in charge of fundamental communications tasks: the task of managing the whole international creative process, for example, is often labeled "translation management" and given to a junior employee with no direct involvement in strategic or branding issues, who then unloads the whole unwelcome task onto an even less qualified and even less brand-aware outside translation service, staffed by academics and linguists rather than copywriters and marketing professionals.

Undervaluing export markets is a vicious circle. If a country is worth exporting to in the first place, then by definition it's worth giving it the same level of attention and quality in communications as the home market.

Until a company learns that all its customers are equally important, no matter where they live, and therefore all require and deserve communications of equal quality, then it will continue to behave as if its export markets were secondary markets. In doing so, it is depriving those markets of their chance to develop into primary markets, and will have endless trouble in building comparable levels of customer loyalty, brand penetration, and profitability.

ON INSOURCING COLLATERAL LOCALIZATION

Producing multilingual collateral material to the required standard is a major headache for many international marketers. It seems clear that the principles of simultaneous origination which I've described are admirable for producing shorter texts—such as TV and press work, mailers, point-of-sale material, and banner advertising—but what happens if it's a 72-page catalog, a customer magazine, an internal newsletter, a fat product manual, a 1,000-page CD-ROM, or a long brochure needing to go into 17 languages?

You wouldn't want to pay for 17 highly-experienced agency copywriters to produce their own, separate versions of pieces like this, especially since adherence to the factual content may be more important than the stylistic virtuosity of the writing. It would cost too much, take too long, and produce too much variety.

On the other hand, translation is so very rarely satisfactory, for the two simple reasons that (1) a translator is never going to get as close to the subject matter as the person who originally researched and created the copy, and (2) commercial translations almost never read as well as original writing.

The scale of the solution depends a great deal on the importance of the issue to the company: most large multinationals *do* have their own internal translation units, but it's a commonly-cited problem that when it comes to the more marketing-oriented texts, the translations which these departments produce tend to be too "literal," and not surprisingly: they can rarely afford the luxury of more than one kind of translator per language, and there is a natural bias towards employing technical translators who specialize in the product area that the company operates in. So valuable man- and woman-hours are then wasted by in-country marketing staff in extensive editing and rewriting of these texts: or worse still, the reworking has to be entrusted to channel partners or other third parties who aren't directly connected to the brand.

For any company which produces multilingual literature on a regular basis, it certainly makes sense to create an internal or tethered structure which can resolve this issue once and for all, and break the company's dependence on expensive and unpredictable outside translation resources.

The quality of work from such sources often depends entirely on the availability of a single individual in each language who happens to have the knack of copy adaptation and knows the business well, and this poses an unacceptable risk for the company and the quality and timeliness of its international materials.

The ideal solution is usually for the company to equip itself to produce its own *texts* but not graphics: this gives it good control over brand values, costs, timing of projects, and the overall quality of its international communications, yet without reducing its freedom to hire from the full range of domestic and international communications agencies for the conceptual work and graphic design.

If the copy adaptation issue is sorted internally by the company, rather than relying on design agencies to manage the entire process (design agencies usually just outsource translations, and generally have even less understanding of the issues involved than ad agencies), then the company can select its outside design talent purely on the basis of their creative work, strategic abilities, and brand understanding, rather than their international credentials or experience.

Setting up an internal literature localization unit doesn't have to be as elaborate or expensive as it sounds. Very often, it's simply a question of getting the *structure* right, and redeploying existing staff in a more "international-friendly" and "creative-friendly" way. Given the marketing function of the work that it will be handling, though, the main issue is simply accepting that it has to be conceived and structured in an entirely different way from the conventional technical "translation pool."

Freelancers can be used, but it's important to be open-minded and imaginative about identifying the right resource for the task in hand. When producing international customer magazines, for example, journalists can often produce better results than translators if they're properly briefed, and given the right creative direction and briefing materials. In countries where advertising hasn't been around for too long—such as Eastern Europe, for example—people who claim to be experienced copywriters, with a couple of years' experience in the branch office of an American ad agency, may actually understand very little about the techniques of popular communication in their country, and you'd be better off hiring a politician, an academic or a rock lyricist. Producing an intelligent copy platform for people to work to, if it's done in the right way, also tends to produce far better end results than simply giving them finished English copy to translate.

Carefully controlling the input and giving the right brief in the right form is obviously important, but proper sub-editing and creative direction of the various drafts of foreign copy is fundamental. This is where really experienced creative heads are most valuable: it does not necessarily have to be their full-time job—such people probably have other responsibilities within the organization—but it's the phase which is most critical in ensuring that the work reads as well in other languages as it does in the original, and preserves its marketing function and trueness to brand as well as readability and elegance.

This phase is very often completely missing in the conventional translation process (translation agencies generally don't provide more than the most cursory quality-control over their work, let alone proper creative direction by senior writers: most of the time texts simply come in from freelance translators and are passed on to the customer without any added value whatsoever).

Monitoring the output is also an important part of making the thing work and keeping it working: so systems have to be set up in order for competent native readers, who properly understand the company's desired brand values, to perform regular audits of samples of the work that's produced, and feed their comments back into the right stage of the briefing or creative direction cycle.

Quite apart from the extra quality control, messaging control, and cost savings which a system like this can give a company, it also communicates some quite important messages, both internally and externally, about the international and cultural competence of the organization: it shows employees, suppliers, and partners in each of the company's export markets that this is an organization which truly has a grip on the practical and cultural realities of doing business in that market—that far from being a helpless foreigner, this is a company with the *right* to do business there.

Oh, and by the way, computers *can't* do translations. At least, not yet: the best estimate is that we're still 10 years away from a program which can perform translations to publishable standard without a qualified translator to revise and edit the results. And since revision is often more labor-intensive than translation (you have three texts in front of you to process instead of two), it's hardly worthwhile except for highly specialized, highly technical documentation.

But even when we do reach the stage where computers can perform linguistically accurate translation, we'll still be a long way away from computers which can adapt texts to suit the cultures of foreign audiences and persuade them to buy a product or believe in a brand.

ON INTERNATIONAL CONTENT CREATION

If the only contact a brand has with its customers is through advertising, direct marketing and promotion of one kind or another, then the dialog can be extremely limited. It can mean that the only time a company's customers ever hear from it is when it's trying to sell them something, and the only time it hears from them is when they're complaining about something: hardly the basis for a long-term, loyal, and meaningful friendship.

As any new-business director will tell you, socializing with clients is almost more important than pitching to them. When you go out for a drink with your clients, and talk about anything other than business, you're building a broader and deeper relationship with them, and showing them that you have wide interests, an attractive personality; and soon enough, if you get on, they begin feel that they know you and trust you.

Then, the selling dialog, when it happens, is simple and direct: if they want or need your product, they'll call you first, and they'll buy it in preference to your competitors' product; and if they don't want it or need it, they know they can tell you why. The honesty of their response becomes, in turn, valuable feedback for your product development cycle.

Friendship marketing tools, such as sponsorship, programming, content-based websites and customer magazines, enable this kind of dialog, the kind which enriches the brand's relationship with the customer, and shows it can give without expecting to receive. This is *essential* if customers are to believe in the brand.

Programming and customer magazines are among the best ways for a brand to meet its consumers in an informal, enjoyable, non-selling environment. They are the mass-market equivalent of the drink after work.

Content is the ideal environment for demonstrating all kinds of good points about a brand. Brands can use content to present themselves as intelligent and interesting companions: thought-provoking and well written articles or well-made documentary strands on a wide range of different subjects are the key to giving this impression.

Most importantly, content providing is a precious opportunity for an international brand to prove that it truly understands its customers, their language, their culture, their country, whilst also sharing its own with them. This is why it is crucial that all international content is genuinely international, and not simply exported material from the "lead" market: if each national version is not immaculately tailored to the local market, the brand risks suffering considerable damage to its image, merely confirming customers' natural suspicion that because it comes from far away, it neither really cares about nor fully understands them or their culture.

This point needs to be stressed. Since there is a tendency amongst many companies to publish content rather reluctantly, to feel cheated if there is no immediate payback, and to see the thing as a rather lightweight selling tool, they are perhaps blind to the serious dangers of doing it wrong, especially if it's an international title. Content can do *serious harm* to the credibility of an international brand if it's not properly done, and it's far safer not to produce content at all if the company isn't fully confident that each title or program will stand up to the best national competitors in each market.

So, with customer magazines, for example, merely translating or "adapting" a lead-market edition into other languages is often little more than a gesture in the direction of proper consumer relevance—the common "80/20" rule applied by many international customer magazine publishers (80% common content, 20% locally generated) probably needs to be turned on its head if the magazine is to give real value to its readers in each market.

When companies become content providers, they suddenly find they have many more brushes and more colors for painting their brand's true portrait than conventional media: as I mentioned before, press and especially television advertising are disciplines which basically stem from a common Anglo-American root, and so are fairly blunt instruments when it comes to dealing accurately with such subtleties as language and culture, and attempting to make a foreign brand look familiar and near to the consumer. But magazines and programming stem from entirely different and much more culture-specific and market-intimate traditions.

Content providing is not a hybrid, low-profile, soft-sell, subliminal promotional device: it is an incredibly powerful *non-selling tool.*

The future of marketing and branding undoubtedly features non-selling tools very prominently, and both consumers and forward-thinking advertisers are turning their backs on the selling-oriented TV presence which has been the bulk of promotional activity in the past.

THE DEER IN THE CLEARING

One of the best things about the internet is that it compels creative marketing to become more creative still: this is as a direct result of the shift from the old mass-media models.

Before, you had a large, imprecisely targeted, captive audience, and the trick of advertising was simply to express your selling message in the quickest, most compelling, most distinctive way, without interfering too much with the content that surrounded the promotional messages. Now media has begun a process of fragmentation into ever finer channels of communication, and the new trick of advertising is about persuading people to visit your channel in the first place: the bait is usually content. Then you can figure out how to get your promotional message across without making it too obvious that you're primarily interested in selling stuff.

Consumers visiting a web site or another brand-owned area are very much like deer visiting a clearing in the forest: once you've built up trust, they might even learn to take sugar lumps from your hand, but they are always poised for flight. The slightest false move on your part, the merest whiff of a suspicion that you want something in return before they're ready to give it, and they'll vanish into the woods, never to be seen again.

Clearly, conventional promotional messages, no matter how creative, aren't designed to perform this task of attraction and retention on their own, because they don't need to: traditional advertising is more an act of *taking* from the consumer rather than of giving, and people won't often make a positive effort to travel somewhere in order to have something taken from them. However, they will travel in order to receive *value*—entertainment, information, stimulation of the emotions in one way or another.

In Chapter 4, I described entertainment, information, and emotion as the necessary *payment* which advertisers need to make in order to "reimburse" the audience for their brief spell of attention. But when the media isn't in front of them, and we need to draw the audience to the media, all this value has to be given away in much higher concentrations, in greater quantities, and at higher quality.

With traditional advertising, we're only asking them to read or listen for a second to a spot rented on a third-party mass medium. In new media (and this is becoming equally true for multichannel cable and satellite television and customer magazines), we're asking them to take the time and effort to travel to our own, brand-owned medium, and *then* read or listen.

Hence the inevitable convergence of content and promotion, of editorial and advertising, and the mutation of sales promotion into friendship marketing, product selling into corporate brand building; and it is this influence, above all, which drives advertisers into becoming real creative artists. In this environment, it is no longer sufficient for advertisers to be mere craftsmen of marketing communications: they need to learn the arts of cinema, music, fine art, graphic design, creative writing, and journalism.

THE INTERNET AND ENGLISH

Smart centralization was practically *made* for the internet. Naturally, all of the large multinational agency groups have "web agencies" and internet design facilities, but their ability to deliver international content and marketing is seriously undermined, it seems to me, by the fact that they have to make use of their geographically-distributed networks in order to produce it—or else subcontract the language work to translation agencies, with the inevitable consequences.

After all, here is a global medium whose content is most naturally produced at a single source, mainly because there never was and never will be a physical or geographical distribution element involved. You make the stuff on a computer, and ship it out worldwide down a phone line, so "local" market presence, arguably an advantage for conventional media, becomes a positive liability for online communications.

What internet content owners and marketing communications providers need more than anything else is a system which enables true sensitivity to world markets and languages to be applied within the immediate ambit of the web-server. Sure, the internet also means that if your foreign writers are based in other countries, they can communicate with "base" just as easily as if they were there, but this is creative work, and creative rules apply. Not being part of the same *physical* team means that the system is condemned to be split into two parts: origination (hierarchically attached to the lead market and lead culture) and post-production "languaging," bolting on the needs of each market at a later stage. And, as is the case with every other medium in the world, this doesn't produce proper culture-sensitive work: it produces a retrofitted hybrid, which consumers don't relate to and which marks down the brand as an imposter and foreigner.

A huge proportion of text on the internet is in English, and there is a tendency for companies to assume that the greater proportion of English-language proficiency amongst internet users worldwide licenses them to avoid the need to provide content in other languages. However, this proportion is diminishing all the time, as internet use spreads rapidly through society—at first, it was just "geeks," the majority of whom were young, well-educated, and often Anglophile, but this picture is changing all the time. Some of the most regular users of the internet in Europe are past retirement age, and, as a group, their knowledge of English tends to be amongst the lowest of any age group: even in the supposedly bilingual Netherlands, for example, the teaching of English in schools only really became commonplace in the 1950s.

As I mentioned in Chapter 1, speaking to your customer in his or her own language is also a question of respect: but there are genuine issues of competency and productivity at stake here. A recent survey[1] carried out amongst corporate software purchasers and end-users in France, Germany, Italy, Spain, and Sweden, clearly shows that being obliged to use nonlocalized software and online information has a severely negative impact on productivity within corporations. This is true of three-quarters of support staff, and nearly two-thirds of middle and upper managers: and only

41% of German middle managers are able to use English-language print materials accompanying such products. The consultants who carried out the research estimate that only 60% of European workers can even begin to cope with English language on the Internet.

If circumstances dictate that, despite our best intentions, it's not feasible to target consumers accurately by language, and much international talk will go on in English (it's far better to communicate in well-written, clear English than bad French or German), it becomes even more important that *what we are saying* is acceptable and accessible to native speakers of other languages.

Managing to communicate to an international audience without the advantage of being able to use that audience's native language is one of the hardest communication tricks to play. And in one sense, there is most definitely a choice of language: there are big differences between the way you write and speak in British or American or Australian or Indian or African English to consumers in those countries, and there are big differences between the different varieties of international English: mid-Atlantic English, Euro-English, neutral English, "Benetton English," beginner's English.

You can tailor your English vocabulary quite precisely to an audience if you know what group of languages they speak. If they speak Romance languages, you favor a lexicon with Latin roots; if they speak Germanic languages, you use a more Anglo-Saxon vocabulary. Part of the trick of being understood worldwide in English is learning which parts of the language are hardest for other people to grasp: for example, phrasal verb forms appear simple to native speakers because they use short words (go to, bring forward, carry out, do over, make up, shut in), but they are actually one of the hardest aspects of the English language for foreigners to learn, and even highly advanced students of English only know a fraction of the thousands of phrasal verbs which native English speakers use every day without even realizing it.

ON THE LANGUAGE OF NPD

As I illustrated in Chapter 3, the issues of language and culture come into play right at the start of the brand development process, and at this point I'd like to show how smart centralization can be applied with equal effectiveness at the earliest stage of new product development (NPD). In fact, in keeping with the model of vertical integration described in the last chapter, the whole process of NPD, brand architecture, communications planning and advertising execution can easily become a unified, turnkey operation.

Serious problems are often caused by the traditional disconnection of these elements. A complaint I frequently hear from brand development agencies and marketing consultants is that they spend their lives developing absolutely core brand strategy for their clients; the client pays them their meager bill, and then marches off to an ad agency, pays it *millions,* and the first thing the agency planners and creatives do is trash all the great positioning work that has already been done, either because they don't understand it, or simply because they didn't think of it themselves and that hurts their pride.

Now I would be inclined to dismiss these complaints as ordinary professional envy, if it wasn't for the fact that I often hear clients making exactly the same complaint. They are *frequently* heard to wonder aloud why their favorite corporate design company, brand development specialist, naming agency, design company, or research bureau can't also do advertising, and simply provide them with a complete service, from brand creation through to marketing communications.

And yet nobody's really achieved it yet. Part of the problem is that many of the "upstream" companies have difficulty moving credibly downstream—their predominant color is brown, and their aura is sober, respectable, and slightly academic, which is all perfectly fine if you're in the research or strategy business: but ad agencies, who are in the *creative talent* business, have to be pretty exciting companies for clients to want to go with them and spend all that money.

By the same token, the executional agencies suffer from the perception that they are bursting with unruly brilliance, but just don't have the strategic discipline or marketing training necessary to move very far upstream. These are gross generalizations, needless to say, and there are several noteworthy exceptions, but by and large, there is a real *and* perceived disjoint somewhere along the continuum between NPD and adverts.

This disjoint creates another golden opportunity for smart centralization.

Many of the same difficulties (caused by the same misunderstandings) occur at the international brand development stage as in the advertising stage: companies developing international market positionings and brand architectures for new or existing products encounter exactly the same problems with the translation of their research stimulus—and feedback—as do the ad agencies with their concept testing. And, perhaps predictably, marketers also place a far greater burden of responsibility on the ability of language to resolve what are effectively creative, strategic and cultural issues, than language is actually capable of resolving.

What often happens is that a core team (and, to be fair, it's more likely to be an international marketing team if this is an experienced exporter) will develop a series of trial positionings, and put these into research in each target country. Trouble is, in order for those positionings to be researched, they have to be translated, and this puts them through a linguistic and conceptual bottleneck.

Then the responses come back from the groups, and they have to be translated back into the original source language, and written into an executive report in the source language: so it all goes back through the same bottleneck a second time.

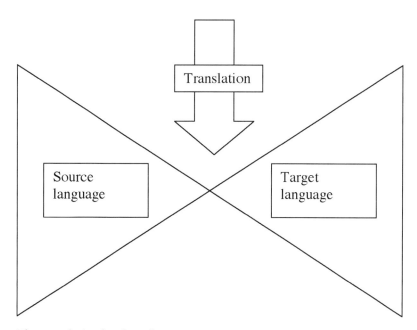

The translation bottleneck.

Clearly, any slip in meaning occurring at any stage in this process is likely to become magnified as the process moves on: a slight mistranslation of one word of the original positioning statement will result in the groups being exposed to the wrong idea; so their responses will be skewed; and in order to bring the account of those responses back into context with the main purpose of the exercise, their translation back into the source language may be accidentally or deliberately modified once again; and the word or words which caused the trouble in the first place may or may not reappear at this stage, and may or may not suffer a similar fate in reverse whilst passing back through the first translation bottleneck.

And then, of course, on the basis of those twice-backtranslated (and culture-stripped) responses, the positioning will be modified (in *English*) to accommodate the new input, that modified positioning will go back through the language bottleneck a third time, picking up more noise and distortion as it goes, and back into research again, and so on, *ad infinitum:* truly, a comedy of errors.

Most people's natural response to this issue is to create systems to ensure that "mistranslations" don't occur—which is how you can easily end up with the kind of expensive, complex and arcane process which I quoted from Usunier's book in Chapter 1.

The idea that the process merely lacks *linguistic accuracy* is missing the point: brand positionings are no less *creative* writing than advertisements (which is to say that they use words not just in their "literal" sense—hardly any writing ever really does this—but play heavily on the echoes and associations of those words within their original cultural context, in order to communicate highly complex and nuanced emotional states).

So, without descending too far into the Whorf-Sapir hypothesis[2] of language determining culture, it is nonetheless perfectly clear that performing linguistic translation of the words is likely to strip the real, desired "meaning" away from the text, and translate the *wrong bit.* The simple fact is that there may well *be* no equivalence to be achieved here: because we all live so tightly wrapped within our own culture, because it's the very air we breathe, we don't even realize most of the time how culture-bound our utterances and creative acts really are.

I've seen brand teams argue for days over whether the best description of their product was *creamy* or *creamy-smooth* (a genuinely important distinguishing aspect of their product), without once referring to the facts that

- The product was never going to be sold in any English-speaking markets, so the detailed discussion of vocabulary was pretty much a waste of time.
- This subtle distinction is quite likely untranslatable into any other language, and in the hands of the trans-

lator would almost certainly end up with the same word whichever of the two they pick.

- The team's familiarity with the expression *creamy-smooth* owes a great deal to the fact that it has often been used in British advertising over the years, so it has some resonance, but it's not a "dictionary" word at all.
- Cream varies enormously from market to market in terms of its consistency, flavor, cost, uses and popularity, so assuming that the translator picks a word which maintains the reference to real dairy cream, it will almost certainly point respondents in other markets to a completely different cultural reference set.
- In many countries, you're not even *allowed* to use words like that to describe a product unless it contains a certain, prescribed proportion of real dairy cream.

Since we're in the kitchen, I will relapse into my culinary similes again. Translating research stimulus is rather like mashing a banana skin and serving it up with sugar and cream, and throwing the banana in the trashcan.

Or, to put it another way, you want those groups to tell you what they think about the hippo, not his ears. The core dilemma may appear to be about finding ways to *express* concepts without *developing* or *executing* them, but this may well be a red herring: after all, as I mentioned in an earlier chapter, consumers will only ever encounter brand positionings once they are expressed in the form of finished communications, so attempting to separate the unseparable may be a waste of time and effort.

For all these reasons, the brand development process is a perfect candidate for simultaneous origination: the same *international* team which collaborates on developing product concepts and positioning concepts which are fit to travel in the first place, is also the best team to develop the best execution of those concepts in their own language from an agreed common brief; those concepts go directly into research without passing through any kind of bottleneck (merely compared against the other country versions for broad consistency and sharing best ideas); they are researched separately; responses come back separately and are "interpreted" for the benefit of the whole international team by their original author; and the cycle is repeated as many times as necessary.

And, lo and behold, if the same creative team is helping to develop and research the brand positionings (and they *can*, because, as you will recall, we've intentionally hired creative people who are also able to think strategically and in pure-ish brand terms), *and* develop the name of the product (as briefly described in Chapter 1), then it makes perfect sense for those same creatives to develop the work into its final, consumer-facing form as advertising and marketing communications, pack copy, and point-of-sale materials.

Smart centralization creates a team which, by definition, can and should be involved throughout the entire brand development process, and thus the damaging and wasteful disconnect between international marketing and international advertising is finally bridged.

Some Conclusions

I hope that a picture has now begun to emerge of smart centralization as an attractive and workable alternative to more traditional ways of creating international brand communications.

At this point, it's probably worth briefly exploring the kinds of companies and the kinds of assignments which such a system is suited to: for it would be vain and foolish to claim that it's the right solution for every need.

As I mentioned in Chapter 5, there are plenty of reasons why a distributed network of some kind is essential for certain kinds of business, although I hope I have also shown that its suitability is not necessarily linked to the simplistic distinction of whether the client company has chosen "standardized" or "localized" communications.

As has been pointed out by many people since Theodore Levitt published his famous article on globalization in 1983,[3] the "globalize/localize" debate isn't a debate at all, because it isn't a simple choice at all—it's a continuum, running between two rather impractical and theoretical extremes, via an enormous range of interesting permutations on the themes of central control and local influence.

As I put it in Chapter 5, it's all a question of how to create the ideal balance between sensitivity to the culture of the brand, and sensitivity to the culture of the consumer.

Intrinsically, the smart centralization model which I have proposed tends towards the "globalization" half of the continuum, whilst the distributed network model tends towards the "localization" half, but to characterize either one as "belonging to" or "targeted at" one or the other would be an oversimplification. Neither model denies that local sensitivity is fundamental from the consumer's point of view; and neither model denies that international marketers (often with good reason) tend to be highly conscious of the need to standardize international communications *to some degree.* In either case, the only issue for debate is *which degree* is most appropriate for the needs of company and consumer.

Having said this, it would merely be another oversimplification to characterize the nature of the debate as "consumer needs versus corporate needs," because the interests of the consumer should be, in every important sense, *identical* to the interests of the corporation.

Other, more practical factors are far more likely to dictate a company's preference for one system or the other.

Cost

It hardly needs stressing that a single office solution will inevitably incur lower administrative costs than a network, and this factor will naturally be reflected in the agency fees:

although as I have pointed out more than once, the vast bulk of the cost of marketing has traditionally been the cost of media (this picture is beginning to change) and the cost of creating communications and servicing the account are hardly the primary issue.

Standardization can still create economies and benefits of scale, as the McCann-Erickson/Coca-Cola example[4] is frequently used to illustrate, and this factor should not be ignored. However, it only becomes of interest when standardization can demonstrably be achieved with no risk of reduced *effectiveness* or contribution to brand stature: if there is even the slightest risk of such an effect, no business on earth would (one hopes) contemplate running it for the sake of marginal cost efficiencies in the order of 2 to 3%. The long-term cost to brand equity, if the risk is found to be real, is liable to outweigh such savings by orders of magnitude.

A more interesting debate about the potential for cost-effectiveness might center around the issue of equity stakes, profit sharing, and payment by results, as discussed in Chapter 7.

Servicing Emerging International Businesses: The "Nursery Slope"
There is no question that first-time exporters can only rarely justify the expense of a fully-fledged network representing their interests in every country. Prudent practice dictates that at the point of entry in a market, it makes more sense to invest in proper distribution, manufacturing quality when relevant, and channel support: in other words, to concentrate on "push" rather than "pull."

To establish an entirely new, foreign brand in a market takes time and money, and unless these values are built organically, on the basis of successful market penetration, it is likely to be an expensive and risky endeavor. It is true that brands can be built artificially as well as organically: it is certainly possible to create the *illusion* of brand equity, or at least brand awareness, entirely through marketing activities. This is a little like putting up an inflatable castle rather than one made of bricks and mortar: it has to be kept pumped full of gas (which costs effort and money), and if you stop pumping even for a moment, the whole thing tends to collapse on top of you.

So any model which enables first-time market entrants to build sensitive and targeted communications platforms in a flexible and cost-efficient way is to be desired. Since, as I have also pointed out, emerging international marketers are unlikely to have their own marketing staff in each country, there is arguably little point in maintaining an advertising agency in that country—and advertising agencies have the power to do much harm to brands as well as much good, so the prospect of having such a weapon in the hands of a distributor, sales manager, retailer or licensee, is something of an alarming prospect for most companies.

Because of their high operating costs, the fully-fledged networks tend to specialize in the task of maintaining market presence for high-spending and well-established consumer brands. This provides a natural vacuum in the market for small international shops which are able to take on the task of helping emerging international brands to establish a presence—a strategic and creative challenge which most agency people would confirm is far more attractive than merely servicing an already established brand.

Speed

As I mentioned in the Introduction to this book, the speed at which business is done increases all the time, and since such a high proportion of emerging international marketers are in technology-related fields, speed of delivery becomes a critical factor. In the PC business, for example, it is perfectly normal for an ad agency to be required to produce a complete pan-European launch campaign for a new model in three weeks or less.

A distributed network, for all the reasons I have described, will find it very much harder to operate internationally at this rate than a single team.

Secrecy

A network agency is a large organization, with many hundreds of people involved at many different levels on anything truly global, and this fact alone can cause concern to a company if the message they wish to communicate worldwide is time-sensitive and needs to be kept absolutely under wraps until the moment of launch.

Nobody can do a proper job of advertising unless they're fully briefed, so attempting to withhold key information from the people who are making the ads until the "last moment" can create disastrous misunderstandings and miscommunication.

So if an automobile or pharmaceutical company is preparing a launch campaign for a top-secret new model or groundbreaking new drug, or two corporations are about to announce a merger, or an oil company gets wind of a vigilante campaign about to break and needs to prepare its public response advertising, the last thing they really need is 600 people in 100 ad agencies all talking about the brief.

In such cases, the ability to prepare a complete global campaign from start to finish within a single office—no e-mails, no faxes, no materials and photographs being couriered around the world, no phone calls except between the client and his agency—is highly reassuring.

Nature of Message

Some kinds of communication are, by their very nature, not intended to be tailored to the *tactical* requirements of individual markets—usually because it isn't a product or service being sold, but simply brand attributes being communicated—and consequently involving a local ad agency might be somewhat counter-productive as well as wasteful.

Typically, if a company is developing a global or regional corporate image campaign, range ads, brand awareness ads or any kind of overall image building work, what is really required is a single campaign, which combines built-in sensitivity to all the relevant cultures (especially important since the messages are likely to be emotional rather than practical) with *knowing avoidance* of individual, functional market detail.

In such cases, ignoring certain individual market characteristics becomes inevitable: but the golden rule is that the more you know, the more you are licensed to ignore. Woe betide the marketer or agency which ignores market needs without thoroughly understanding them first.

In such cases, smart centralization is ideal: it's like having a small creative hotshop whose domestic market happens to be Planet Earth.

Youth Marketing

As I mentioned in Chapter 5, networks often find it extremely difficult to maintain strong creativity across borders. The ones that work best together as networks tend not to be the creative hotshops; yet the more creative networks tend, by their nature, to find it much harder to work together as a coherent international unit.

All this creates an unwelcome dilemma for the marketers who need, for the very survival of their brands, to inhabit the absolute cutting edge of youth culture in many different countries.

A number of the networks have responded to this need by acquiring highly-rated creative shops in various countries, and linking them into the network. The main problem, however, is not usually the *origination* of radical creative work (after all, even if the "lead" office of a network is unused to producing work of this kind, they can always bring in freelance creatives who are more suited to it): the problem is *making that stuff travel*, or, more to the point, making stuff that *can* travel.

Looked at from one angle, such an acquisition might appear to make perfect sense: it combines an established creative agency brand with a tried and trusted international delivery system, which, in theory, will combine to produce international creative excellence.

The trouble is that the stuff which the creative shop naturally produces—and the very reason why the network bought it in the first place—simply *doesn't fit down the pipeline.* If we entirely leave aside the issues I have explored about the basic unreliability and leakiness of that pipeline, and assume for the moment that it works perfectly, we are still left with a fundamental problem that pipelines are round and real creative work is spiky. By the time the idea bumps and clatters out the other end, all of its points have simply broken off.

Once again, what you *really* need is a creative shop that can draw its inspiration from the markets it is serving in order to match its fundamental concepts to those markets— to find the uncommon ground which links those consumers together and makes them respond to this global brand in the first place. Then you need an executional model which is flexible and international enough to communicate the uncommon ground in ways which are just as different as they need to be, and no more, to bring that concept into being in all of those markets.

In other words, you need to eliminate the pipeline by fixing international communications *at source.*

I call this "locking the package." Many companies in the business of international marketing tend to assume that once their domestic communications product is locked, it's safe for export.

Of course, as I hope I have succeeded in pointing out, nothing could be further from the truth. Locked at home means *dangerously unlocked* for the rest of the world: more can happen to threaten the integrity, effectiveness and quality of that creative product as it attempts to leap over language and culture barriers than ever happens between brief and domestic execution.

The degree of control given by locking the creative product in its final market versions at source means that you can confidently send your brand out into the world, knowing that you've given it the best possible chance of survival, and success, in the cultural jungle.

Crucially, in order to achieve this, you need a shop which is *small enough* to cluster around the brand and behave like a true creative team, rather than a multinational communications ministry.

Business to Business

A while ago, I had a visit from the global marketing director of a large industrial component manufacturer — the largest in the world in its highly specialized field.

Needless to say, the name of the company was one which is almost completely unknown to the average consumer.

But that doesn't matter, because the average consumer doesn't buy the product, and doesn't need to know that they exist. (Unless, of course, the company considers itself an *ingredient brand* and decides that a little "pull" from the end-user might usefully augment the "push" they normally give into the process chain — but that's a subject for another book.)

He had a pretty substantial budget to spend on advertising, too: much of it was range and product advertising in industry books, but some of it was to run in the global financial and business press, in order to boost brand awareness amongst senior influencers in client companies.

I asked him why he didn't go to a network agency, since he had substantial local needs in many countries, and certainly wasn't short of money, and he gave me an interesting reply. He said, "Oh, I've been to see some of the networks. It's perfectly obvious that they like my money but they don't like my *product.*"

He went on to describe how he'd made an appointment to see one of the big agencies, and found that his meeting was with an account manager who admitted that she didn't know what his company actually made. It was only when he explained to her how big his advertising budget was that she went out and called the new business director to come and join them.

The problem? Brand awareness. Unless you're a household name, most of the networks really aren't that interested.

It's difficult enough for networks to service smaller international accounts properly without having to cope with a major technical learning curve as well—for a network to have to learn a whole new product language, a whole new marketplace, manufacturing process, distribution cycle, which are as far from consumer packaged goods as you can imagine, is often impossible to contemplate. Moreover, such advertisers usually spend the bulk of their media budget on lower-cost specialist publications, so the agency's fee, which may well be linked in some way to media spend, makes a pretty unattractive package for the average top-twenty global shop.

Leaving yet another disinherited category of international advertiser, desperately in need of an alternative solution.

Non-Physical Products

The one factor which more than any other is driving marketers to reassess the old models of export marketing, distribution and geography-based promotion, is the fact that the internet is more than a global channel of brand and content communication.

It's also a practically free and interactive global *distribution* channel for entire product and service categories: anything you can fit down a wire and transmit or acquire digitally or virtually, from software to stock photography, from advertising to industrial design, from news coverage to marketing consultancy, from banking and insurance to library catalogs, from stocks and bonds to lotteries and sweepstakes.

Suddenly, whole swathes of export marketers can perceive a not very distant day when they can completely dispense with their export manuals, their distribution partnerships, their in-country marketing staff. And it really is fruitless to deny that in such a future, a full-service, fully-staffed advertising agency in every foreign market seems more and more of an anomaly.

But the companies which leap too far along the standardization route, seduced by the dangerous fiction of millions of global, English-speaking consumers, all united in the American-led internet fraternity, are behaving as the front riders in a seller's market always behave. Whilst their marketplace is in a state of under-supply and rapid growth, such grossness can even reap dramatic results, but it won't last. The world is no longer as it was in the 1950s, when product ruled, and brands meant little to the hordes of grateful, eager, global consumers. Not too many people now inhabit the bottom levels of Maslow's hierarchy of needs, and brand awareness is only temporarily suspended in high-growth markets: it hasn't gone away.

Competition will multiply and accelerate faster in this sector than it has ever done in any other commercial field before, and even as I write, internet marketing is starting to form itself into the familiar patterns of customer loyalty, brand equity, and fine targeting.

But the fact seems indisputable that new structures are needed in order to achieve the same old ends in a radically different environment.

A WORD ABOUT COURAGEOUS TRAVELERS

There's no denying that the size and geographical distribution of classic network agencies is, at first glance, a source of great comfort for potential clients.

As I have said, "abroad" is a frightening place: all that scaremongering about language and culture has had its effect on us, and we feel we desperately need a guide. Guides have to know the territory and speak the language; and the bigger, stronger, and more experienced that guide is, the more likely we are to hire him, even if he's rather expensive. Actually, the fact that he's rather expensive is nothing if not further reassurance that we've done the right thing.

There's also the question of who to blame if things go wrong. International marketing has been presented for so many decades as a terrifying battlefield, littered with the remains of our incautious or ill-prepared predecessors. We feel we need a guide whose back is broad enough to share responsibility for the success of the expedition—then, at least, if the worst happens, we can always limp back home and say to people, "I can't understand it: I didn't skimp, I hired the best guide in the country." Then we're exonerated in the eyes of our countrymen.

There's undeniably a great deal of simple, intuitive logic in the notion that if you need to sell your product in another country, then you need someone in that country to help you sell it. Even the most diehard proponent of naif standardization wouldn't deny that it's reassuring to have somebody over there to make sure that your work is appearing when, how, and where it should.

Market expertise is, in any circumstance, a basic requirement of effective marketing. The trouble is that people almost always leap instantly from this truism to the assumption that market expertise and *physical market presence* are synonymous and indivisible.

This is the assumption I challenge. So much of what is happening around us as we rush into the third millennium seems to favor those who are bold enough to bend the old, old rules of geography and economics to their own advantage.

With this thought in mind, let us proceed to my final chapter.

9

Where Do We Go from Here?

Whatever people may say, the world is still a big place.

You can feel this when you're in an airplane, flying high over a desert, and you imagine yourself set down, a speck in the middle of a vast, empty landscape. Who knows how long it would take you—days? weeks?—to walk from the rock you can see from your window to the mountain you can see from the window in the row in front of you—if you ever made it at all. And in all that time, you wouldn't meet a soul, perhaps wouldn't see a single sign of civilization.

A few minutes pass, your meal has arrived, you've stopped worrying about rocks in the desert, and you're 100 miles over the mountains and well into the next landscape.

The way we travel in the modern world, it's easy to forget what distance means. Traveling by land, you're aware of every stone of the road, and that sense of distance fundamentally alters your perception of the place you get to. When you travel by plane, you get into a kind of elevator, you get out again, and you've arrived. It's as if you've hardly moved: it's as if the place has come to you, rather than you needing to come to the place.

The way we now travel conspires with many other gradually changing circumstances to diminish our respect for the size and variety of our planet. It sometimes makes us guilty of believing that if you only scratch the surface, you'll find that most places, and most people, are pretty much the same.

As I hope I have shown in this book, it's really not that simple at all. The harder you scratch, the more examples you find of genuine, ineradicable, unavoidable, glorious, solid *difference;* then if you dig again, and dig deep, you may be lucky and find seams of true commonality. It's complex, it's contradictory, and it's confusing: long may it remain so. It's one of the things that makes living on this planet so interesting.

But much of the difference that we find derives from the fact that, over the centuries, some countries have fared differently from others—some have managed to keep peace better than others, some have governed more fairly or less wisely than others, some have done nothing but mind their own business, and some have attained levels of prosperity which others can barely even dream of.

Why this should be is neither within the scope of this book to explore, nor within my competence to explain, but I do believe that it is within our competence to influence the way these circumstances continue to evolve in the future.

These matters may seem out of the province of a book about international advertising, but they are not: I believe that the future prosperity of every country in the world is intimately linked to the degree to which that country manages to accede to and control the instruments of commercial communication and brand power.

My model of a brand strategy and communications agency characterized by the twin axes of smart centralization and "transcultural competence" has both a medium-term and a long-term aim. In the medium term, it simply aims to provide international companies with an intelligent alternative to the traditional global brandbuilding structures and techniques. This model is already in existence and under constant enhancement at World Writers, but I encourage others to follow suit, to model their own businesses on however many aspects of it they choose, and to modify or develop other aspects themselves: it's freeware, if you like.

I believe that this sector of the communications industry, of small-to-medium sized independent international agencies, currently little more than a niche, will grow extremely rapidly over the next few years, and there will be plenty of business for everyone.

But in the longer term, I see the smart centralization model as forming just one segment of a larger organization: a business which doesn't exist yet, and which one might call the *globalization company*. The purpose of a globalization company is simply to bring together, in reality or virtuality, all of the advice, support, and systems required to turn domestic brands into global brands, or to develop global brands from nothing.

This will involve other small, globally-minded businesses like World Writers, naturally from all over the world, with expertise in compatible fields such as finance, technology, distribution, professional services, human resources, graphic and product design, public relations, and lobbying, which together will form the total toolkit necessary to build global brands with the minimum of fuss and expense, and the maximum possible creativity, originality, efficiency, flexibility, and sensitivity to the culture of consumers worldwide.

And the companies, institutions and governments to whom we offer this model will all be in countries with "emerging" economies.

NEW GLOBAL BRANDS FOR THE NEXT MILLENNIUM?

In Chapter 3, I mentioned that there is a "Top Ten" list of countries which produce the lion's share of global brands, and that at least part of their success, and certainly (from the consumer's point of view), their "license to brand," derives from that privileged provenance.

However, the story doesn't end there, and there are many other countries around the world which have equally strong brand prints, and as yet no commercial brands exploiting those equities.

Brazil is one very striking example: a country which, arguably, has one of the strongest and best-defined brand images in the world. Ask people in Europe, Asia, Africa, or America what Brazil means to them, and they will babble fluently for hours about music, football, carnival, youth, pleasure, ecology, samba, coffee, beaches, sex, and so on, without having ever had any direct personal experience of the place at all.

In other words, it's a classic global youth brand: the kind of attribute set which companies like Nike and Pepsi would *die* for. Even the negative elements in Brazil's brand print are exactly the kind which are most likely to stimulate and challenge the prickly, contrary nature of the teenage consumer: drugs, pollution, corruption, violence, prostitution.

Brazil is not alone in possessing such a wealth of natural branding resources. There are some extremely powerful provenance brands in Asia which are largely unexploited—and I don't just mean the more obvious "national produce" images of Japan, Taiwan, Singapore, Korea, and Malaysia as technology and automotive producers. Given the still-growing trend amongst Western consumers to downshift, at least in their imaginations, and to re-explore "wiser" civilizations, their remedies, their philosophy, their art, and culture (consumer behavior pundits have termed this *asianization*), it surely follows that countries like China, Thailand, India, Indonesia, and the African nations are sitting on a treasure-house of latent brand value. Perhaps smaller countries like Myanmar, Tibet, Sri Lanka, Laos, and New Guinea, with their strong individual cultures, are more niche brands just waiting for the right product line.

And what of the emerging markets in Eastern Europe, the Baltics, and Central Asia? I mentioned Lithuanian raincoats, and it doesn't take long to make a fine shopping-list of global brands from the post-Soviet world: sailing apparel from Estonia, retro-styled Czech sunglasses, a Bulgarian nightclub chain, Russian binoculars, Polish youth fashions, post-industrial furniture from Latvia for style-conscious, middle-class American homes: obviously, such brands would first need to address current perceptions of poor manufacturing quality, but the *cultural* potential is vast.

So how long do we have to wait before the world's markets are flooded with Brazilian surfboards, fashion labels, fizzy drinks, sporting goods, fast-food outlets, ecological healthcare products and coffee shops? When can we expect the Chinese stationery brands, the Sri Lankan jewelry, the Malaysian tennis rackets, the Estonian freezers?

Perhaps not so long. Naturally, launching a global brand requires flair, confidence, and *chutzpah*—especially if you don't come from a Top Ten country. It requires objectivity to an unusual degree: the ability to see yourself as others see you, and to accept that this is, at least in commercial terms, more important than the way you see yourself. It requires government support. It requires free trading. It requires a competent and internationally-minded marketing department and a strong advertising resource.

And it requires constant investment in the country brand itself, which in turn requires commitment, collaboration and great synergy between the main purveyors of the country's image in the global media: usually the national Tourist Board, the national airline and the major food producers, because these are the routes by which the national brand is most commonly created and exported.

Country brands can be built and maintained in many ways, and there's ample scope for creativity here. For example, by encouraging—even paying—a world-class movie director to set and shoot his or her next global blockbuster in your country, you are giving millions of people the chance of a vicarious tourism experience. In effect, it's an interesting spin on the idea of product placement: rather than placing your product within the movie, you place the movie within the product.

Until a few years ago, I would also have said that building a global brand requires lots of cash to buy media: because until the new media revolution happened, this was the *sine qua non* of building global brands. You just couldn't think of building a global brand for less than $50 or even $100 million a year: quite simply, as in all extremely mature and heavily exploited markets, every media vehicle had its own value calculated to the *n*th degree, and there were no bargains.

But since the revolution, we find ourselves in an entirely new world, in an immature and as yet very imperfectly understood market. And in immature markets, there are bargains everywhere, for anyone who knows how to recognize them: because even the owners of some of the new channels of communication have yet to realize the true value of what they're offering.

There's no doubt that selling brands, rather than goods or commodities, is one of the quickest routes to prosperity for any developing nation. Most of the "emerging" countries I've mentioned are enmeshed in a pattern of third-world behavior which keeps them firmly in the third world: selling unprocessed goods to richer nations at extremely low margins, and allowing those nations to add massive "value" by finishing, packaging, branding, and retailing to the end user. This pattern serves to deplete the third-world country's resources whilst keeping their foreign revenues at break-even level. Not for nothing does the *Economist* call some of them the "submerging" economies.

The irony of the expression "added value" never fails to strike me in these contexts. In advertising and marketing circles, we use it so frequently and so thoughtlessly, it is all too easy for us to overlook what a grotesque piece of doublespeak it really is. As a matter of fact, value is the one thing we're *not* adding: what we're adding is, objectively speaking, valueless stuff—packaging, advertising, brand values, gloss—in order to justify charging a greater premium on the cost of raw materials and the manufacturing and finishing process, and in order to compete with other similar products for the consumer's attention and admiration.

Branding, if you want to be cynical about it, is little more than creating a distortion field in the mind of the consumer which enables the brand owner to charge more money than the product is actually worth: it's a technique for corrupting one's sense of value. There has seldom been a more powerful metaphor for this process than Nike's *Air* technology, where the manufacturer explicitly and openly charges an additional price premium because of the presence of air in the product — a commodity which, more than any other, is known to be free.

Branding, from the consumer's point of view, is *detracting* value, not adding it. It's what oils the wheels of commerce and as a card-carrying member of the IAA (whose remit is to protect the right to advertise), I should really be defending it: but sometimes the vocabulary we use is a little too euphemistic to stomach. I suggest that we should be more straightforward, and call it "added attraction."

Creating and selling international brands in this way is the classic trick of first-world nations — indeed, some of the world's richest nations have precious few commodities to export — and one which many poorer nations would do well to emulate. What all rich nations have is expertise in handling the tools of mass communication.

Brands are, arguably, the ultimate ecological export, since like the Nike product they're made of air, and are infinitely sustainable: but just as importantly, they are the real creators of wealth in the modern age, the most powerful development tool a country can acquire. This, it seems to me, is the best counter-argument to the contention that branding is theft.

It is also conceivable that if consumers in developing markets are faced with the choice between yet more brands from the Top Ten nations, and new brands from other emerging nations — "colleague countries" with no shady colonial past — they might just feel more comfortable with the latter.

Ethics, of course, have a crucial role to play in marketing, even when we're merely talking about a single-market situation: whether it is right (and "fair") for the wealthy to extract more money from the less wealthy by using yet more of their money to create that distortion field in the mind of the consumer, and other such well-rehearsed debates. In the case of *global* marketing, the dilemmas become far more pervasive and far more pronounced: whether it is right and fair for a wealthy *country* to extract more money from a poorer country by the same means, when the wealth gap is far more pronounced, and where, moreover, consumers may be completely unaccustomed to and "uninoculated" against the techniques used to create the value distortion field.

A simple formula is irresistible:

- If a company in a rich country sells brands to rich consumers at home or in other rich countries, nothing really happens: money simply circulates within a more or less closed system, and there's little to criticize on moral grounds.
- If a company in a rich country sells brands to poor consumers in the same or other rich countries, there is a risk of exploitation and a further widening of the wealth gap.
- If a company in a rich country sells brands to consumers in a poor country, the risk of exploitation is far higher, partly because the cultural vulnerability of the consumers is greater.
- But if a company in a poor country sells brands to consumers in a rich country, the overall balance begins to be redressed, and justice is done.

Global brands as the ultimate distributor of wealth? It's an intriguing thought.

We now live in a world where, increasingly, mass communication is no longer in the hands of the state, and no longer the province of religion, or non-commercial broadcasting. The only voices which the vast majority of people now really listen to, at least in the Western world, are the voices of marketing, entertainment, and the commercially-funded media. Even the tradition of political communication, leading to democratic elections, is gradually being replaced by a marketing-based model, where the candidate is literally *sold* to the electorate: this particular American legacy is rapidly spreading through-out the Western world.

The so-called "CNN effect" seems to further confirm the power and significance of the media as the planet's loudest voice — television news can shape world events in a faster and more decisive way than politicians ever could.

This great power, as with all power, can be used for good or for ill. The fact that it appears to be a force for democrati-zation, and that it is in the hands of the many, rather than the few, cannot alone guarantee its moral rectitude: on the one hand, it does make every world leader instantly and globally accountable for his or her actions; on the other hand, it can become an instrument of mob rule. After all, post interactive television, who's to say that acts of foreign policy might not be influenced, or even decided, by instant global referenda?

Mary Goodyear[1] has defined the "consumerization con-tinuum" as developing from the *Seller's market* (typified by under-supply, manufacturer power, and volume commodity sales), to *Marketing* (increasing competition and choice, with brands becoming a reference point), to *Classic branding* (intense competition, where brands acquire and depend on personality), to *Customer-driven marketing* (where a saturated marketplace makes brands icons, and advertising becomes symbolic), and finally to *Post-modern marketing* (where a loss of belief in authority and pressure from vigilante consumers drives companies to become their brands, and where brands become policy).

I wonder whether there isn't a sixth stage beyond "post-modern" marketing, where brands become instruments of global change. After all, it is already the case that 5 of the world's top 10 *economies* are corporations, and it is said that the large advertising groups like Omnicom are so wealthy they can affect the value of the dollar on world currency markets simply by moving their cash around.

The tools of global influence and analysis that we the marketers, and the content-providers (our hosts, clients, and customers, with whom we are locked in an ever-converging dance), have learned to use and refine over the last century, are now recognized as being the most powerful tools that anyone can wield. These are tools which can eliminate poverty at a stroke, or they can destroy the planet. They can make poor countries into rich countries, or spell the instant ruin of great corporations, pulling dependent national economies with them.

These are the tools which, ultimately, smart centralization and "transcultural competence" can render affordable, accessible, and useable to the countries which actually *need* more prosperity, and need self-sustaining, export-based economies, more than they need handouts. As the African saying has it, "The hand which receives is always beneath the hand which gives."

There's nothing terribly new about the economic theory that brands create sustainable wealth, and there's nothing terribly new about the marketing theory that countries have brand values which can transfer to products produced in those countries.

What may be new is the combination of the two, and it leads to an irresistible conclusion: the commercial forces which have done most to further the unequal division of wealth in the last millennium could prove to be the same forces which finally begin to redress the balance as we move into the next.

As we go about our daily work in advertising and marketing jobs, let's try to keep at least part of our thoughts fixed on that horizon.

We have a great power to do good.

Notes

CHAPTER 1

1. Roger Bennett. *International Marketing*, 2nd edition. London: Kogan Page, 1998.

2. Actually, this is completely the wrong word. Transliteration simply means to spell out a word phonetically using the letters of one alphabet when it originates in another (for example, spelling the Greek word *kudos*, the Hebrew word *kibbutz*, or the Russian word *glasnost* in the Roman alphabet instead of their native Greek, Hebrew, and Cyrillic forms). Now, I don't wish to be pedantic, and I'm all for people giving old words new senses if the language appears to need it, but I simply can't understand why people would pick a word that sounds so much like *literal translation* when what they wish to convey is precisely the opposite.

3. Franklin R. Root. *Entry Strategies for International Markets*. San Francisco: Jossey-Bass, 1994.

4. Jean-Claude Usunier. *Marketing across Cultures*, 2nd edition. London: Prentice Hall, 1996.

5. This car was originally called the Ritmo (rhythm) in Italy, but renamed for export, presumably because Ritmo didn't convey much to non-Italian speakers. It seems odd, though, that an Italian manufacturer chose Strada (road) — a piece of cod-Italian equal to the worst efforts of the Japanese. Fiat was also the perpetrator of a little station wagon in

the 1960s charmingly called the Rustica (countrywoman). It took a little while before they discovered that British people liked to pronounce this *rusty car*—a little close for comfort, given the deservedly bad reputation Italian cars used to have for corrosion when shipped outside of their native Mediterranean climate.

6. I can only presume that Nokia wishes to conceal the fact that it is a Finnish-owned multinational, which is a shame, because I'm sure there is much appropriate equity to be gained from the intelligent and enlightened management of such an unusual provenance. (See the section on country of origin as brand in Chapter 3.)

7. David Crystal. *The Cambridge Enyclopaedia of the English Language.* Cambridge, England: Cambridge University Press, 1995.

CHAPTER 2

1. Paul A. Herbig. *Handbook of Cross-Cultural Marketing.* New York: The International Business Press, 1998.

2. Daniëlle Campo. *International Advertising without Networks?* Utrecht, the Netherlands: Hogeschool van Utrecht, 1998.

3. Jon Steel. *Truth, Lies and Advertising.* New York: John Wiley & Sons, 1998.

4. Geert Hofstede. *Cultures and Organizations—Software of the Mind.* New York: McGraw Hill, 1997.

5. Fons Trompenaars and Charles Hampden-Turner. *Riding the Waves of Culture.* New York: McGraw Hill, 1998.

6. F. Kluckhohn and F.L. Strodtbeck. *Variations in Value Orientations.* Evanston, IL: Row, Peterson, 1961.

7. Marieke de Mooij. *Global Marketing and Advertising—Understanding Cultural Paradoxes.* Sage, 1998.

8. Marieke de Mooij. *Advertising Worldwide.* Upper Saddle River, NJ: Prentice Hall, 1994.

9. Jean-Claude Usunier. *Marketing across Cultures*, 2nd edition. Upper Saddle River, NJ: Prentice Hall, 1996.

10. David S. Landes. Quoted in *The Wealth and Poverty of Nations*. New York: Norton, 1998.
11. Lafcadio Hearn. *Glimpses of Unfamiliar Japan (1894)*. London: Jonathan Cape, 1927.

CHAPTER 3

1. David S. Landes. *The Wealth and Poverty of Nations*. New York: Norton, 1998.
2. Roger E. Axtell. *Gestures*. New York: John Wiley & Sons, 1991/1998.

CHAPTER 4

1. Jonathan Bond and Richard Kirshenbaum. *Under the Radar*. New York: John Wiley & Sons, 1998.
2. The survey, carried out in late 1998 by the international research house GfK Great Britain, received 16,691 responses in 14 European countries.
3. *The Economist*, April 5, 1999.
4. Henri Bergson. *Le Rire, Essai Sur La Significance Du Comique*. Paris: 1900.
5. Jean de la Bruyère. *Les Caractères*, 1688. Paris: Classiques Garnier, 1962. (My paraphrase).
6. Quoted from *Role Conflict and Personality*, S.A Stouffer and J. Toby (*American Journal of Sociology*, LUI-5, 1951) by Fons Trompenaars and Charles Hampden-Turner in *Riding the Waves of Culture*. New York: McGraw Hill, 1998.

CHAPTER 5

1. Gundersen Partners, L.L.C. *Anatomy of a 21st Century Marketer*. 1999.
2. Of the total of 73 global account moves and 37 European moves in 1998, totaling around $4.5 billion in media spend,

the average spend was around $40MM. Seventy-five per-
cent of these clients were spending below $50MM. (Data
from Advertising Age International Special Report, January 1999.)

CHAPTER 6

1. Geert Hofstede. *Cultures and Organizations — Software of the Mind*. New York: McGraw Hill, 1997.
2. Philip M. Parker. *Religious Cultures of the World, A Statistical Reference*, Vol. 1. Westport, CT: Greenwood, 1997.
3. Edward de Bono. *Serious Creativity*. London: Harper Collins, 1992.
4. Frances Gillson, quoted in *Mini Sagas*. London: Sutton, 1997.
5. See Craig Raine. *A Martian Sends a Postcard Home*. Oxford, England: Oxford University Press, 1979.
6. Thomas Hatton. Quoted in *Mini Sagas*. London: Sutton, 1997.

CHAPTER 7

1. See http://www.the-ceres-community.com.

CHAPTER 8

1. Equipe European Survey, quoted in *Language International*, February 1999.
2. Edward Sapir. "The status of linguistics as a Science" and other writings. *Language*, vol. 5, 1929.
3. Theodore Levitt. "The Globalization of Markets." *Harvard Business Review*, May–June 1983.
4. McCann-Erickson claimed to have saved their client $90 million over their tenure of the business through produc-

ing standardized global TV campaigns; however, because they had the account for 20 years, this amounts to an average of just $4.5 million per year, a mere blip compared with the media expenditure throughout the same period.

CHAPTER 9

1. Mary Goodyear. "Divided by a common language: Diversity and deception in the world of global marketing." *Journal of the Market Research Society,* 38(2), 1996.

Index

A

Abbott, David, 120
Acceptance, 202–203
Account handlers, 181, 209, 249
Accounts, 249
Accuracy, 250–252
Achievement/ascription orientation, 67
Acquired languages, versus native languages, 47
Acts of communication, creation by non-nationals, 62–63
Added value, 304–305
Advertising:
    core message of, 152
    cultural differences in function of, 142
    cultural focus of, 3
    cultural provenance of, 120
    culture and, 58–59
    emotive, 138–143
    entertainment value of, 143–146
    function of, 9–10
    as knowledge business, 262–263
    and marketing, bridging gap between, 257–258, 288
    multi-local, 159
    sharpness of, 58
    simplification of, for export, 142–143
    world, 189
Advertising agencies. *See also* Agency networks; Independent agencies
    service orientation of, 247–250
    stake in client businesses, 254–255
    types of, 246

Advertising industry, international competence of, vii
Affective externalizations, 67
African television, perception of, 132
Age, and receptivity to wit, 145
Agency networks, viii, 158–159, 162–164, 181
    accuracy of, 250–251
    benefits of, 160–162
    brand awareness of, 295–296
    versus centralization, 289–297
    disadvantages of, 162–167
    dysfunction of, 167–168
    fees of, 170
    global coverage of, 161, 179
    individual offices of, 171–172, 176
    international brief preparation process, 205–206
    interoffice interaction, 177–178
    negative learning in, 211
    network solutions for, 178
    politics of, 169
    production and pre-production processes, 245
    security provided by, 297–298
    small-size, 179–181
    speed of service, 166
    structure of, 174–176, 184
    suitability of, 288–289
Alfa Romeo 164, 24
AMC Matador, 23
America:
    enjoyment of advertising in, 141
    expectation of superior work from, 176
    as provenance brand, 109

American brands, English for, 49
American creativity, 141–142
American culture, 73–75
American English:
    versus British English, 75–76
    naming conventions in, 32
American international businesses,
    69–73
    Britain as intermediary for, 70–71
Americans:
    Japanese interactions with, 74
    perception of Europe, 74–75
    world view of, 72–73
Approval process, 236–238
    complexity of, 228–229
    management of, 231–234
Archetypes, 92, 94
    adherence to, 96–97, 129
Art directors, 191
Ascription orientation, 67
Asia, provenance brands of, 302
Asianization, 302
Asians, 83
Atatürk, Kemal, 77
Australia, provenance brands from,
    104
Automobiles, names for, 25–27
Avis, 150–151

B

Backtranslations, 12–15
Baltics, emerging markets of, 302–303
Bartle Bogle Hegarty, 148
Basque, 80
Beauty, in diversity, 85
Behaviors, 100
Beliefs, 100
Benetton, 138–139
Bergson, Henri, 145
Bernbach, Bill, 120, 134, 152
Bilingualism, versus fluency, 16
Bowerman, Bill, 34
Brand attributes, home culture defini-
    tion of, 97
Brand awareness, 295–296
    and the internet, 297
Brand books, 99
Brand development, simultaneous origi-
    nation for, 287–288
Brand equity, using provenance for, 109
Brand essence:
    communication of, 93–94
    describing, 94

Brand extensions, 107–109
Brand identity, 108
Brand images, 104
    consistency of, 12
Branding, 305
    classic, 307
    cultural clichés for, 27
    and global change, 307–308
Brand management, 96
Brand managers, 95
Brand owners, and perception of prove-
    nance, 102–103
Brand pairings, 107–109
Brand personality, 95
Brand prints, 302
Brands:
    archetypes of, 92, 94
    consistency of, 96–97
    local cultural immersion of, 109–110
    pride of origin, 112–113
    provenance of, 102–103
    richness of, 95–97
    self-confidence of, 110
    standards for, 89–91
    survival of, 95
Brand USA, 109
Brazil, brand image of, 302
Briefs. *See also* International briefs
    consistency of, 12
Britain:
    advertising infrastructure of, 70
    creatives versus suits mentality,
        207–209
    enjoyment of advertising in, 141
    expectation of superior work from,
        176
    as intermediary for American busi-
        ness, 70–71
British ad agencies, client service tech-
    niques, 233
British creativity, 141–142
British culture:
    global superiority complex of, 19
    masculinity of, 70
    and provenance of brand names, 107
British English, 75
    versus American English, 75–76
    dialects of, 79–80
British management style, 195
Broadcast work:
    casting and directing, 251–252
    glamour of, 270
Budgets, 170

Business strategists, advice from, 257–258
BVP, 226

C
Cannes festival, 146–149
Cars, names for, 25–27
Casting agencies, 251–252
Central Asia, emerging markets of, 302–303
Centralization, 173–174, 235–236. *See also* Smart centralization
country managers, effect on, 237–240
of marketing department, 117
CEO, personality of, 100
Chaos, advantages of, 203
Chevrolet Nova, 22
Choices, 153
Class, cross-cultural communication of, 225–227
Classic branding, 307
Clichés, 218
Clients:
ad agency stake in, 254–255
agency knowledge of, 257
needs of, 158–159
relationships with, 276
respect for, 249–250
Client service:
culturally adapted, 232–233
etiquette for, 232
Cloning, 124–125
CNN effect, 307
Coca-Cola:
brand provenance of, 109
Russian campaign, 61–62
Colgate-Palmolive, 242
Collaboration, 166–167
Collateral materials, multilingual, 272–276
Collectivism, 67
Comedy, 145–146
Commands, in slogans, 38
Commerce, respect for, 76
Communication. *See also* International communications
corporate, 92
interoffice, 166
Communitarianism, 67
Communities, 254–255
Companies, structural change in, 117
Competition:
as driver of consistency, 117
in internet marketing, 297

Competitive advantage, 99
from provenance brands, 105
Competitiveness, of quality advertising, 41
Computers, translation by, 276
Concentrated value, 40–41
Conceptual creativity, 150–152
Confucian dynamism, 67
Conrad, Joseph, 63
Consensus, 201–203
Consistency, 12, 96–97
agency network enforcement of, 160–161
drivers of, 113–117
measuring, 123–126
of positioning, 121–122
purpose of, 126–130
and quality control, 117–120
of voice, 261–262
Consultants:
for cultural mergers, 65
on multicultural teams, 258
threat of, 157
Consumer communication briefs, 94
Consumerization continuum, 307
Consumers:
attention to commercial messages, 133–134
attraction to Web sites, 279
belief in big brands, 95
brand provenance, assumptions about, 102
brand provenance, perception of, 105
demonstrating understanding of, 10
exposure to advertising, 134
homogenization of, 77
information for, 135–138
linguistic preferences, 47–49
loyalty, and brand positioning, 115–116
observing and analyzing, 63
perception of brands, 101
reaction to advertising, 141
respect for, 46–50
Content, 277–278
Context, 101
Coordination, agency network enforcement of, 160
Copy:
accuracy of, 250–252
purpose of, 9
simultaneous origination of, 230
subtleties of, 5
translating (*see* Translation)

Copywriters, 191
  bilingual, 16
  freelance, 274–275
  qualifications of, 180
Copywriting, 7–8, 10, 58–59
  from briefs, 11
Corporate communications, versus
    product marketing, 92
Corporate cultures, 68
Corporate identity, consistent visual
    appearance of, 128
Corporate messaging, 35
Corporate mission, 100
Corporate strategy, brand representa-
    tion in, 99
Corporate vision, 100
Costs:
  of global brands, 304
  of networks versus centralization,
    289–290
Cost savings, resulting from consistency,
    121–122
Countries:
  brand images of, 104, 108
  clichés assigned to, 27
Country brands, 303–304
  Top Ten, 108
Country managers:
  approval from, 237–238
  decreased responsibility of, 238–240
Creative direction, 275
Creative directors, 169, 192
Creative integrity, 252–254
Creative process, for international cam-
    paigns, 228
Creative proposals, 232
Creatives, 191
  dealing with clients, 207
  integrity of, 253
  knowledge of client business realities,
    257
  on strategy team, 213
  versus suits, 207–209
  tolerance levels of, 196
Creative stars, 193–194
Creative team. *See* Multicultural teams
Creative work, as common property, 231
Creativity, 132–135
  conceptual, 150–152
  culturally relevant, 266
  executional, 151
  exportability of, 293–294
  international, 149–152
  and the internet, 278–279

  monocultural approach to, 188–189
  multicultural approach to, 189–190
  mystery of, 253
  versus originality, 149–150
  standards for, 163–164
Cross-market testing, 244
Cuckoo brands, 102
Cultural analysis, 64
Cultural differences:
  explicit acknowledgment of, 194–197
  perseverance of, 77–80
Cultural directors, 192–193
Cultural erosion, 42
Cultural fluency, 61
Cultural freeware, 104
Cultural identity, preservation of, 77–80
Cultural misunderstandings, 119
  results of, 217–218
Cultural provenance, 120
Cultural references, inaccurate, 7
Cultural refreshment, 199
Cultural richness, 85
Cultural sensitivity, 80–87
  acquiring, 82
  to brand and consumer, 183, 289
  for human resources management, 93
  and multilingualism, 244
Cultural testing, 210
Culture, 52–55
  and advertising, 58–59
  clichés assigned to, 27
  filtering effect of, 57
  5-D model of, 66–67
  formal teaching of, 56
  global, 84–85
  versus human condition, 152–154
  of individuals versus national, 65
  invisibility of, 55–57
  Kluckhohn-Strodtbeck Framework,
    68
  and language, 61–62
  and language, separating from, 21–22
  learning, 54
  as means of perception, 56
  mixing, 85
  and natural selection, 85–86
  planning with, 63–69
  popular, 59
  themes underlying, 152–154
  Trompenaars model of, 67–68
Culture mapping, 64–69, 209–210
  for mass marketing, 66
  usefulness of, 65–66
Customer magazines, 277–278

D

Daewoo, 109
De Bono, Edward, 212
Decentering, 15
Dedication, of ad agencies, 248
Defensive networks, 177
Demographics, 60
De Mooij, Marieke, 68–69
Design agencies, 274
Developing countries, selling brands, 304–305
Development process, changes in, 230–231
Differences, 300
  encouraging, 206–207
  explicit acknowledgment of, 194–197
  perseverance of, 77–80
Diffuse expectations, 67
Dilemmas, 153
Direct mail, 268–270
Direct marketing, 262–266
  cultural appropriateness of, 266–267
  direct mail, 268–270
  international, 265
Director of music, 191
Disappointment factor, 33
  elimination of, 239
  employee disappointment, 271
Disaster checking, 30
Disasters, avoiding, 20–22
Disaster stories, 17–18
  with names, 22–25
Discourse, subject and mode of, 113
Disney Company, 103
Distribution channels, internet as, 296
Diversity:
  beauty of, 85
  maintaining, 197–201
Dixons, 102
Domestic agencies, 181
  structure of, 183
Domestic campaigns:
  flexibility of, 229
  popular culture in, 60
Domestic products, names of, 29
Double-entendre, 41–42, 148
Dulux, 140
Dutch culture, femininity of, 70

E

Eastern culture:
  characteristics of, 192–193
  representation of, 191–193

Eastern Europe, emerging markets of, 302–303
Efficiency, of ad agencies, 179, 248
EFIGS (England, France, Italy, Germany, and Spain) region, 204
EMEA (Europe, Middle East, and Africa) region, 204
Emerging marketers:
  consistency of marketing, 122
  needs of, viii
  servicing, 290–291
Emerging markets, 302–303
Emotional triggers, of brand provenance, 104
Emotions, advertising with, 138–143
Employee disappointment factor, 271
Empowerment, communication of, 40
English. *See also* American English; British English
  for brand names, 31
  fluency in, 49
  as a foreign language, 48
  in foreign markets, 36–37
  foreign words adopted in, 42–44
  for internet text, 281–282
  master ads in, 236
  mastery of, 50
  for planning meetings, 217
  for taglines, 41–46
  tone of voice, 38
Entertainment of consumers, 143–146
Entry strategies, 11
Environment, internal/external control of, 68
Error-checking software, 251
Ethics, 306
Ethnocentricity, 71
Etymology, of brand names, 31
European Direct Marketing Association, 264
Executional creativity, 151
Exporting, naïve rule of, 11
Export markets. *See also* Foreign markets
  brand building for, 99

F

Fashion, 161
Fear, 18–20
Feedback, market, 185, 277
Femininity/masculinity, 67
Ferrero, 225
Fiat, 309–310
Figures of speech, 218–219

Filth, 148
Finns, sense of humor, 144
First-time exporters, consistency of
    marketing, 122
5-D model, 64, 66–67
Flexibility, of ad agencies, 248
Fluency:
    versus bilingualism, 16
    cultural, 61
    and tagline comprehension, 37
Ford Focus, 24
Foreign brands, special status of, 86
Foreign languages, slogans expressed
    in, 36
Foreign markets:
    emotive advertising in, 140–141
    English taglines in, 41
    English use in, 47–48
    undervaluing, 272
Foreign versus local, 73
Formal/informal address, 38–39
Formality, of service, 248
France, foreign language regulation in, 37
Freedom of expression, 129
Freelance talent, 200
    copywriters, 274–275
    translators, 251
Free writing, 11
French:
    intellectualism of, 39–40
    taglines in, 37–38
Friendship marketing, 277, 280

G
Gates, Bill, 32
Gender, and receptivity to wit, 145
Gerber disaster story, 51–52
Germany:
    enjoyment of advertising in, 141
    function of advertising in, 142
    humorous advertising in, 143
Gillette, 60
Glamour:
    of English in foreign markets, 45
    of foreign language taglines, 36–37
Global brands:
    as distributor of wealth, 306
    launching, 303
    media costs of, 304
Global culture, products of, 84–85
Global influence, tools of, 308
Globalization, vii
    competition-driven, 117
    versus localization, 289

of media, 159
    price-driven, 116–117
Globalization companies, 301
Global marketing, ethics of, 306
Global marketing managers, 123–125
Global superiority complex, 19
Global trade, vii
Gnatworks, 179–180
Goodyear, Mary, 307
Government support, for international
    advertising, 303
Grammar, 7–8, 55
Greyhound Buses, 107–108
Groucho Marx syndrome, 111

H
Hall, Edward T., 53
Hampden-Turner, Charles, 64–65
The Headquarters for Combating Vice
    and Promoting Virtue, 144–145
Hearn, Lafcadio, 83
Hegarty, John, 120
Heinz, 263
Herbig, Paul, 53
Heritage, authentic, 106
Hierarchies, 97–99
High-speed industries, viii
Hofstede, Geert, 19, 64
Hofstede model, 194
Hollywood, promotion of Brand USA,
    109
Hopkins, Gerard Manley, 85
Horizontal integration, 256, 262
Horlicks, 13
Human condition, versus culture,
    152–154
Human resources management, cultur-
    ally sensitive, 92
Humility, of international brands,
    112
Humor:
    in advertising, 143–146
    universal, 147–149

I
Ideas:
    consistency of, 12
    level of acceptance of, 202–203
    strength of reaction to, 202–203
Identity, 100
    corporate, 128
    cultural, 77–80
    personal, 84, 86
    proper sense of, 112

Index

Ignorance, 81
Image building, 292–293
Images:
  standardization of, 128
  versus words, 127
Imperatives, in slogans, 38
Independent agencies, 162. *See also*
  Multicultural teams
  international capability of, 180
  purposes of, 300–301
  sector growth of, 301
Independent networks, 176–178
  collaboration between agencies, 178
Individualism/collectivism, 67
Individualism/communitarianism, 67
Inequality, cultural view of, 66
Influence, global, 308
Information, for consumers, 135–138
Ingredient brands, 295
Inspiration, 219
Integration, 255–258
  horizontal, 256, 262
  linear, 283
  vertical, 255–258
Intellectual protectionism, 105
Intercultural relations, 56
Intermediaries, for multinational corporations, 69–70
International advertising agencies, 158.
  See also Agency networks; Independent agencies
  collaboration within, 166–167
  hiring policies, 93
  innovation in, 157–158
  interoffice communication, 166
  motivation of, 164–167
International advertising campaigns,
  11–12
  approval phase, 228–229
  budgets of, 170
  creative direction for, 275
  creative process for, 228
  culture, incorporating into, 60
  versus domestic campaigns, 241
  editing, 275
  execution of, 228–231
  freelancers for, 274–275
  government support of, 303
  internal creation of, 275
  last-minute changes to, 229
  power of, 215
  pre-production phase, 229
  product-based, 138
  production phase, 229

  skills for, 227–228
  team effort for, 231
  testing, 229, 240–242, 244
  trafficking, 229
International Advertising Festival,
  146–149
International brand development, complexity of, 91–92
International brands, 106–107
  humility of, 112
International briefs, 275
  core idea description, 216
  development of, 228
  market description, 216
  preparation of, 205–209
International businesses:
  agency network servicing of, 160
  American, 69–73
  emerging, 290–291
  fears of, 18–20
  identity of, 99–101
  valuable qualities of, 57
International businesspersons, cultural
  insensitivity of, 18–19
International capability, 177, 180
International communications:
  consistency of, 114–117, 121
  and cultural mixing, 85
  detail orientation of, 270–272
  hierarchical approach, 97–99
International creative teams. *See* Multicultural teams
International creativity, 149–152
International research companies, 244
Internet:
  advantages of, 201, 278–279
  and brand awareness, 297
  and dual positioning, 116
  as global distribution channel, 296
  and globalization process, 159
  smart centralization on, 280–282
Internet marketing, 297
Intolerance, 81
Intranational brands, 107
Iran, regulation of humor in, 144–145
Irony, 225–226
Italian agencies, client service tech-
  niques, 233–234
Italian language, car names in, 25–27
Italy, English language use in, 44–45

J

Jack Daniel's, international marketing
  of, 110

Japan, provenance brands from, 105
Japanese culture, American interaction with, 74
Japanese language, brand names in, 27
"Just Do It" campaign, 36–41

K
Key markets, cultural characteristics of, 210–211
Key truths, 60–61
Kickbacks, 235
Kluckhohn-Strodtbeck Framework, 68

L
La Bruyère, 149
Language:
    borrowing of foreign words, 45–46
    culture, separating from, 21–22
    and culture, 61–62
    function in advertising, 2
    inaccurate, 7
    pollution of, 42
    preservation of, 79–80
Language barriers, 20
Laughter, cultural expression of, 144–145
Lead agencies, 59, 164, 175, 179–180
    support of, 171–172
Legal checks, on brand names, 30
Legislation, promotional, 213, 226–227, 267
Levi's, provenance of, 107
Levitt, Theodore, 289
Linear integration, 283
Linguistic accuracy, 286
Linguistic evolution, 43–44
Linguistic preference, 47–49
Literature, corporate, in-house creation of, 273–276
Local cultures, immersion of brand into, 109–110
Localization, versus globalization, 289
Local market presence, and the internet, 280
Local politics, and brand names, 28
Local references, 62
Local versus foreign, 73
Locking the package, 294
Long-term orientation, 67
Lowe Howard-Spink, 111
Loyalty, and brand positioning, 115–116

M
Madonna, 113
Management, of multicultural workplace, 195–197
Management consultants:
    on multicultural teams, 258
    threat of, 157
Management theory, culture-based, 65
Market entrants:
    servicing, 290–291
Market expertise, versus physical market presence, 298
Market feedback, 185, 277
Marketing, 307
    and advertising, bridging gap between, 257–258, 288
    and appropriateness of names, 34
    consumer-driven, 307
    versus corporate communications, 92
    direct, 262
    ethics of, 306
    friendship, 280
    post-modern, 307
    third-party, 122
    to youth, 293–295
Marketing across Cultures (Usunier), 14
Marketing department:
    centralization of, 117
    expenditures of, 261
    influence and responsibility of, 238–239
Marketing directors, cultural awareness of, 54
Marketing events, direct marketing around, 268–270
Market needs, ignoring, 293
Market penetration, 290
Market position, in foreign markets, 11
Market research, 49, 60–61, 124
Markets. *See also* Foreign markets
    characteristics of, 213
    cost of entry into, 134
    emerging, 302–303
Martha's Vineyard Sign Language, 80
Martianism, 223
Masculinity/femininity, 67
Mass communications:
    control of, 306–307
    tools for handling, 305
    use of country brand images, 108
Mass marketing, culture mapping for, 66

Mazda Bongo, 27
McCann-Erickson, 166, 312–313
Means of expression, 150
Media:
  globalization of, 159
  power and significance of, 307
Media advertising, 263. *See also* Advertising
Message delivery systems, consideration during planning, 216
Messages:
  nature of, 292–293
  visual communication of, 12
Microsoft, 32
Mindshare, competition for, 47–48, 62, 135, 261
Mitsubishi:
  Fuso Fighter, 27
  Pajero, 23
  Starion, 24
Modernization, 77
Motivation, of advertising agencies, 164–167
MS-DOS, 32
Multicultural teams, 190–193
  approval process within, 239–240
  balancing, 193–197
  brand development by, 288
  client staff on, 257
  consensus within, 201–203
  knowledge of client business realities, 257
  maintaining diversity within, 197–201
  permanent members of, 200–201
  physical interaction of, 201
  team dynamics, 212
  team spirit of, 196
Multi-local advertising, 159
Music, importance of, 191

N
Naïve rule of exporting, 11
Names, of brands:
  and brand provenance, 107
  creation of, 33
  cultural context of, 23
  culturally and linguistically sensitive, 29–32
  development of, 30–31
  disappointment in, 33
  excellence of, 35
  in foreign languages, 22–29
  function of, 33–35

  meaning of, 31
  and politics, 28
NASA, promotion of Brand USA, 109
Nashua, 102
National acts, creation by non-nationals, 62–63
Native languages:
  versus acquired languages, 47
  versus bilingualism, 16
  formal teaching of, 55–56
  use on internet, 282
Nature, cultural view of, 68
Netherlands, as intermediary for multinational corporations, 69–70
Networks. *See* Agency networks
Neutral/affective externalizations, 67
New brands, establishing, 290–291
Night starvation, 13
Nike:
  Air technology, 305
  brand development, 34
  Dutch market research, 78
  provenance of, 106–107
  tagline of, 36–41
Nissan:
  naming conventions of, 27–28
  Swingroad, 27
  Vanette Escargo, 27
Nokia:
  "Connecting People" tagline, 41–42
  provenance of, 310
Nonverbal communication, 127
"Not invented there" syndrome, 235–236

O
Objectivity, and international advertising, 303
Office politics, avoidance of, 196
Ogilvy, David, 120, 134, 137, 143
Ogilvy & Mather, viii
Old Kentish Sign Language, 80
Ollander-Krane, Jason, 254–255
Omnicom, 308
Oppression, as result of political correctness, 81
Originality, versus creativity, 149–150
Original text, 8
Overseas, concept of, 72
Overseas offices:
  as delivery systems, 180
  as lead agencies for regional work, 179–180

P

Packaged goods, international advertising of, 161
Parallel translation, 14–15
Particularism, 67
Pasta, provenance of, 103–104
Payment by results, 256
Payment by stakeholding, 254–255
Payment with emotion, 138–143
Payment with entertainment, 143–146
Payment with information, 135–138
Pepsi:
    "Come alive with Pepsi" campaign, 17
    provenance of, 106–107
Perceptions, cultural influence on, 56
Perfetti company, 102
Personal identity, discovering through travel, 84, 86
Personality, 65
    complexity of, 95–96
    versus culture, 65–66
Physical market presence, versus market expertise, 298
Pizza, provenance of, 103–104
Planning, 211–212, 214
    with culture, 63–69
    message delivery system consideration, 216
Plato, 92
Political bias, cultural influence on, 57
Political communication, 307
Political correctness, 81–82, 195
    versus world advertising, 190
Politics, and brand names, 28
Polynational brands, 107
Popcorn, Faith, 115
Popular culture, use in advertising, 59
Positioning:
    consistency of, 115, 121–122
    creativity of, 286
    dual, 115–116
    expression of, 150–151
    modifying, 285–286
    niche, 115
Positioning statements, simplicity of, 94
Postcards from the World, 197–198
Power distance, 66
Power systems, cultural perception of, 68
Precision, of ad agencies, 251
Pre-production phase, 229, 245–246
Price-points:
    consistency of, 115
    increasing, 116–117

Pride of origin, 112–113
Print ads:
    consistency of, 126–127
    glamour of, 270
Production phase, 229, 245–246
Products:
    names of (see Names, of brands)
    non-physical, 296–297
Programming, 277–278
Promotional legislation, 226–227, 267
Pronouns, formal and informal, 38–39
Proofreaders, 251
Provenance, 48–49, 102–103
    associations of, 103–106
    building and maintaining, 105–106
    cultural, 120
    disguising, 109
    disloyalty to, 112
    levels of, 106–107
    rediscovering, 112–113
    use of, 109–112
Provenance brands, constant investment in, 303–304
Publicis, 61
Purpose of copy, 9

Q

Quality:
    of advertising, 41
    density of, 40–41
Quality control, and consistency, 117–120
Quandaries, 153

R

Raine, Craig, 223
Raw names, 30
Ray, Phil, 12–13
Reaction, strength of, 202–203
Reebok, provenance of logo, 107
Reliability, of ad agencies, 248
Religion, sociocultural groupings based on, 204–205
Religious fundamentalism, 79
Research, 60–61
    exaggerated facts in, 49
    local, 124
Research questionnaires, translation for, 14–15
Respect, for consumers, 46–50
Retired persons, on multicultural teams, 198
Richness, 95–96
Rock music, English lyrics for, 44–45
Rolls Royce "Silver Mist," 22

Romance languages, versus English, 44–45
Russia, marketing to, 61

S
Saab 900SE, 24
Sainsbury's, 104
Saisho Electronics, 102
Sayings, 218
Scandinavia:
    femininity of, 71
    marketing of, 118–119
Schadenfreude, 148, 153
Schwarzenegger, Arnold, 113
Second-language skills, 227
Secrecy, 292
Self-confidence, 248
    and ability to communicate, 19
    of brands, 110
Seller's market, 307
Service orientation, 247–250
Simultaneous origination, 230
    for brand development, 287–288
Singer, provenance of, 112
Skills, 100
Slogans, 35–41
Smart centralization, viii–ix, 181–185, 227, 308
    benefits of, 188
    on the internet, 280–282
    multicultural teams for, 190–193
    and vertical integration, 256
Social issues, in advertising, 138–139
Sociocultural groupings, 204–205
Sony, provenance of, 107
Sound design, importance of, 191
Specific/diffuse expectations, 67
Speed of delivery, 291
Speed of service, 166
Sri Lankans, 76
Stakeholding, payment by, 254–255
Stallone, Sylvester, 113
Standardization, economy of, 290
Status:
    achievement of, 67
    cultural perception of, 68
Steel, John, 63
Stephenson, Robert Louis, 79–80
Stories, 149, 219–222
    storylines of, 222–224
Strategic planning, 211–212, 214
Strategy:
    executions of, 213–214
    media- and cultural-neutrality for, 215

Strategy team, cultural representatives on, 211
Students, on multicultural teams, 198
Style brands, acceptance and rejection of, 139
Sun Microsystems, London campaign, 111
Suntory, provenance of, 107
Supranational brands, 107

T
Taglines, 35–41
    double meanings, 41–42
    English for, 41–46
    in foreign languages outside home market, 36–37
    globalizing, 35–36
    power, tone, and style of, 36
    translation of, 36
Talents, 100
Targeting, 11–12
Taste, 119–120, 161
Technology. See also Internet
    for multicultural team communications, 201
    for production, 245
    and speed of service, 166
Television, for cultural refreshment, 199
Television news, impact of, 307
Testing, 229, 240–242, 284
    cultural, 210
    purpose of, 242
Third-party marketing, 122
Thompson, J. Walter, 158
Threats, 153
Time, cultural perception of, 67–68
Tolerance, 82
Tone:
    consistency of, 12
    impact of, 38
Toscani, Oliviero, 139
Toubon, Jacques, 37
Toyota MR2, 24
Trademarks, 31
Trafficking, 229
TrainCrash words, 32
Transcultural competence, 308
Translation, 3–7
    backtranslation, 12–15
    of collateral materials, 273
    by computers, 276
    copywriter qualifications for, 180
    errors in, 14

exact, 8
false ring of, 9
inaccuracy of, 13
literal, 4
of subtleties, 5
of taglines, 36
Translation bottleneck, 284–285
Translation equivalence, 14
Translation management, 272
Translators, 8–10
Transliteration, 309
Travel, benefits of, 84
Trompenaars, Fons, 19, 64–65, 83, 152–153, 195
Trompenaars model, 67–68
Trott, Dave, 253
Trusted foreigners networks, 123–124
Truth, Lies and Advertising (Steel), 63
Turkey, modernization of, 77
Turnkey operations, 283, 288
TV campaigns:
    consistency of, 126–127
    revision process for, 231
TV commercials, 133–134
    production of, 40
Typesetting, 230–231
Typographical mistakes, 250–252

U
Uncertainty avoidance, 67
Universalism/particularism, 67
Usunier, Jean-Claude, 14, 68–69

V
Value:
    added, 304–305
    concentrated, 40–41
Value distortion field, 305–306
Values, 100
Verbal humor, 147–148

Vertical integration, 255–258
    and smart centralization, 256
Videoconferencing, 201
Video work, casting and directing, 251–252
Visual communication of message, 12
Voice, consistency of, 261–262
Volkswagen Rabbit, 27

W
Warmth, of ad agencies, 248
Web sites, attracting consumers to, 279
Western culture:
    advance of, 77
    characteristics of, 192–193
    representation of, 191–193
Westernization, 77, 84
Wieden & Kennedy, 37
Wisdom, preservation of, 219
Wit, 145
Women, receptivity to wit, 145
Words:
    cultural sensitivity, expressing with, 128
    culture-specific, 12
    versus images, 127
    space considerations for, 230
    standardization of, 128
World advertising, 189
    versus political correctness, 190
World market, 77
World Writers, 189–190, 301
    creative team of, 190–191
    use of English, 217

Y
Yin/yang symbol, 193
Young & Rubicam, viii
Youth marketing, 293–295

About the Author

Simon Anholt grew up in Holland and England, in a family where English, Dutch, French, German, and Finnish were spoken. He went on to study modern European languages, linguistics, and literature at Oxford University, and after graduating in 1984 went to work at McCann-Erickson's London office as a copywriter. This was followed by stints at Wells Rich Greene in New York, Chiat/Day in Los Angeles, DPZ in São Paulo and Rio de Janeiro, Clarion Advertising in Delhi and Bombay, and McCanns in Tokyo, Honolulu, Hong Kong, Singapore, Jakarta, and Manila.

This "bird's-eye view of planet advertising" gave him the inspiration for his company, World Writers, which he founded in London in 1989. World Writers has provided the international strategic, creative, cultural, account management, and production dimension to many of the best international campaigns—from Nike, Coca-Cola, Pepsi, Adidas, Levi's, Timberland, Benetton, Sony Playstation, and MTV, to General Motors, IBM, Microsoft, Boeing, British Airways, Procter & Gamble, American Express, and Hewlett-Packard.

Simon Anholt is widely recognized as one of the world's leading consultants to companies and agencies who wish to build global brands, and is a frequent speaker at international marketing conferences and a regular contributor to many branding and advertising publications and academic journals.